Michigan

Dixie Franklin
with Bill Semion and Dan Stivers
Photography by Dennis Cox

COMPASS AMERICAN GUIDES
An imprint of Fodor's Travel Publications

Compass American Guides: Michigan

Editors: Bland Crowder, Kristin Moehlmann, John Morrone
Designer: Frances Rizzo
Compass Editorial Director: Paul Eisenberg
Compass Creative Director: Fabrizio La Rocca
Compass Senior Editor: Kristin Moehlmann
Production Editor: Linda K. Schmidt
Photo Editor and Archival Researcher: Melanie Marin
Map Design: Mark Stroud, Moon Street Cartography

Second Edition
ISBN 1–4000–1483–2

The details in this book are based on information supplied to us at press time, but changes
occur all the time, and the publisher cannot accept responsibility for facts that become outdated
or for inadvertent errors or omissions.

This book is available for special discounts for bulk purchases for sales promotions or premiums.
Special editions, including personalized covers, excerpts of existing books, and corporate
imprints, can be created in large quantities for special needs. For more information, write to
Special Markets/Premium Sales, 1745 Broadway, MD 6-2, New York, New York 10019, or e-
mail specialmarkets

Compass American Guides, 1745 Broadway, New York, NY 10019
PRINTED IN CHINA
10 9 8 7 6 5 4 3 2 1

Dedicated to my family and others whom I love, in memory of the good times.

CONTENTS

Sidebars and Topical Essays

Literary Extracts

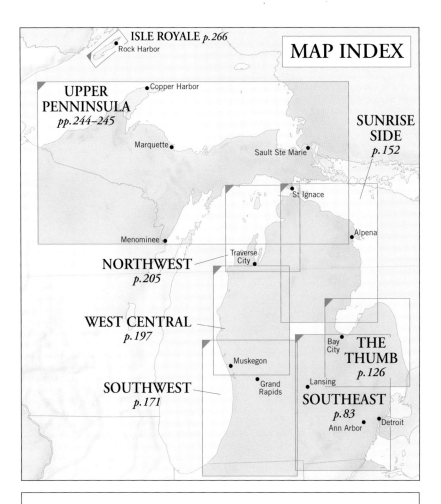

ISLE ROYALE *p. 266*
• Rock Harbor

MAP INDEX

UPPER
PENNINSULA
pp. 244–245
• Copper Harbor

Marquette •

Sault Ste Marie •

SUNRISE
SIDE
p. 152

Menominee •

St Ignace •

Alpena •

NORTHWEST
p. 205

Traverse
City •

WEST CENTRAL
p. 197

Bay
City •

THE
THUMB
p. 126

Muskegon •

Grand
Rapids •

Lansing •

SOUTHWEST
p. 171

SOUTHEAST
p. 83

Ann Arbor •

Detroit •

Maps

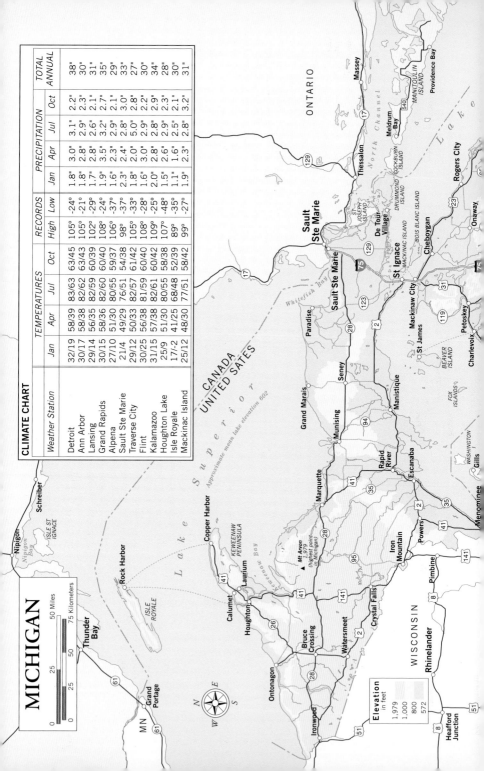

MICHIGAN

CLIMATE CHART

Weather Station	TEMPERATURES				RECORDS		PRECIPITATION				TOTAL ANNUAL
	Jan	Apr	Jul	Oct	High	Low	Jan	Apr	Jul	Oct	
Detroit	32/19	58/39	83/63	63/45	105°	-24°	1.8"	3.0"	3.1"	2.2"	38"
Ann Arbor	30/17	58/38	82/62	63/43	105°	-21°	1.8"	2.8"	2.9"	2.3"	30"
Lansing	29/14	56/35	82/59	60/39	102°	-29°	1.7"	2.8"	2.6"	2.1"	31"
Grand Rapids	30/15	58/36	82/60	60/40	108°	-24°	1.9"	3.5"	3.2"	2.7"	35"
Alpena	27/10	51/30	80/55	59/37	106°	-37°	1.6"	2.3"	2.9"	2.1"	29"
Sault Ste Marie	21/4	49/29	76/51	54/38	98°	-37°	2.3"	2.4"	2.8"	3.0"	33"
Traverse City	29/12	50/33	82/57	61/42	105°	-33°	1.8"	2.0"	5.0"	2.8"	27"
Flint	30/25	56/38	81/59	60/40	108°	-28°	1.6"	3.0"	2.9"	2.2"	30"
Kalamazoo	31/15	57/38	82/61	60/42	109°	-25°	2.0"	2.8"	2.8"	2.9"	34"
Houghton Lake	25/9	51/30	80/55	58/38	107°	-48°	1.5"	2.6"	2.9"	2.3"	28"
Isle Royale	17/-2	41/25	68/48	52/39	89°	-35°	1.1"	1.6"	2.5"	2.1"	30"
Mackinac Island	25/12	48/30	77/51	58/42	99°	-27°	1.9"	2.3"	2.8"	3.2"	31"

Elevation
in feet
1,979
1,000
800
572

CANADA
UNITED STATES

ONTARIO

WISCONSIN

MN

Lake Superior

Approximate mean lake elevation 602

Mt Arvon
1,979
(highest point
in Michigan)

KEWEENAW PENINSULA

ISLE ROYALE

Keweenaw Bay

Whitefish Bay

North Channel

MANITOULIN ISLAND

50 Miles
75 Kilometers

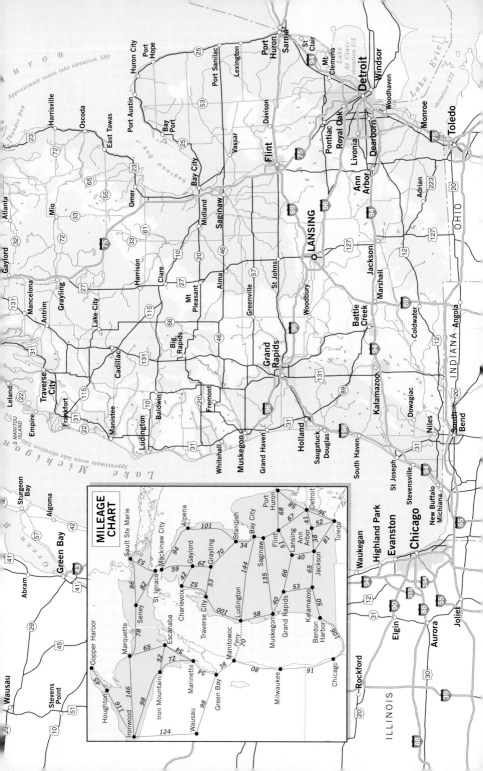

O V E R V I E W

Michigan is more than cars. The north is a landscape of lakes too wide to see across, moss-covered paths winding through deep forest, gurgling streams rippling fresh and clean over their pebbled beds, and waterfalls plunging headlong down rocky cliffs. Flat, fertile farmland rolls through the southeast, broken by the steel and concrete of industrial centers—especially Flint, Battle Creek, Lansing, and Grand Rapids. Ann Arbor, home to the University of Michigan, is one of the liveliest towns in the state. And finally, dominating the eastern edge of the state, Detroit is an economic powerhouse with global industrial reach.

DETROIT, MOTOR CITY

Appropriately, there's a steady roar of honking horns, screeching brakes, and slamming limousine doors in the city that put the world on wheels. Greater Detroit boasts the "high" culture of museums, opera, orchestras; a setting that enables the simple pleasures of riverfront dining, strolls through woodland parks, and dancing at outdoor festivals; and a fascinating, sometimes turbulent industrial history that resulted in palatial mansions, crowded ethnic enclaves, and the chart-breaking sounds of Motown.

SOUTHEAST

Southeastern Michigan is mostly farmland and flat as a pancake—until you get to the Irish Hills. Formed by the eroded deposits of glacial moraines, these rolling hills are distinctive for their spreads of oak trees and lakes. The state capital, Lansing, rests at the center of largely rural area.

ANN ARBOR

A quintessential college town, Ann Arbor (or "A^2," as some refer to it), entertains as well as educates. Museums, cinemas, and a plethora of theaters vie with Kerrytown restaurants and U of M football and basketball for the visitor's attention. Galleries and funky shops abound, and, with one of the highest concentration of used- and rare-book shops in the United States, A^2 is a mecca for book lovers.

South Pier Light at South Haven, along the Lake Michigan shore in southwest Michigan.

THE THUMB

Here, big cities give way to small towns and wide-open farmland punctuated by silos and cider mills. From the end of the breakwater at Port Austin, you can watch the sun rise over Lake Huron and return in the evening for the sunset over Saginaw Bay.

SUNRISE SIDE

Fishing boats bob in Saginaw Bay. Marinas crowd the river mouths. Lighthouses date back to the 1840s. Inland, forested hills dramatically define the horizon. Canoes float down the Rifle and Au Sable rivers.

SOUTHWEST & WEST CENTRAL

From the Indiana border to the Straits of Mackinac, you'll see ribbons of yellow sand and the blue waters of Lake Michigan, green forests, villages accented with harbors, lighthouses, vineyards, and rivers. The world's breakfast cereal capital, Battle Creek, vies for attention with the sculptures in Grand Rapids, the artist-colony feel of Saugatuck-Douglas, and the long, beckoning beaches of Warren Dunes State Park.

NORTHWEST & MACKINAC ISLAND

This triangle of Michigan contains some of the best beaches, hiking trails, and venues for boating and canoeing, plus some of the most fascinating historic sites in the country. Take the ferry out to the Manitou Islands, or visit Mackinac Island, almost a living museum.

UPPER PENINSULA

Lakes Michigan, Huron, and Superior wrap their shores around the Upper Peninsula. Country roads lead to parks, beaches, waterfalls, and trails; between hikes, stop for a cup of coffee at one of the many roadside restaurants, where communal tables invite friendly conversation. The wilderness here is unforgettable, especially on Isle Royale, with its ancient drama of wolf and moose.

In Petoskey, on Little Traverse Bay in northwest Michigan, you can meet your friends at the clock tower in Bay Front Park.

LANDSCAPE & HISTORY

Through aeons of scraping and heaving, shoving and receding, the great glaciers of various ice ages sculpted North America. By the end of the most recent ice age—known as the Wisconsin, approximately 10,000 years ago—a great swath of continent had been leveled. Close to the center of that landmass, a glacier carved out a massive lake and deposited in its middle two 300-mile-long peninsular ridges—one running north to south, the other east to west—separating the one body of water into five. These, the Great Lakes, are easily identified on any map of the United States or satellite picture of North America. Schoolchildren learn early to produce an image of these peninsulas: two hands, palms up, thumbs extended, index finger of the right hand almost touching the pinky finger of the left—the distinctive features of the state of Michigan. The mitten-shaped right hand is Michigan's Lower Peninsula, with its characteristic "Thumb." The left hand is Michigan's Upper Peninsula, or the "U.P." (Residents genially refer to themselves as "Yoopers.") This pair of hands is washed by four of the five Great Lakes, and the resulting shorelines—including magnificent, if sometimes treacherous, beaches, dunes, and sandstone cliffs—stretch longer than the entire Eastern Seaboard of the United States.

Situated between the 41st and 48th parallels, Michigan is midway between the equator and the North Pole and shares its borders with Ohio, Indiana, Wisconsin, and Ontario, Canada. The landscape is a collage of flat farmland to the south and roller-coaster hills and valleys to the north.

As the legend on the Great Seal of the State of Michigan so aptly states, "If you seek a beautiful peninsula, look about you."

■ GEOLOGY

On the shores and ridges of the Keweenaw Peninsula (the far northern extension of the U.P.) or on the distant Isle Royale, you can kneel down and touch some of the most ancient rock on earth: the Precambrian stone is at least 2.5 billion years old. Volcanic eruptions deep beneath ancient seas deposited copper, iron, silver, gold, gypsum, and dolomite. In turn, glaciers, relentlessly grinding stone and ice, stacked the resulting sand in thick layers that eventually hardened into yet more

Miners Castle at Pictured Rocks National Lakeshore in autumn.

Keweenaw Peninsula in autumn, as seen from Brockway Mountain Drive.

stone. The geologic history can be read in the multi-tinted strata of the 200-foot sandstone cliffs of Pictured Rocks National Lakeshore, along the southern shore of Lake Superior between Munising and Grand Marais.

■ GEOGRAPHY: LAKES, PLAINS, AND FORESTS

Four of the five Great Lakes—Superior, Michigan, Huron, and Erie—define Michigan's boundaries, and taken together create a shoreline more than 3,200 miles long. In a straight line from the northwest tip of the Keweenaw Peninsula to the southeast corner at the Ohio border near Toledo, the state measures 456 miles. By highway it's about 640 miles, the same as the distance from Detroit to New York City.

The topography changes from flat plains in the agricultural south to forested hills north of Saginaw Bay, with summits exceeding 600 feet in the northwest corner. Across the Straits of Mackinac, the eastern half of the Upper Peninsula is dotted with low hills that give over, about midway across the peninsula, to the hills and ranges that we in Michigan refer to as mountains.

The shoreline of Lake Superior freezes in winter.

■ CLIMATE

Because of the Great Lakes, Michigan's climate is classified as semimaritime, even though the state is more than 600 miles from the nearest ocean. The great bodies of fresh water create the famous "lake effect," cooling the westerly flow of air during the summer and warming it during the winter. This causes an average 10-degree moderation of temperature along the shore in all seasons and imposes a kind of "climate-control system" near the lakes. Inland, however, temperatures reach the extremes for which the upper Midwest is known—try a record low of -51 degrees F in Vanderbilt and a record high of 112 degrees F in Mio, inland towns that lie 30 miles apart on the Lower Peninsula.

In spring, lake-effect breezes extend the growing season, encouraging bumper fruit harvests along Lake Michigan's eastern shores. The same effect in winter brings prodigious snowfalls: the average annual snowfall on the Keweenaw Peninsula is 200 inches (over 16 feet).

Climate has a dramatic effect on the people of Michigan, influencing work schedules, travel plans, education, and recreation. Those in the maritime industry are especially challenged by frozen waterways and sudden winter storms.

■ WATER, WATER, EVERYWHERE: THE GREAT LAKES

A Michigan old-timer once told me that I "hadn't arrived" until I started towing a boat behind my car. Not surprisingly, most Michiganians do, as the state is surrounded by 40,000 square miles of Great Lakes and laced with 37,000 miles of rivers and streams. It has more than 11,000 inland lakes and countless bogs, fens, and marshes. These inland waters contain more than 150 major waterfalls and more than 3,000 islands, some large enough to boast lakes of their own.

Altogether, the Great Lakes hold one-fifth of the world's fresh surface water. Along Michigan's coastline are 85 boating harbors; safe harbors are never more than 15 shoreline miles away. Stand anywhere in the state, and you're always within 85 miles of a Great Lake and within 6 miles of a lake or stream.

■ LAKE SUPERIOR

Undisputed queen of the Great Lakes, Lake Superior is the Midwest's ocean, and at 31,800 square miles the largest body of fresh water in the world. It is a lake too wide to see across, an inland sea with cliffs and sandy coves, a sea without the smell of salt but with tide-like seiches governed by the winds. Stand a 1,000-foot freighter on end at Superior's deepest point, and it would disappear. Superior writes her own tales in which peaceful, glass-smooth dawns can explode into storms whose waves can ascend 200-foot cliffs to fling huge boulders like beach balls or, more dreadfully, reach up and drag huge freighters down to her depths.

■ LAKE HURON

Emptying into the St. Marys River (yes, that's how it's spelled) at Sault Ste. Marie, Superior starts the waters of mid-America on a 2,000-mile journey to the Gulf of St. Lawrence. They flow first into the 223-mile-long and 183-mile-wide Lake Huron, the third-largest Great Lake. Early explorers forging through the wilderness from Montreal called Huron "La Mer Douce," the Sweet Sea. The rocky shore with long stretches of white sand hugs a lake of azure blue. But don't be fooled: three underwater preserves mark the graves of scores of ships that met their fate in Huron's stormy embrace.

■ LAKE MICHIGAN

At 307 miles long, Lake Michigan is the world's sixth largest and the only Great Lake entirely within the boundaries of the United States. Its 2,730 miles of shoreline (including islands) are shared with Indiana, Illinois, and Wisconsin. Every shoreline city boasts a harbor, and this lake is liberally strewn with beaches of "singing" sand—with silica so fine it whispers a sighing, singing sound under every footstep— including the world's highest freshwater dunes, towering up to 600 feet as part of Sleeping Bear Dunes National Lakeshore.

■ LAKE ERIE

Only 241 miles long, most of Lake Erie's coastline is claimed by New York, Pennsylvania, Ohio, and Ontario, Canada. Michigan's share of its waters are shallow and gray, with cattail marshes dotted with lotus blossoms in the fall.

■ INLAND LAKES AND RIVERS

Inland lakes tend to be serene, surrounded by green forests and sheltered bays. The largest is Houghton Lake, at nearly 32 square miles. Six other lakes are 20 square miles or more. Common names range from the descriptive, such as Long, Little, Big, Round, Bass, Mud, Crooked, and Silver, to the native, such as Gogebic, Michigamme, and Ponemah. For hundreds of years the many peoples indigenous to the Great Lakes region used Michigan rivers as water highways. The largest of these rivers—the Grand, Kalamazoo, Manistee, Muskegon, and St. Joseph—all flow into Lake Michigan.

■ FIRST INHABITANTS

The history of the indigenous Michigan cultures is as fascinating as it is appalling. Native American Michigan culture inspired Henry Wadsworth Longfellow to write *The Song of Hiawatha,* and it was here that two of the Native Americans' greatest leaders, Pontiac and Tecumseh, rose to prominence and waged their final, doomed battles against European encroachment.

The earliest inhabitants arrived in the Great Lakes area about 11,000 years ago. These were nomadic hunter-gatherers, pursuers of mastodons, woolly mammoths, and migratory game along the edges of the receding glaciers.

Of the Old Copper Culture, whose shallow diggings can still be explored at the tip of the Keweenaw Peninsula and on Isle Royale, we know virtually nothing. Around 7,000 years ago, these early settlers discovered they could extract high-grade copper by heating the ore. They then fashioned the metal into tools and various utensils. Objects wrought from this exceptionally pure copper have been found as far away as New York, Illinois, Kentucky, and the Gulf of Mexico, indicating early and widespread trade with other tribes. The shallow-pit mines on Isle Royale in Lake Superior, 22 miles from the nearest mainland, further indicate that these early metalworkers were capable of safe and extended Great Lakes travel.

About 3,000 years ago the first Mound Builders arrived, called the Adena people. They were succeeded by the Hopewell people, who were architects of more complex mounds and were widely dispersed throughout the Great Lakes area.

The above sketch, made by J. C. Tidball around 1850, shows how the artist imagined copper was mined by people of the Old Copper Culture.

This depiction of Indians on a Lake Huron island (circa 1845) was painted by Paul Kane based on sketches made during his travels through the Great Lakes region.

■ MODERN TRIBES

In the 1600s, when French explorers first saw the lake that the local Indians called Michiganong, or Michigama, they found an indigenous population that had been in place for less than 1,000 years and knew nothing of its predecessors. Michigan, like all the Ohio Valley and Great Lakes region, was a territory in flux. The Iroquois (the Five Nations to the east) had pushed the Algonquian-speaking tribes out of the eastern forests into the Ohio Valley and the Great Lakes area. These Algonquin tribes—whose language was closely related to that spoken by the Indians encountered by the first British colonists—in turn pushed the Sioux out of the Ohio Valley onto the Great Plains.

The Algonquins had formed a loose confederation called the Three Fires, consisting of the Potawatomi, Ottawa, and Chippewa (Ojibwa) tribes. The Potawatomis resided largely in southwestern Michigan, where the rich soil promoted the cultivation of beans, corn, and squash, and there built elaborate permanent villages. Farther north, the Ottawas built semipermanent villages where they also grew crops; but during the summer fishing season they would move entire villages to their favorite waters. The Chippewas, a largely nomadic people of the far north country, hunted, fished, and gathered berries and nuts, which they added to ground, dried meat to make pemmican. Although these people were considered "savages" by the Europeans, their cultures were highly developed and very competitive—a fact that the Europeans were quick to seize upon in building Indian alliances during the era of the fur trade.

The widespread and intricately interwoven nature of these tribes and subtribes prompted Bruce Catton, the preeminent modern Michigan chronicler, to write:

> You can study the names of the tribes until your face is blue without adding much to your knowledge, because, essentially, they were all much the same people: Chippewas (or Ojibways, Outchibous, Otchipwe, or what you choose) and Ottawas, and the blend of Potawatomis, Fox, Saux, and Massauaketon that are often lumped together as the people of the Fire; the Miamis, sometimes called the Omaumeg; and the remnants of the Hurons, driven from their Georgian Bay homeland by the cruel Iroquois, to whose family they once belonged, given now to living about Detroit, known of late as the Wyandot.

As was true for all the other indigenous peoples in the New World, contact with the Europeans spelled doom for Michigan's Indian inhabitants—but not without a long and valiant struggle. Although the region's two great warrior-chiefs—Pontiac, an Ottawa, and Tecumseh, a Shawnee—were separated in history by more than half a century, they both formed broad confederations of Indian tribes and threw their lot in with the European nation most likely to achieve their aims, which more and more would include, ironically, stopping the westward advance of European settlers.

On the one hand, toward the end of the French and Indian War (1754–63), Pontiac, frustrated by the loss of trade with the French (the English had cut off the shipping lanes) and outraged at British encroachment on Indian land, formed a powerful Indian alliance that sided with the French against the British. The alliance involved nearly every Indian tribe from Lake Superior to the lower Mississippi in a plan that called on each to attack the nearest fort—what became known as Pontiac's Rebellion. Pontiac himself attacked the British-held fort at Detroit, while his allies attacked a dozen more forts and captured all but four. In the end, the Indians were forced to retreat, however, having won from Britain only a proclamation that strictly limited white settlement in Indian territory. (The utter disregard of this treaty by white settlers would trigger decades of Indian warfare.)

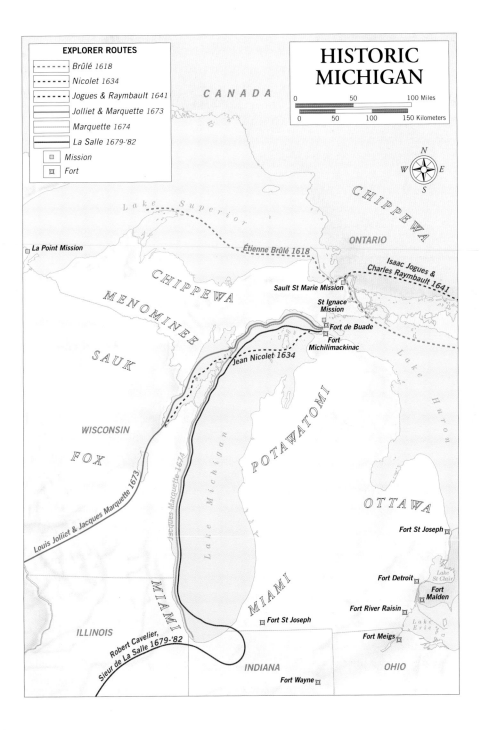

HISTORIC MICHIGAN

EXPLORER ROUTES

- ------- Brûlé 1618
- ------- Nicolet 1634
- ------- Jogues & Raymbault 1641
- Jolliet & Marquette 1673
- Marquette 1674
- La Salle 1679-'82
- ☐ Mission
- ⌧ Fort

0   50   100 Miles
0   50   100   150 Kilometers

CANADA

Lake Superior

CHIPPEWA

ONTARIO

La Point Mission

Étienne Brûlé 1618

Isaac Jogues &
Charles Raymbault 1641

CHIPPEWA

MENOMINEE

Sault St Marie Mission

St Ignace
Mission

Fort de Buade
Fort
Michilimackinac

SAUK

Jean Nicolet 1634

Lake Huron

WISCONSIN

FOX

Lake Michigan

POTAWATOMI

Jacques Marquette 1674

Louis Jolliet & Jacques Marquette 1673

OTTAWA

Fort St Joseph

Lake
St Clair

Fort Detroit

Fort
Malden

MIAMI

MIAMI

Fort River Raisin

Lake Erie

ILLINOIS

Robert Cavelier,
Sieur de La Salle 1679-'82

Fort St Joseph

Fort Meigs

INDIANA

OHIO

Fort Wayne

N
W   E
S

On the other hand, during the War of 1812, Tecumseh, a legendary orator who had built an even more powerful confederation than Pontiac's, sided with the British against the Americans. He saw the war between the United States and Great Britain as an opportunity to stop the continued expansion of white settlement and avenge the massacres of his people. The participation of Tecumseh and his allied Indian nations in the critical battles of Detroit (August 1812) and the River Raisin (January 1813) was instrumental in making them British victories. Only with his death at the Battle of the Thames in Canada in October 1813—won by the Americans led by Gen. William Henry Harrison, later U.S. president—did the influence that the Indians exerted throughout the region during the early days of exploration and settlement finally cease. Tecumseh's courage and ferocity in this and earlier battles exacted such a toll on American troops that he is widely considered to have almost single-handedly prevented the U.S. conquest of Canada.

■ TRAPPERS, TRADERS, EXPLORERS, PRIESTS

In 1634 Jean Nicolet set out from Quebec on a mission ordered by Samuel de Champlain, lieutenant governor of New France, to explore the recently claimed

An imaginary representation of the death of Tecumseh at the Battle of the Thames in 1813.

The Charismatic Tecumseh

The implicit obedience and respect which the followers of Tecumseh pay to him is really astonishing, and more than any other circumstance bespeaks him one of those uncommon geniuses which spring up occasionally to produce revolutions and overturn the established order of things. If it were not for the vicinity of the United States, he would, perhaps, be the founder of an empire that would rival in glory that of Mexico or Peru. No difficulties deter him. His activity and industry supply the want of letters. For four years he has been in constant motion. You see him today on the Wabash and in a short time you hear of him on the shores of Lake Erie or Michigan, or on the banks of the Mississippi and wherever he goes he makes an impression favorable to his purposes.

—William Henry Harrison, letter to William Eustis, August 7, 1811, from *Tecumseh, A Life,* by John Sugden, 1997

lands to the west. Champlain, the French navigator-mapmaker turned politician who later became famous as the father of the fur trade, was primarily obsessed with finding a faster trade route to China—the fabled Northwest Passage.

China and her awe-inspiring riches had long captured the imagination of entrepreneurial merchants and covetous kings, thanks to the late-13th-century travels of Marco Polo and his reports of lavish silks, spices, gold, rubies, and porcelain. Great riches would reward the man who could circumvent the existing routes, then plagued by bandits, pirates, and enemy nations. In the person of Jean Nicolet, Champlain believed he had found the man to open a new water route to the Pacific. He equipped Nicolet lavishly for his mission to the Far East (which common knowledge held lay just beyond the Great Lakes), including giving him an elaborate Chinese robe of fine damask, colorfully embroidered with flowers and birds.

Passing from Lake Huron through the Straits of Mackinac, Nicolet traversed Lake Michigan, hugging the shores of the Upper Peninsula until he reached Green Bay. Spotting a group of people camped on the shore and presuming his mission accomplished, he donned his glorious robe, stood up in his canoe, fired two pistols in the air to announce his grand arrival, and stepped ashore before an astounded group of Winnebagos.

Hoping to find a water route to the Far East, explorer Jean Nicolet landed near Green Bay in 1634 and mistakenly assumed that the Winnebago Indians he met onshore could show him the passage to Asia.

While Nicolet failed to find the trade route to the Far East, he fared better than the more daring Étienne Brûlé, who, in 1610, at the age of 18, had been sent by Champlain into the wilderness to study the land and its people. A decade later, the group of Hurons with whom Brûlé was living guided him west to St. Marys River at what is now Sault Ste. Marie, where some historians credit him with being the first European to set foot on Michigan soil. For years, Brûlé led a charmed life. Some said he became more Indian than the Indians themselves as he adopted their lifestyle and learned their language. In 1632 his luck ran out. According to legend, a violent disagreement broke out, whereupon Brûlé was beaten to death and eaten by his chosen tribe (not such an ignominious fate, as ritual cannibalism was a sign of great respect among the Three Fires peoples).

■ THE BLACK ROBES

Hot on the heels of explorers in search of wealth and adventure came fervent and intrepid missionary priests, whom Indians dubbed the "Black Robes." In search of souls to convert, many met martyrdom instead. The first Jesuits came at the invitation of Champlain; in 1641 Fathers Isaac Jogues and Charles Raymbault traveled to the present Sault Ste. Marie to conduct the first Christian religious services ever held in Michigan.

Among other Jesuits who left indelible marks on Michigan were Claude Jean Allouez, who established the first mission in Michigan at Sault Ste. Marie; Claude Dablon; Bishop Baraga ("The Snowshoe Priest"); and Jacques Marquette.

Exploration and conversion traveled hand in glove. On May 17, 1673, fur trader, navigator, and mapmaker Louis Jolliet, along with Father Marquette and five other Frenchmen, pushed off from St. Ignace in search of the legendary "Messipi," the big river of Indian lore. A month later their canoes were swept into the mighty Mississippi. Elated, they rode it all the way to the mouth of the Arkansas River before it became ruefully evident that they had failed to find the long-sought water route to the Pacific.

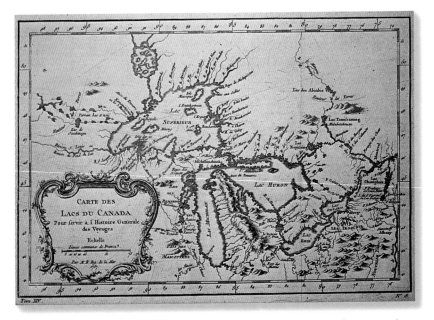

Evidence of the high quality of French surveying techniques, this 1757 map by Jean Nicolas Bellin is remarkably accurate.

■ FRENCH AND INDIAN TRADERS

Champlain, disappointed in his quest for the Northwest Passage, found his treasure right where he stood—and it was beaver fur. In trendsetting France, beaver hats had ascended to the height of fashion. No European man of distinction was considered ready to appear in public until he had donned an elegant chapeau made from the soft fur found under the tough outer guard hairs of the beaver pelt. The Three Fires nation, traders by ancient tradition, took naturally to the French, who offered knives, beads, blankets, iron kettles, trinkets, guns—and whiskey—in exchange for the prized pelts. Soon canoes full of furs were headed down the major waterways to the trading outposts.

But this traffic soon kindled another ancient tradition: raiding. The Iroquois, allies of the British and traditional enemies of the Three Fires, began plundering the convoys, striking terror into the hearts of all who were forced to run their gauntlets. The French replied by constructing forts: at the Straits of Mackinac, at Detroit, at Fort St. Joseph (near the present city of Niles), and at Sault Ste. Marie.

Even with the relative safety of the forts, the logistical problem of transferring immense quantities of furs remained, a problem solved by the colorful *voyageurs* boatmen. Primarily French-Canadians, these short, muscular men who spoke a patois only they could understand, traversed the lakes and rivers in large canoes, paddling them hundreds of miles a day to the cadence of their songs.

The French-Canadian boatmen of the fur trade, known as voyageurs, *were hardy men, transporting furs hundreds of miles across rivers and lakes in canoes.*

Father Jacques Marquette and Louis Jolliett, the first Europeans on the upper Mississippi, traveled down the river to the mouth of the Arkansas in 1673.

■ BRITISH

The British, casting covetous eyes on both the fur trade and the potential for a Northwest Passage, marshaled Indian support to foment the French and Indian War. A confused enterprise at best, the conflict relied on deep hatred among the various tribes, who were adroitly manipulated by both sides to meet either French or British ends. The great Ottawa chief Pontiac, for instance, enlisted the aid of his Indian allies on the side of the French, motivated in part by the participation of the Iroquois, the Ottawas' ancient rivals, on the side of the British. For the Europeans, the true prize of the war was domination of New France, what is now eastern Canada, and the conclusion to that quest came with Gen. James Wolfe's defeat of the Marquis de Montcalm on the Plains of Abraham outside Quebec City in 1759 and the resulting surrender of Quebec to the British. With the Treaty of Paris in 1763, France ceded all her territories to Britain, and the British assumed occupation of the forts, took over the fur trade, and began a policy of coexistence with the French, underlined by an attitude of mutual disdain, that endures to this day.

An early-19th-century watercolor showing Native Americans spearing beaver.

■ SETTLEMENT

One effect of the fur trade had been the widening of the ancient Indian trails into roads—roads that thus opened the land to settlement. At first only a few log houses sprang up among the wigwams surrounding the trading posts at Detroit, the Straits of Mackinac, and Sault St. Marie. Then came homesteading on a larger scale—farmers clearing the land and planting crops in ever-expanding waves from the core-city forts.

Early on, in 1701, a 43-year-old French army officer, Antoine de la Mothe Cadillac, had convinced French royalty that the Great Lakes area was ready for organized settlement. With the aid of a hundred soldiers and workers, Cadillac built a 12-foot-high, 200-foot-square palisade at the spot where the Detroit Civic Center now stands. For additional protection for his soldiers occupying the cabins, he enticed friendly Chippewa, Ottawa, Huron, and Miami Indians to set up villages nearby. Cadillac's wife, Marie Thérèse, soon joined her husband to become the first white woman to brave the Michigan wilderness.

Although Michigan was made part of the Northwest Territory in 1805, the claim of the United States to the region was not fully clear until the end of the War of 1812. Nevertheless, homesteaders continued to make the long wagon treks across Ohio to Michigan, settling mostly in the fertile southern plains. The completion of the Erie Canal in 1825, connecting Michigan via Lake Erie to Buffalo, New York, sparked settlement in earnest. In less than five years, Michigan's population tripled to 31,639.

■ THE END OF THE FOREST

Hard on the settlers' heels came the lumbermen who, having exhausted the forests of Maine and the Northeast, saw new fortunes in the deep forests of Michigan, which stretched from the southern edge of Saginaw Bay north to Lake Superior. Hundreds of thousands of 300-year-old white pines, towering 200 feet or more and measuring 5 feet in diameter, created a mixed hardwood and pine canopy under which the hottest, brightest day of summer turned cool and dark. (A remnant of this awesome forest can be glimpsed at Hartwick Pines State Park near Gaylord and Estivant Pines Sanctuary at Copper Harbor.) Growing amid the white pine were Norway pine, jack pine, spruce, white cedar, hemlock, and tamarack. In groves along the southern meadows stood beech, oak, hickory, sugar maple, and ash.

A souvenir plate commemorating the 1825 opening of the Erie Canal.

■ WHITE PINE TREASURE

White pine mattered most to lumbermen. Surveyors in the mid-1800s estimated standing pine at 150 billion board feet—enough to build a floor that would cover Michigan's entire land area, with enough left over to resurface the state of

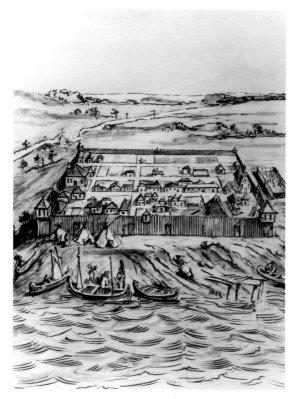

The city of Detroit began with the building of this fort in 1701.

Rhode Island. French-Canadians signed on as lumberjacks, along with workers from New England, New York, Pennsylvania, and Ohio and from countries across Europe, especially from Scandinavia.

The lumber industry began in the Saginaw River valley; then, like a mass of slow-moving locusts, the loggers inched westward to the Grand River valley, along the rivers to Lake Michigan, and northward into the Upper Peninsula. The riverine system that so favored canoe travel also served as the water highway for the buoyant pine. In less than 50 years the pine forest was gone, the value of its timber exceeding that of the goldfields of California and Alaska combined.

Michigan trees helped build America's cities and rebuild them, as in the case of Chicago, after disastrous fires. The great cities of the treeless plains benefited particularly from the beautiful, easy-to-work lumber streaming out of Michigan.

The introduction of the crosscut saw and railroads that could reach into the farthest corners of the state hastened the end. Cutover land fell to unpaid taxes, resulting in hundreds of acres reverting to the state. Land speculators encouraged ill-fated farming on inhospitable lands. Farmers failed, regrouped, made the best of it. Cherry trees flourished on the cutover land, Michigan-made furniture became world famous, and the discovery of new resources such as iron and copper spurred the growth of powerful new economies.

The decimation of the white pine forests had pricked the national conscience. In the 1930s the Civilian Conservation Corps began replanting trees and working to control erosion. Today Michigan grows twice as much timber each year as it harvests, and prides itself on having created a sustainable forest-products industry. As of 2004, the state's 276 sawmills, 14 veneer mills, eight pulp and paper mills, and 18 miscellaneous wood-using plants employ 150,000 people and contribute $9 billion annually to Michigan's economy.

■ MINERALS IN THE EARTH

Great Lakes Indians had known about Michigan's copper for centuries. French and British explorers had heard the stories and observed the crude mining pits on the Keweenaw Peninsula and at Isle Royale but paid them little heed. They missed other buried troves as well: iron, gold, silver, gypsum, limestone, salt, petroleum, coal, dolomite, peat, sand, and gravel, plus natural gas and oil.

In 1844 state land surveyor William Austin Burt noticed his magnetic compass swinging wildly as he traveled along Lake Superior. His curiosity over this

Loggers pose for a photo in Hermansville, circa 1900.

Gypsum mining at Alabaster, Michigan, in the late 19th or early 20th century.

discovery led him to outcroppings of iron, but it stopped there. Although his inventiveness did drive him to create a "solar" compass—on display at the Marquette County Historical Museum—others were more ambitious. Enlisting the aid of Chippewa chief Marji-Gesick, prospectors were led to hunks of iron protruding from the roots of an upturned tree on the banks of Teal Lake at the present city of Negaunee. This finding ultimately led to the three great iron ranges of the Upper Peninsula: the Marquette, Menominee, and Gogebic.

Today these ranges are largely mined out and silent. Two open-pit iron mines still operate on the Marquette Range: the Tilden and Empire, managed by the Cliffs Michigan Mining Company. Employing about 1,450 workers, they produce about 22 percent of the nation's ore. The abandoned mine shafts are now the abodes of hundreds of thousands of bats during their winter hibernation.

■ TRANSPORTATION AND INDUSTRY

Soldiers were the first to widen the original Indian and fur trapper trails into roads, paving them with hardwood timbers. Many of Michigan's modern roads follow these same tracks that were forged by the area's earliest residents.

After Michigan became a state in 1837, towns developed rapidly. Rails were driven into the wilderness, opening the way for more settlers, more logging, and more industrial development. On June 22, 1855, the Soo Locks at Sault Ste. Marie lifted the first steamer, the *Illinois,* up the 22 feet between Lake Huron and Lake Superior, thus bypassing a half-mile portage around St. Marys Rapids.

One of the lingering and most delightful legacies of the Great Lakes shipping boom during the lumber era is the lighthouse. Of Michigan's 116 lighthouses (more than in any other state), 12 lighthouses and one lightship now house museums, all of them unfailingly capturing the romance of the inland seas.

■ THE HORSELESS CARRIAGE

In the late 1800s, Ransom "Ranse" Olds, son of Pliney Olds, was tinkering in his father's gas-fired boiler engine shop, comparing ideas with his friend Frank G. Clark, who had grown up working in his own father's carriage shop. By 1887 they

Copper ingots stacked in rows await transport on this dock in Houghton, circa 1910.

(above) View of the St. Clair River *(1863)*, *by George B. Gardner, shows the* Forester, *an excursion boat that made thrice-weekly trips between Port Huron and Detroit. Bands on board provided music for dancing. (opposite) Point Betsie Lighthouse in late winter.*

had combined the two establishments and built a gas-fired horseless carriage, and proceeded to chug their way down Lansing streets. In 1897, Olds and his partners built the first Oldsmobile, producing four "carriages" that first year.

Meanwhile, Henry Ford had satisfactorily tested his invention of a self-propelled quadricycle, his first step toward developing what would become Michigan's favorite automobile of the era. By 1908 Ford was producing Model Ts that sold initially for $850. "You can have any color Model T you want, as long as it's black" was Ford's famous quip. The public drove away with black. A year later Michigan laid its first rural concrete highway. In 1915 the world's first traffic light was installed in Detroit. The first center stripe was painted on Dead Man's Curve at Marquette in 1917, and the first urban freeway was built in 1942.

Michigan can also boast of automotive pioneers John and Horace Dodge, David D. Buick, William C. "Billy" Durant of General Motors fame, and others. Automobiles, related industries, and the manufacture of transportation equipment in Michigan continue to lead the economy.

(above) A Model T assembly line circa 1913. (opposite) The Lake Superior shore in autumn.

■ BACK TO NATURE

Homesteaders had hardly settled into their cabins when the first tourists arrived from Chicago seeking to experience wilderness, to breathe fresh air, to fish and hunt. Tourism came early and came to stay. Mackinac Island welcomed the tourists most spectacularly, with its Grand Hotel and fantastic Victorians, followed by Marquette, Petoskey, Sault Ste. Marie, and St. Ignace. Even during the hardest of times, people sought Michigan's sunny shores and quiet lakes. Today it seems that one can enter a reviving and balmy quietude just steps away from almost any road or tour a downtown humming with activity.

Welcome to Michigan.

THE REAL MICHIGAN

Michigan is perhaps the strangest state in the Union, a place where the past, the present and the future are all tied up together in a hard knot. . . . It killed the past and it is the past; it is the skyscraper, the mass-production line and the frantic rush into what the machine will some day make of all of us, and at the same time it is golden sand, blue water, green pine trees on empty hills, and a wind that comes down from the cold spaces, scented with the forests that were butchered by hard-handed men in checked flannel shirts and floppy pants. It is the North Country wedded to the force that destroyed it.

—Bruce Catton, *Michigan, A History,* 1974

D E T R O I T

by Bill Semion

Detroit is unique in the American experience. It's the only major American city in which you can stand downtown and look *south* at Canada. Another great bit of trivia: Detroit is the only major U.S. city to have been occupied by a foreign power, when during the War of 1812 William Hull, governor of the Michigan Territory, turned the city over to the British without firing a shot.

After the War of 1812, Detroit sought more settlers from the East Coast— although letters from soldiers stationed in Michigan did little to inspire the folks back home to come west. In 1814 Gen. Duncan McArthur posted this personal letter from Detroit: "The banks of the Detroit River are handsome, but nine-tenths of the land in the Territory is unfit for cultivation."

By 1817, however, Detroit newspapers that promised a more positive future had made their way east, and soon the rush was on, with Detroit the major point of entry. Roads and rails were laid for travel to the interior. Steamboats such as *Walk-in-the-Water*, a popular 330-ton sail-rigged steamship, chugged across Lake Erie from Buffalo.

The annual Old Car Festival at Greenfield Village in Dearborn, in metropolitan Detroit, is a sort of homecoming for classic autos.

The steamship Walk-in-the-Water *is shown in Detroit Harbor in a 1820 painting.*

The Territory of Michigan received a sizable land grant, part of which was appropriated as an endowment for schools suggested by a Judge Woodward. Today's students at the University of Michigan can be thankful that his idea for their institution was adopted, but not the name once proposed— Catholepistemiad. Former territorial governor Lewis Cass himself stumbled over the name, calling it "Cathole . . . what's its name."

In 1825 completion of the Erie Canal, connecting the Hudson River and Lake Erie, helped facilitate water travel. While many settlers remained near Detroit, even more unlashed their wagon wheels from the ships' masts, reassembled their gear, and headed west. One newspaper reported that from dawn to dark a wagon was pulling out every five minutes. The first road, if the muddy trail through the wilderness can be called a road, followed the Old Sauk Trail used by generations of Indians. By 1835 two weekly stages were running the Chicago Road (today's U.S. 12) from Detroit to Fort Dearborn.

■ STATEHOOD

The new state constitution of 1837 expressly forbade slavery in Michigan, strengthening the territorial ban that had been in place since 1787. Detroit became a focal point for the Underground Railroad, which enabled slaves fleeing north from southern states to reach Canada, where freedom lay within a mile's reach across the Detroit River.

As settlers streamed into Michigan, shysters popped up like ticket scalpers at a sports event, offering maps and touting land—below market value—in towns that existed only on paper, if they existed at all.

Just as spurious were the banking institutions that appeared overnight, sometimes boosting their reserves by borrowing from each other when inspectors were due. With the crash of 1840, some wildcat banks went on the dodge in an effort to escape note holders. In *Detroit: Dynamic City,* Arthur Pound writes:

Detroit on Election Day, November 1837: Stevens T. Mason (at left, in top hat) becomes Michigan's first elected governor.

A 1900 panoramic photochrome print of Detroit, then known as "the most beautiful city in America."

> As banks went out of business, and those with sound money took to hoarding, there presently was not enough money left in circulation to carry on even the greatly decreased volume of trade. As a result of being cursed with too much money, Detroit was presently cursed with too little. Companies were forced to use due-bills; the city issued shinplaster script; wooden bowls were used for small change. "Don't take any wooden money" remains in the Michigan idiom as a depression counterpart of the pithy boom phrase "land-office business."

In 1847, still mistrustful of the British nearby in Canada, legislators decided to relocate the state capital, though Detroit fought the move. Perceiving the partisan opinions on a site for the capital, one legislator proposed a *tiny* town yet unnamed (a cluster of homes and a sawmill) on the Grand River as a neutral alternative. If *one* side couldn't win outright, then *no* side should win, he argued. The capital moved to what is now Lansing.

■ CIVIL WAR

By the outbreak of the Civil War, Detroit had left the fur trade and farming far behind, having turned instead to the manufacture of steam engines, wagons, buggies, and ships, as well as copper smelting and the production of salt. The change was just in time. When Fort Sumter fell to Confederate troops, President Abraham Lincoln sent out an urgent call for military support. Because the state treasury was empty, the city of Detroit lent $50,000 to the war effort and called on its citizens for matching funds. Within two weeks Detroit's First Michigan Infantry was

This 1862 broadside offered impressive incentives for those signing up with the 20th Michigan Infantry Regiment. Each volunteer would be given $100 and 160 acres of land, as well as a monthly stipend for his family.

training at Fort Wayne. A month later 780 new soldiers boarded steamships, then trains for Washington, proudly reporting in as the first western regiment. The Fifth Michigan Infantry received its colors in September 1861, and under the name the Fighting Fifth fought in many battles, among them Fredericksburg, Chancellorsville, and Gettysburg. Detroit alone furnished 6,000 men—one out of every eight citizens.

■ CITY OF INDUSTRY

After the war the wounds and diseases of returning soldiers attracted the attention of medical men, pharmacists, and chemists. One company (later renamed Parke, Davis & Co.) began in 1867 to manufacture drugs to address the soldiers' needs, and as other firms followed suit Detroit became a center for the manufacture of quality pharmaceuticals.

Detroit was still a major shipping port, manufacturing products for the Great Lakes maritime industry, both for building and repairs. At the end of the 19th century its factories were producing railroad cars, horse-drawn streetcars, stoves, furnaces, engines, and other products based on raw materials such as lumber, copper, and iron. Household products ranged from beer to paint to cigars to shoes. The popular Governor Cass had called Detroit the "City of Muscle," and it was flexing it with factories. Under the pall of factory smoke, citizens built libraries, colleges, theaters, a fine opera house, and grand estates along the river.

Subsequently, Henry Ford and his innovative assembly lines made Detroit the world's first truly modern industrial city and, more importantly, vaulted it into prominence as Motor City—the one and only. By 1904 Detroit had already established itself as the world's leading auto producer, but it was not until 1908, when Ford's assembly lines produced an *affordable* Model T, that the city attained an unassailable dominance.

In revolutionizing personal transportation, Ford also revolutionized labor, offering a $5 minimum wage for an eight-hour day, thereby launching the largest economic immigration the world had yet seen and creating the ethnic mix that remains Detroit's essential strength today.

DETROIT GOES TO WORK

In 1941 the WPA guide to Michigan described the change the nascent automobile industry brought to the once quiet, tree-shaded city of Detroit.

Bulky Georgian mansions frowned over iron fences on Woodward and Jefferson Avenues and Detroiters took modest pride in calling theirs "the most beautiful city in America." Then came Ford. Not only Ford, but Buick, Durant, R. E. Olds, the Fisher brothers. . . . The automobile, which was to change all America, wrought its first profound changes in Detroit. The city grew at an unprecedented pace, its pulse beat quickening to the staccato rhythm of the riveters, as steel swung into place and grimly functional factories reared up almost overnight. . . . Detroit grew as mining towns grow—fast, impulsive, and indifferent to the superficial niceties of life. Niceties could wait. Meanwhile, there were automobiles to be made.

Detroit rolled up its sleeves and went to work. The old Georgian mansions were converted into rooming houses. Trees were chopped down so that the streets could be widened. The title of "most beautiful city" became hollow. But who cared? . . . Detroit grew. It absorbed suburbs and, when it could not absorb them, grew around them. Young fellows flocked in from the farms of Michigan, Tennessee, Georgia, Poland, Italy, Hungary, Greece—from all over the old and the new world.

Detroit had a special need for young men. The high-speed machines, in which auto parts were cut and shaped, and the throbbing conveyor belts, on which the finished cars were assembled, needed the suppleness of youthful fingers, the nervous alertness of youthful brains, and the stamina of youthful bodies. Detroit needed young men and the young men came.

—Michigan Writers' Project, *Michigan: A Guide to the Wolverine State*, 1941

The workforce of Detroit's Hudson Motor Company in 1909, the year it was founded.

By 1913, 43 auto companies, plus all their attendant parts manufacturers, were operating in Detroit. The following year 26 new auto firms were in production. By 1933, although competition, mergers, and buyouts had reduced that number to only seven—led by Ford, General Motors, and Chrysler—an industrial sprawl was evident across Detroit from the riverfront to the suburbs and nearby towns.

Over the course of its 300 years Detroit has become both hard-bitten and sophisticated. It is a town of dirty fingernails, where assembly-line workers and executives alike take their families to the Detroit Institute of Arts (DIA) to admire Monet's paintings, Rodin's sculptures, and the worker-oriented murals of Diego Rivera. It is still the world's motor capital, and despite its smudges and black eyes, it is a city that has had as profound an effect on American culture as any other in the United States.

■ DETROIT TODAY

There is a saying in this one-industry city: "When the nation catches a cold, Detroit gets pneumonia; when the nation prospers, Detroit is on a boom." Thus it has weathered booms and recessions, depressions, race riots, wars, and strikes that led to the formation of the United Automobile Workers of America and other unions. After the riots of the late 1960s, industrial flight from downtown, and the impact of competition from Japan and Germany, the city seemed caught in an endless downward spiral.

Now, there are signs of an upturn. Although the dread of yet another downturn in the automobile industry lurks in the background, a vibrancy is being felt in Detroit that has not been evident for almost a half century. After decades of talk, new building is finally returning to downtown. The side-by-side **Comerica Park,** home of the Detroit Tigers, and **Ford Field**, where the Detroit Lions play, have spurred some companies to reenter the city. Burned-out hulks of homes from earlier eras are being razed, 21st-century housing and other developments taking their place. The venerable Eastern Market area, where many residents shop for fresh vegetables on Saturday mornings, winter and summer, is getting a face-lift. Nowhere is this renewed vitality more evident than in the area of entertainment. The elegantly restored **Fox Theatre** is a prime example, as are the 14 major downtown theaters and concert halls, among them the recently refurbished **Orchestra Hall**; the elegant **Detroit Opera House,** with an orchestra pit that accommodates 100 musicians; and the **Fisher Theatre**, which hosts the best of Broadway's touring companies.

Along lower Woodward, shops and restaurants are undergoing rapid remodeling. Pocket parks are gracing the streetscape, and other improvements are coming, along with progress on the long-hoped-for Riverwalk. A giant replica of Motor City Madman Ted Nugent's guitar dominates the entrance of the Hard Rock Cafe Detroit, an anchor for the retail shops that include Compuware's new world headquarters on Monroe Street. Rivertown (the city's former warehouse district) and Greektown are still favorite dining destinations for local residents and tourists. On summer weekends Hart Plaza regularly hosts a variety of events. Although some prefer the malls in outlying neighborhoods, downtown specialty stores attract shoppers who come also for the festivals, sporting events, museums, the waterfront, and the casinos.

But perhaps the most significant symbol of Detroit's rebirth is the colossus called the Renaissance Center.

In 1974, with the nation enduring economic recession and an oil embargo, Henry Ford II announced the building of four identical 39-story office towers surrounding a 73-story skyscraper that would soar above the Detroit River and the city like a phoenix rising out of its ashes—the Renaissance Center.

When it was completed, pedestrians along Jefferson Avenue stared up at three-story berms designed to hide exterior heating and cooling systems and saw battlements instead. Despite the architects' attempts to give it a friendly appearance, the RenCen, as it was quickly dubbed, looked like a fort, a walled-off safe zone in the middle of a hostile city. Inside, the design wasn't much more successful. The maze of towers was nearly impossible to navigate. Developers tried everything from color-coded painted lines on the floor to information booths where people could get directions.

General Motors' purchase of the RenCen in 1996 is making an impact on the complex as well as on downtown Detroit. Upgraded building support systems are integrated into the structure itself; the offensive berms have been removed. Offices of General Motors World Headquarters occupy the four smaller towers, while the central tower is occupied by the 72-story Detroit Marriott Renaissance Center, where every guest room is guaranteed a view of downtown Detroit, the Detroit River, or Windsor, Ontario. Shoppers and diners browse among the shops and food court in the building's first- and second-floor atrium. (See "Detroit" in the "Lodging & Restaurants" chapter.) *Jefferson Avenue between Brush Street and Beaubien Boulevard.*

(preceding pages) Ford Field, home of the Detroit Lions, in downtown Detroit. (above) The city skyline, with the RenCen on the right, as seen from the Canadian side of the Detroit River.

■ **RIVERWALK** *map page 51–see inset*
Detroit has ambitious plans for its downtown waterfront; a Riverwalk and a network of parks are now under construction, with completion anticipated in 2006. A highlight of the plan is Tri-Centennial Park, the first new urban green to open to the public in Michigan in more than a century. Eventually two other parks will connect a 3-mile complex of biking and hiking trails that will stretch from Belle Isle's MacArthur Bridge to Joe Louis Arena. Complementing this greening of the waterfront will be a new harbor for cruise ships and pleasure boats, situated near General Motors World Headquarters. A portion of Riverwalk is finished and open and has met with the public's approval, but as for its completion, the initiative has seen so many ups and downs that most Detroiters are assuming an attitude of "wait and see."

■ **MARINERS' CHURCH** *map page 51–see inset*
Remember the line in Canadian singer Gordon Lightfoot's ballad "Wreck of the *Edmund Fitzgerald*," in which he sings about the "maritime sailors' cathedral"? This is it. Nestled amid the noise and hubbub of downtown near the RenCen, this Gothic-style limestone church holds regular Anglican services. Once a year, the Great Lakes fleet is blessed and the *Fitzgerald* remembered. As the song describes, the church's bells echo 29 times along the busy Detroit River, one for each man who went down aboard the ore freighter in 1975. *170 East Jefferson Avenue; 313-259-2206; www.marinerschurchofdetroit.org.*

■ **JOE LOUIS FIST AND STATUE** *map page 51–see inset*
This is quite a sight. Hanging from a 24-foot-high black triangle on the Jefferson Avenue median immediately east of Woodward across from Hart Plaza is a 24-foot-long bronze sculpture of an outstretched muscular arm and clenched fist, directed horizontally toward the river. It's the fist of Joe Louis, former heavyweight boxing champ, who grew up in Detroit. Some say it is a fist of anger; others, a fist of power and pride. Whatever the interpretation, the sculpture effectively communicates the devastating power of the legendary "Brown Bomber." To see a powerful full-view sculpture of Louis, stroll three blocks west to Cobo Center at One Washington Boulevard, where a 12-foot-tall replica of the boxer takes a fighter's stance in the lobby.

The Renaissance Center and the Detroit People Mover.

■ **GREEKTOWN** *map page 51–see inset*

When looking for fun downtown, I inevitably head for Greektown. So named when Greek immigrants laid claim to the area as the nucleus of their community in the 1880s, the city's most popular entertainment district is alive both day and night with tourists as well as city residents. Exuding much the same vibrancy as can be found in faraway Athens, the neighborhood is where elderly gentlemen meet for morning coffee in many small cafés; where grocers sell hard-crusted Greek bread, feta cheese, and Greek wines; and where storekeepers stand on the sidewalk hawking the wares that wait inside.

On a favorite two-block stretch of Monroe Street, you hear "Ooopa!" shouted continually from the numerous Greek restaurants as waiters ignite *saganaki* (flaming cheese appetizers) to the delight of diners. Take your pick of these restaurants; you can hardly go wrong. Other recommendations are included in the lodging and dining section of this book, but here are a few of my favorites:

New Hellas Café

Walk through the glass-and-wood doors and step into the soul of Greektown. Opened in 1901, New Hellas is one of the original Greek restaurants and has been

(above) The Joe Louis Fist in downtown Detroit. (opposite) Catching up on the news in Greektown.

continuously owned by the same family. All the dishes are great, from the appetizers to the braised lamb shanks and rice pilaf. Don't let the idea of marinated squid scare you from trying it—it's terrific. And the *saganaki* here is a must. *583 Monroe Avenue; 313-961-5544.*

Pegasus Taverna
More epic Greek meals await. Try the combo platter of lamb, shrimp, gyro sandwiches, stuffed grape leaves, artichokes, and eggplant. *558 Monroe Avenue; 313-964-6800.*

Fishbone's Rhythm Kitchen Café and Sweet Georgia Brown

New Hellas Café.

Okay, so they're not Greek. But two contrasting restaurants fit in well with the fun. **Fishbone's** (400 Monroe Avenue at Brush Street; 313-965-4600) dishes up spicy and authentic New Orleans–style meals, including jambalaya and alligator appetizers, on tables festooned with several types of hot sauce, from mild to wild. If you're looking for a quiet, romantic spot, go elsewhere, as it can get a bit loud. The upscale **Sweet Georgia Brown** (1045 Brush Street; 313-965-1245) is the newest place to see and be seen. The menu is more lobster tails than Southern fare, until you come to desserts such as Georgia peach cobbler served warm over house-made peach ice cream.

■ DETROIT'S CONEY ISLANDS
About a half dozen blocks from Greektown and west of Woodward, it's "coney" central for Detroit's hometown meal. The original Coney Island hot dog normally just comes with mustard, say the Coney Island folks, who should know. But when it reached Detroit, residents made it into what it is today, so ours is a Detroit original. I can still remember my family heading for our favorite coney place after attending anything from the symphony to the auto show downtown. We'd sit at tables with scenes straight out of Edward Hopper's classic painting *Nighthawks* and listen as waiters in white paper caps and white aprons delivered coneys and bowls of steaming, cumin-laced, meaty chili to our table, accompanied by my favorite drink of choice, Orange Crush, thick with orange flavor and bits of orange dancing in the bubbles.

Two restaurants have been serving 'em up for more than 75 years. Operating almost around the clock since the 1920s, these two places were started by the same Greek family. The only difference between the **Lafayette Coney Island** and the **American Coney Island** is that the Lafayette does not serve beer and now closes four hours of the day. But the American, in addition to serving beer, has a bit more elbow room. Don't be surprised if you're the subject of some friendly competition for business by waiters who often step outside these two neighboring establishments looking to nab the hungry in search of a quick, inexpensive, and tasty meal that has Detroit written all over it.

Inside at a counter stool or table you may rub elbows with prominent lawyers, judges, the cop on the beat, or a visiting celebrity. It's about as eclectic a mix of diners as you'll find anywhere, but everybody knows what to order: a tube steak fixed with onions and mustard—never, never ketchup—and always with chili, slathered on by the counter cook with such dexterity you'd think he'd done it nearly all his life (and some of them have). Or you could get yours with a streak of yellow mustard, topped by a spoonful of onions, if you wish. Or try a combo of a coney and a bowl of chili, thick and spicy, a meaty sauce you can chew. However you order yours, pay attention! It's all done so fast you might miss the show.

Waiters have a unique way of placing your order, shouting it out to the front in their own unique lingo. In coney-ese, "six on four, two no onions, two chilis, and a burger" means six coneys on four plates, two without onions, with two bowls of chili and a hamburger—but not an ordinary pressed burger. Coney burgers are made with loose beef, topped again with chili and served traditionally on a hot-dog bun or sometimes, with a nod to more modern tastes, a burger bun. All finished? Now you have tasted "down-home" Detroit. *Lafayette, 118 West Lafayette Avenue; 313-964-8198. American, 114 West Lafayette Avenue; 313-961-7758.*

■ **BELLE ISLE** *map page 51, F-3*

Floating high like an emerald yacht in the middle of the Detroit River a few miles north of the RenCen, Belle Isle has been in the hearts of Detroiters almost since Cadillac arrived, although their first intention wasn't to make it a park.

Settlers let pigs loose on the island (ostensibly to eat the rattlesnakes there). Then they had to contend with the pigs until city fathers recognized the island's possibilities. In the late 19th century, Frederick Law Olmsted, the designer of Central Park, transformed Hog Island into Belle Isle. It quickly became a 985-acre

playground for the city, where the pigs, long since gone, were supplanted by deer hiding in secluded woods.

Nowadays Detroiters shake their heads at the mention of Belle Isle. In recent years the park has known neglect and felt the pinch of budget cuts. Those with fond memories look to the future when, with any luck, their playground island will find new life.

On the island's south side, the **Dossin Great Lakes Museum** pays homage to the city's nautical past. Two cannons from the War of 1812's Battle of Lake Erie guard the entrance. Inside, you can listen to live communications from passing ships on the radio in the wheelhouse of a former Ford Motor Company ore carrier. *100 Strand Drive; 313-852-4051.*

■ **FISH AND FLOWERS**
It may not be the largest aquarium on the Great Lakes, but the **Belle Isle Aquarium** (313-852-4141) is one of my favorites. Perhaps I feel that way because

(opposite) Fireworks explode above the harbor during the Freedom Festival, behind the head of the Spirit of Detroit *statue. (above) Scott Fountain in Belle Isle Park.*

DETROIT—THE HARD-BOILED POINT OF VIEW

You might call Elmore Leonard the poet laureate of Detroit. Except that he's no poet. The University of Detroit alumnus now living in the suburb of Bloomfield Hills is an ex-advertising copywriter turned crackerjack author of urban-jungle thrillers that manage to be both caustic and comic. What Raymond Chandler did for Los Angeles noir and what Chester Himes did for Harlem, Elmore Leonard and his streetwise cops and misfits do for Detroit. In the excerpt below, one of those misfits, Clement Mansell, tools around town following a crime spree and has a few choice observations about his home turf.

The Detroit River looked like any big-city river with worn-out industrial works and warehouses lining the frontage, ore boats and ocean freighters passing by, a view of Windsor across the way . . . .

But then all of a sudden . . . here were the massive dark-glass tubes of the Renaissance Center, five towers, the tallest one seven hundred feet high, standing like a Buck Rogers monument over downtown. From here on, the riverfront was being purified with plain lines in clean cement, modern structures that reminded Clement a little of Kansas City or Cincinnati—everybody putting their new convention centers and sports arenas out where you could see them. . . . Clement would swivel his gaze then over downtown and come around north—looking at all the parking lots that were like fallow fields among stands of old 1920s office buildings and patches of new cement—past Greektown tucked in down there—he could almost smell the garlic—past the nine-story Detroit Police headquarters, big and ugly, a glimpse of the top floors of the Wayne County jail beyond the police building, and on to the slender rise of the Frank Murphy Hall of Justice, where they had tried to nail Clement's ass one time and failed. Clement liked views from high places after years in the flatlands of Oklahoma and feeling the sky pressing down on him. It was the same sky when you could see it, when it wasn't thick with dampness, but it seemed a lot higher in Detroit.

—Elmore Leonard, *City Primeval: High Noon in Detroit,* 1980

I am a fisherman. Focus is on freshwater fish found in Michigan and others imported from around the world. It also features a coral reef exhibit with stingrays, electric eels, and saltwater species. Next door is the domed **Anna Scripps Whitcomb Conservatory** (313-852-4064), which houses more than 2,000 species of blooming tropical plants. Clumps of orchids dot the pathways. *Conservatory and Inselruhe Avenues.*

■ **AMERICAN POWER BOAT ASSOCIATION GOLD CUP**

Watching a boat speed by at 200 mph down this stretch of the river in early July raises my heartbeat to almost the same speed. Now sponsored by Chrysler Jeep, the race is one of the city's biggest events, drawing close to half a million fans, who watch as a dozen hydroplanes test the waters and themselves.

Hydroplanes are built to skip across the water's surface. Most are powered by jet turbine engines and send rooster-tail sprays high into the sky. They run at around 225 mph in the straits, but the course is trickier than most on the circuit due to the waves that kick up along portions of Belle Isle and cause the craft to bobble and bounce. The races can be viewed for free from a limited stretch of Belle Isle or for a fee from stands and the grass on the mainland. *17640 East Nine Mile Road, Eastpointe; 586-774-2722; www.gold-cup.com.*

■ **CANADIAN NEIGHBOR**

Perhaps it's partly the lure of another country with different customs and different currency, *eh?* Whatever it is, **Windsor, Ontario,** draws me over and under the mile-wide Detroit River time after time. The **Detroit Windsor Tunnel** was a marvel

A hydroplane races in the APBA Gold Cup.

when it opened in 1930, and it remains so—the first and only vehicular subway built between two nations (the "chunnel" between England and France is for trains only). Two pieces of official identification (i.e., passport, driver's license, birth certificate) for passengers of all ages must be shown at both ends. *100 East Jefferson Avenue, next to the Renaissance Center; 313-567-4422; www.dwtunnel.com.*

Return via the **Ambassador Bridge**, completed one year after the tunnel, from which you can see freighters and other traffic coursing up and down the river, and the skyline of Detroit stretching as far as the eye can see. *Porter Street and I-75; 313-849-5244; www.ambassadorbridge.com.*

Windsor dotes on its riverfront parks, especially **Dieppe Park**, graced with gardens and a promenade along the river. While browsing through the Canadian shops with their fine British linens and woolens, remember the duty you may have to pay at customs. (Acquaint yourself with customs rules on refundable VAT tax and tax breaks for longer stays.) Or check out the duty-free shops at both ends of the bridge and tunnel. I recommend the fine restaurants, such as the **Park Terrace** in the Hilton Hotel (277 Riverside Drive West; 519-973-4225), which provides a spectacular view of the Detroit skyline from every table. At the **Mason Girardot Alan Manor** (3202 Peter Street; 519-253-9212), an antiques-filled 1877 Victorian mansion, the chef's Ottoman, Mediterranean, and French cuisine makes good use of fresh herbs and vegetables from the restaurant's own gardens.

■ UNIVERSITY CULTURAL CENTER *map page 51, B-1*

Many of Detroit's cultural attractions are conveniently clustered in an area 4 miles north of downtown, where Wayne State University and the sprawling Detroit Medical Center campus create a mini-downtown known as the University Cultural Center.

Although Detroit isn't spoken of as a Midwestern arts community in the same breath as, say, Chicago, the **Detroit Institute of Arts** is the nation's fifth-largest fine arts museum, with more than 100 galleries devoted to masterpieces from the classical era to the Renaissance, from the Impressionists to contemporary artists. The collections of the Ford family and of other auto tycoons stock the walls, as do traveling exhibits from museums around the world. *5200 Woodward Avenue; 313-833-7900; www.dia.org.*

The **New Detroit Science Center**, one of the top-draw attractions for families with children, is located just behind the DIA. With extended laboratories, new science stages, and an enhanced IMAX Dome Theatre, this is where children of all ages learn how science can be fun. *5020 John R Street; 313-577-8400; www.sciencedetroit.org.*

Sunlight streams through the multifaceted glass-domed ceiling, painting rainbows across the terrazzo floor of the **Charles H. Wright Museum of African-American History.** A three-part multimedia display orients us to eight "historical stations," with images, quotes, facts, statistics, and artifacts that bring to life the centuries-long plight of African-Americans in American history. Some exhibits are painful to examine, such as the replica of Dr. Martin Luther King's Birmingham jail door and a ballot box used by "colored" people. Others are victorious, such as the flight suit of NASA astronaut Mae Jemison. *315 East Warren Avenue, behind the science center; 313-494-5800; www.maah-detroit.com.*

The **Detroit Historical Museum** captures the breadth and scope of the city's history, from Cadillac's landing on the river's banks to the city's ongoing role in industry. There's even an exhibit on now-closed Hudson's department store, once

This 1941 aerial photo shows the Detroit River, with Canada on the left and Detroit on the right. The Ambassador Bridge can be seen in the distance.

(above) Children's Day at the Children's Museum in the Detroit Cultural Center. (opposite) The lobby of the Fox Theatre.

the queen of downtown emporiums. My favorite is "Streets of Old Detroit," a cobblestone walk through history and past reproductions of 17th- and 18th-century shops. Upstairs is the interactive "Motor City" display, which showcases a section of an assembly line where a car body drops onto a chassis. *5401 Woodward Avenue; 313-833-1805; www.detroithistorical.org.*

■ THEATER

Detroit is a great city for theater. From professional companies and college repertories to neighborhood ensembles and comedy troupes, Detroit's stages are alive with everything from opera to Shakespeare.

Opened in 1928, the Fox Theatre was one of the grandest of them all in an era when Hollywood studios owned their own picture palaces. Fortunately, after years of decline, the Fox was rescued from destruction by a $12 million renovation by its current owners, Little Caesar pizza mogul Michael Ilitch and his wife, Marian. Today it's home to the sounds of musicals, concerts, and other programs. The interior, a fusion of Hindu, Persian, and Chinese motifs, resembles a setting for an oriental

spectacular, with faux marble columns, gilt, and elaborately carved gargoyles holding court over the immense 5,000-seat auditorium. *2211 Woodward Avenue; 313-471-3200; www.olympiaentertainment.com.*

Resplendent with marble and decorative works of crystal and bronze, the opulent and remodeled Fisher Theatre is another vintage 1928 movie and vaudeville house that now attracts Broadway plays and their stars for live performances. *3011 West Grand Boulevard; 313-872-1000; www.nederlanderdetroit.com.*

The Gem and Century Theatres, two auditoriums under one roof, have weathered more than a century since 1903 and remained together: through hits and closings, movies and vaudeville, and in 1999 a five-block move through the streets of Detroit to make way for the Ford Field and Comerica Park sports stadiums. The two halls now offer some of the city's best musicals and comedies in an intimate setting. *333 Madison Avenue; 313-963-9800; www.gemtheatre.com.*

■ **BABY, BABY, WHERE DID OUR LOVE GO?**
Are you a fan of the Four Tops, the Temptations, the Supremes? Did you dance to the tunes of the Imperials or Martha Reeves and the Vandellas? They're all remembered at the **Motown Historical Museum** located in "Hitsville USA." A main attraction is Michael Jackson's sequined glove. Check out the two small houses where Berry Gordy Jr. started it all, including the kitchen table where he wrote many of his songs, and the patched-together studio where the Motown Sound was born. *2648 West Grand Boulevard; 313-875-2264; www.motownmuseum.com.*

■ **SPORTS**
From a field that once held the shells of long-neglected 19th-century mansions rises an entertainment complex. For decades both the Detroit Tigers and the Lions played in one stadium, the Tiger Stadium on Michigan Avenue. Now two stadiums provide cheek-by-jowl entertainment from April to December.

Comerica Park is more like a mini-amusement park than a venue for baseball. The 40,000-seat open-air stadium features the league's largest scoreboard, street-level viewing (even sidewalk umpires can call the game), a Ferris wheel, a carousel, and statues of famous players who wore the Olde English "D" on their caps. *2100 Woodward Avenue; 313-471-2000; www.detroittigers.com.*

Ford Field commands an equally dramatic setting for football as defined by the Detroit Lions. Between plays in the 65,000-seat stadium, a giant glass wall affords

MOTOWN: MORE THAN MUSIC

For a particular group of American roughly those born between 1958 and 1968, in or near a Northeastern or Midwestern city, Detroit's most significant product was not a Chevrolet or a Ford or any other car. For us, "Motown"—derived from "Motor City"— calls up visions of scratched-up 45s with faded blue maps on the label, pale blue sequined gowns, and subtle, stylish dance moves. A Motown hit is as likely to be etched in our memory as our first crush. (And in my case, my first crush *was* a Motown star— Michael, youngest of the foxy Jackson 5.)

The Supremes in concert in 1965. From left to right: Florence Ballard, Diana Ross, and Mary Wilson.

Our fandom is strong, but our opinions are not monolithic. For instance, I believe that a life without Stevie Wonder is not worth living, while others say the same of sultry Marvin Gaye. Some prefer Smokey Robinson's vulnerable, sweet falsetto; others, Edwin Starr's angry, percussive bass. When it comes to slick moves, I'd vote hands down for the Temptations, but the Four Tops have their adherents, as do Gladys Knight's pair of Pips. Energetic and earthy types work it out to the Vandellas; the fashionably fabulous prefer to swoon over the Supremes.

For most of us, hearing these songs today inspires fond, sweet recollections; it's hard to resist singing along. The setting in which the Motown Record Corporation came to be, however—the turbulent, racially charged Detroit of the 1960s—reads a little differently from the upbeat memories most of us acquired as children. From its 1958 founding until its 1973 relocation to Los Angeles, Motown was deeply intertwined with both the changing automobile industry and the civil rights movement. The African-American community in which Motown founder Berry Gordy Jr. grew up was one long established in Detroit, largely because of the auto industry. In 1914 Henry Ford announced a $5 daily wage, drawing many black Americans from the South. "I'm goin' to Detroit, get myself a good job/ I'm going to get me a job, up there in Mr. Ford's place" went one frequently played blues tune. The migration resulted in a large black community whose members shared similar backgrounds and musical traditions; they could also commiserate about their dreary jobs—as in Joe L. Carter's lyrics, "Please, Mr. Foreman, slow down your assembly line. No, I don't mind workin', but I do mind dyin'." Blues singer–Chrysler assembler Bobo Jenkins also drew rhythmic inspiration: "That whirlin' machinery gives me the beat. Every song I ever wrote that's any good has come to me standin' on that line."

Likewise, when Berry Gordy Jr. worked a short stint on the line at Ford's Wayne assembly plant, he found himself composing songs to fight the oppressive machine beat. He learned about something else, too: mass production. Seeing shiny new cars roll off the line, one after the other, Gordy realized that the concept could be applied at the record company he hoped to start. And apply it he did. In 1959, with $800 borrowed from his family, he and songwriter partner Raynoma Mayberry Liles rented a converted house on West Grand Boulevard. The highly talented musicians they'd attracted—Gordy, who already managed the Miracles, had a gift for pulling talent—went with them and optimistically dubbed the barebones studio "Hitsville, USA."

This nickname rang true two weeks after they moved in, when their song "Money (That's What I Want)"—an appropriate tune for the ambitious company—hit Number 2 on the charts. While Detroit could claim many companies owned and operated by African-Americans, Berry Gordy's company was the first to aim for and achieve great crossover success. One key was the attention he paid to "packaging" his acts, especially in the case of the Supremes, for whom choreographers, hair and makeup stylists, fashion consultants, even elocutionists were hired to provide the right polish. And befitting a Detroit company, Motown used the auto industry to sell the product. Marvin Gaye posed next to his Cadillac. Martha and the Vandellas were filmed riding in the new Ford Mustang, itself specifically marketed to the vast number of young drivers. Groups were filmed in automobile assembly plants for local appeal. Finally, songwriters paid special attention to the advent of the car radio, writing short songs more likely to be played by radio stations—especially by white radio stations. In 1983, 80 percent of all Mustang purchasers asked for radios in their cars—proof, perhaps, of Motown's marketing savvy.

Meanwhile, ironically, increasing automation in the auto industry was leaving a disproportionate number of African-Americans out of work in this one-industry town. Black Americans were still denied access to the executive ranks and were discriminated against on the job. The civil rights movement, gaining momentum in the South, had different issues to wrestle with in the industrial North. Since 1953, urban renewal projects had demolished 10,000 buildings in the city; 70 percent of the occupants displaced were black. By the early 1960s Detroit's black political action groups were prominently staging protests over job discrimination and segregation.

As the economic clout of Motown Records increased, activists looked to Gordy and his company for support. In 1963 Martin Luther King visited Detroit and led the Great March for Freedom. Berry Gordy recorded King's Detroit speech and released it on Motown's pioneering spoken-word label—Black Forum—just in time for the Great March on Washington. But the words of Detroiter Malcolm X, who spoke in Detroit just a few months later, were too controversial for Black Forum: Malcolm advocated separatism and nationalism, while Motown's political line was integrationist—its financial gains were dependent upon crossover. Nonetheless, in the years that followed Motown became the sound of Detroit of the '60s. Martha and the Vandellas' 1967 hit "Dancing in the Street" became a rallying cry for urban protests, even though its singers insisted it was just a "party song." Later in the decade Stevie Wonder and Marvin Gaye challenged the Motown standard of lightweight hits and created albums of social protest; Edwin Starr's version of "War," contrary to executive predictions, was a smash hit.

While Motown was truly of Detroit, by the end of the 1960s internal differences at the company put it at odds with its community. Although the assassination of Martin Luther King had inspired Gordy and his executives to participate in civil rights causes again, for many this was not enough. The Dodge Revolutionary Union Movement (DRUM) was challenging the status quo in the auto industry and inspiring worker movements all over town. Artists wanted more songwriting freedom as well as more equitable royalty payments. Berry Gordy began to acquire small Detroit-born-and-raised record labels, and in 1973 he moved Motown to Los Angeles. No longer in spirit or place in Motown City, the company was no longer the family it had been. You can even tell by the record label: after the relocation, the map on the label was faded back, with the star marking Detroit barely visible.

—Julia Dillon

The Detroit Tigers at the ballpark in 1908.

an unobstructed view of the Detroit skyline. Ford Field also hosts other sports and non-sports events. (Guess which famous Detroit family owns the team.) *Adams and Brush Streets at St. Antoine; 800-616-7627; www.detroitlions.com.*

■ CASINOS

In the late 1990s Michigan legislators cleared the way for Detroit casinos; bells started flashing on gaming machines right on the heels of the final vote. By the fall of 2000 three casinos with wheels spinning, slots clicking, live entertainment, and dining were in operation near the heart of the city. The art-deco-style **MGM Grand Detroit Casino** (1300 John C. Lodge Drive; 877-888-2121; www.detroit. mgmgrand.com) is reminiscent of Las Vegas and is further enhanced by photos of Hollywood's classic stars. There's live entertainment, and dining ranges from plush to buffet; you can also catch your favorite televised sporting events. The **MotorCity Casino** (2901 Grand River Avenue; 313-237-7711; www. motorcitycasino.com), where the decor is a stylized interpretation of Detroit's industrial history, offers the biggest gaming area; its breakfast buffet, beginning at 2 A.M., tends to attract a younger crowd, who stay and play or enjoy the music.

The **Greektown Casino** (555 East Lafayette Avenue; 888-771-4386; www. greektowncasino.com) gambled on filling the space previously occupied by Trappers' Alley (a four-story marketplace that itself occupied a 19th-century tannery) and it succeeds, evoking the feel of the Greek Islands and the bustle of Greektown just outside its door.

■ **EASTERN MARKET**

Wake with the dawn to join farmers for breakfast at restaurants in **Eastern Market** as they set up their stalls of tomatoes, potatoes, petunias, live chickens, and other market goods fresh from local farms. Then wander through shops of nose-tingling spices, freshly ground coffee beans, and baskets hanging from the rafters. Eastern Market has been a Detroit tradition since 1841. *Russell Street between Mack Avenue and Gratiot Avenue; 586-393-8800; www.easternmarket.org.*

■ **METRO DETROIT** *map page 83*

Detroit is ringed by successful, vibrant suburban communities that stretch for miles. Here are highlights of the best:

■ **DEARBORN** *map page 83, D-4*

In the early 1900s Henry Ford started collecting "things"—no simple collection of stamps or books for this unusual man, but entire homes, farms, and laboratories where inventions had been made that forever left an impact on

Produce stalls at the Eastern Market, shown here in full swing on a Saturday morning.

the world. He set crews to dismantling and shipping his acquisitions to his 90-plus acres of former farmland in Dearborn, and what he couldn't buy he had workmen reproduce in every detail. This collection would become part of the historical experience now known as Greenfield Village; the more portable items went to the Henry Ford Museum next door. Now, with the two sites combined and revitalized, they are collectively called the **Henry Ford**. Besides the village and the museum, the attraction includes an IMAX Theatre, the Benson Ford Research Center, and the Ford Rouge Factory Tour.

Perhaps nowhere else is there such a collection of 19th- and 20th-century Americana as there is in **Greenfield Village,** which preserves more than 80 historic structures that illustrate the country's evolution from a rural to an industrial society. Costumed characters roam the grounds to present old-time medicine shows or other depictions of how life used to be, or at least how we imagine it was. For an introductory overview you can board an authentic steam train or one of Henry Ford's Model Ts, passing reassembled farms including the Firestone complex, where tire inventor Harvey Firestone grew up. In another spot stands a replica of Thomas Edison's Menlo Park laboratory. Ford so revered his camping friends Edison and Firestone—they practically invented the pastime, including what might have been the first recreational vehicle—that during the celebration of the 50th anniversary of the invention of the lightbulb Ford ordered the chair that Edison had sat in nailed to the floor of Edison's studio to exhibit it for all eternity.

Down the street stands the Wright Cycle Co., where the first practical airplane was conceived and built. (The building was imported from Ohio.) Other exhibits include the Suwanee Steamboat, an antique carousel (that still wheezes out a merry tune), and the Eagle Tavern, a former stagecoach inn on the old route between Detroit and Chicago. African-American contributions are remembered with a replica log cabin of inventor George Washington Carver, along with a cabin depicting how slaves lived.

The **Henry Ford Museum,** housed in a building whose facade replicates Philadelphia's Independence Hall, is also dedicated to American life. A highlight is the restored Cleveland Avenue bus that the seamstress Rosa Parks rode in Montgomery, Alabama, on December 1, 1955. A volunteer is usually on hand to tell the story of how Parks boarded the yellow-and-white bus, never dreaming that this was the day she would refuse to give up her seat to a white passenger and spark the civil rights movement that changed America. The surge and pull of soaring aircraft are nearly palpable at the "Heroes of the Sky" permanent exhibit, a salute to America's first century of aviation, with 15 history-making planes displayed as though in flight. Calling attention to aviation's first 40 years are replicas of the Wright brothers' flyer and Charles Lindbergh's *Spirit of St. Louis.* In "The Automobile in American Life," a ramp guides visitors past a moving caravan of the automobile's development, represented by more than 100 classic models, including the only surviving 1896 Duryea—the first mass-produced vehicle made in the nation—and the Ford GT cars that swept Le Mans. A replica of a drive-in, an original vintage service station, and an original classic roadside diner in gleaming chrome are in this building, along with an example of one of the first Holiday Inns. The museum includes some of the equipment used by Ford and his camping cronies Thomas Edison, Harvey Firestone, and John Burroughs. Other displays include the Lincoln in which John F. Kennedy was riding when he was assassinated, as well as the rocking chair in which Abraham Lincoln was sitting when he was shot.

A replica of Thomas Edison's laboratory stands in Greenfield Village.

(above) Henry Ford, circa 1925. (opposite) An exhibit at the Henry Ford Museum.

For the first time since 1980, the **Ford Rouge Factory Tour** is again being conducted. Developed between 1917 and 1928, the Ford Rouge plant was designed for the manufacture of automobiles from "raw ore to assembly," with everything done on site, and became one of the world's largest automotive complexes. The two-hour tours, which begin with a 15-minute bus ride from the Henry Ford Museum to Ford Rouge, take in historic landmarks, videos, and a walking tour above the assembly line where Ford F-150s are made. Reservations are recommended.

To reach the Henry Ford from downtown Detroit, take Jefferson Avenue east and merge onto John C. Lodge Freeway north, then west on I–94 to Dearborn Avenue and Oakwood Boulevard. *20900 Oakwood Boulevard; 313-982-6100; www.thehenryford.com.*

Fair Lane

Henry Ford grew up in Dearborn. After making his vast fortune—and wanting a more private place than his Detroit mansion—he returned to Dearborn to build an estate, Fair Lane, beside the Rouge River a few miles upstream from the Ford Rouge complex and 2 miles from his birthplace. The 56-room home, built in 1914 of Ohio limestone, resembles an English castle in overall design, but in its Prairie School architectural details it shows the influence of Frank Lloyd Wright, who had been the architect originally chosen. (Wright's personal life intervened when he eloped to Europe with his new bride, and the project was taken over by his former student Marion Mahony Griffin.) Although it was not as lavish as some mansions of its time—Ford and his wife insisted on moderation—intricately carved wall panelings were done in mahogany and oak and, oddly, the home was built with seven bedrooms and 15 baths. Today some of the furnishings on display are original. Tours of the mansion and grounds include the restored and working river powerhouse that provides electricity to the mansion. The 1920s camper Ford used

Henry Ford: An American Magnate

In every sense of the word, Henry Ford was a complex man. On the one hand, he may have contributed more than any other individual besides his friend and mentor Thomas Edison to the reality of the modern world. On the other hand, he fought to suppress and control a society that would remain forever at arm's length. He could be talkative and entertaining but could suddenly stop in mid-sentence and blurt out, "That's not what I was thinking at all," excusing himself to disappear into his laboratory, sometimes for days, until he emerged with a new engine element, new car design, factory layout, rail locomotive, or other pioneering idea.

Born on July 30, 1863, in Dearborn, he was the oldest of six children born to first-generation Irish farmers William and Mary Litogot O'Hern Ford. Not rich but far from poor, the family fared well. Ford's legendary curiosity was demonstrated at an early age. Fascinated by the vapors rising from the boiling water in the tea kettle on the kitchen stove, Henry plugged up the spout. With no outlet for the steam, the kettle exploded, shooting hot water in all directions. His practical side began as he tinkered with farm tools. He was fond of recounting the July day in 1876 when he saw his first self-propelled steam engine working a farmer's field.

Fifty years later Ford was producing 57 percent of the automobiles sold in the United States and around half the cars sold worldwide. As an adult Ford allowed no one to use his first name, but he was proud to affix his last name to the affordable Model T and Model A automobiles. The slender 5-foot, 9-inch, long-legged industrialist baffled even those who knew him best. When he set the industrial world on edge with his production line for the Model T, paying $5 for an eight-hour workday, he built nearby housing complexes where workers lived to keep his factories moving. Workers grumbled at Ford rules that came with living there. Inspectors knocked at regular intervals, inquiring into lifestyles with questions that some took as intrusive. As in other matters, it was Ford's way or no way.

In 1915, as World War I dragged on, Ford's political leanings led him to finance a pacifist expedition and lease the sailing ship *Oscar II*, which he proclaimed the "Peace Ship." On December 4 he boarded her and set sail for Norway on a self-proclaimed mission to end the war, pledging to be "home by Christmas." The effort failed, but Ford later said, "At least I tried." Years later, with the advent of World War II, his pacifism took a backseat to full-out, one-an-hour factory production of B-24 "Liberator" bombers at Willow Run.

In 1916 the *Chicago Tribune* attributed to Ford the incorrect information that employees who left their jobs to serve in the National Guard would lose their jobs.

The next day a *Tribune* editorial followed up by calling him an "ignorant idealist." Ford sued, and the trial—staged in Mount Clemens—made headlines around the world. Well aware of Ford's lack of interest beyond the inventive, experts drilled him for hours about his general knowledge. He saw little value in the drills, since he said he could pay workers to locate such information for him in five minutes. Badgered by lawyers, with journalists frantically taking notes, Ford calmly sat in the witness chair, his long legs crossed as he sharpened his pocket knife absently on the bottom of his leather shoe. When asked what this nation was before its discovery by the Europeans, he kept sharpening his knife and without a glance upward, said, "Dirt, I guess." The jury settled against the *Tribune,* but awarded Ford only six cents in damages.

The common people loved his folksy responses—and bought more Fords. After the trial Ford seemed more conscious of education and history. He built schools, experimental farms, small-town factories, and hospitals. He developed an obsessive collection of historical memorabilia, and housed it in the Henry Ford Museum and Greenfield Village at Dearborn. An avid camper, Ford took long auto trips—in Model Ts, with a Japanese chef—with Thomas Edison, Harvey Firestone, and naturalist John Burroughs. An avid hiker, he was out morning and afternoon, ending the day around a campfire telling rambling stories and tall tales.

Exasperated with the newspapers of the day, he published his own *Dearborn Independent,* in which he aired his anti-Semitic and anti-labor views. In 1933 Ford led the fight against the fledgling United Auto Workers (UAW) unionization efforts led by Walter Reuther. Hiring an army ironically called the Service Department (some claim it numbered up to 2,000), Ford took on the union organizers. In 1937, the conflict erupted in the "Battle of the Overpass," where Ford's goons viciously attacked Reuther and other UAW officials who were handing out union flyers near a Ford plant gate. Photojournalists captured the incident, and it outraged the nation. Courts ordered Ford to cease interfering with union activities, and the UAW contract was signed in 1941.

Ford was notorious for avoiding his office, preferring instead the noise and clatter of his assembly line. To escape the social whirl of Detroit, he built his Fair Lane estate at Dearborn. Then, prompted by his love of dancing, he organized grand balls that were the rage of society. In 1945 Ford's grandson, Henry II, took his 81-year-old grandfather to Greenfield Village and watched him climb aboard his original "quadricycle" horseless carriage for a ride along the streets of the man-made colonial America. In 1947 the man who idolized Thomas Edison and his electric lightbulb, the man who did the most to create the world on wheels, died quietly by candlelight.

with friends Edison and Firestone is on display, as is a prototype electric car Ford built with Edison. A walking tour meanders through the restored gardens created by renowned designer Jens Jensen. *4901 Evergreen Road at the southern end of the University of Michigan-Dearborn campus; 313-593-5590; www.henryfordestate.com.*

■ ROYAL OAK *map page 83, D-4*

Opened in 1928, the **Detroit Zoo** was nationally acclaimed and copied for its barrier-free exhibits that use dry or water moats to keep animals confined and thus provide better views. Make reservations in advance for the trackless train and a narrated tour around the 125-acre grounds—it's a great ride.

The newest exhibit to open is the 4.2-acre "Arctic Ring of Life," in which visitors watch bears cavort through a 70-foot-long clear underwater tunnel, the world's only underwater Polar Passage. The Arctic tundra is re-created with an open sea and pack ice as well as an Inuit village of the early 1900s. In 2004, as part of the zoo's breeding program, Norton, a 17-year-old, 800-pound Polar, came calling with honorable intentions and wistful eyes toward Barle, a fetching 17-year-old female. Other favorite exhibits include the Penguinarium and the Chimps of Harambee (where visitors can view chimpanzees in natural settings and up close from blinds); among the new galleries are an aquarium with Pacific Ocean fish, and a butterfly-and-hummingbird garden. *From downtown, take I-75 north to I-696 and watch for the zoo signs near the Woodward Avenue exit. Ten Mile Road and Woodward Avenue; 248-398-0900; www.detroitzoo.com.*

■ BLOOMFIELD HILLS *map page 83, C-3*

Cranbrook Educational Community, in suburban Bloomfield Hills, is my favorite place to visit in the area north of Royal Oak. There is much to see, especially the 40-acre gardens built by George Gough Booth and Ellen Scripps Booth, both part of the *Detroit News* editorial families. Their personal interests are reflected in educational institutions they established here at Cranbrook: **Cranbrook Art Museum,** which focuses on exhibits of contemporary works; private schools; and the **Institute of Science,** among whose natural science displays are many rare specimens, including Michigan's only skeleton of Tyrannosaurus rex. I am captivated by the house and gardens, both of which are National Historic Landmarks. Designed in 1908 for the Booths by Albert Kahn, the house follows the English Arts and Crafts style, with much detailed hand-carved woodwork, and is furnished with centuries-old tapestries and antiques. Sculptures, stone walls, brooks, waterfalls, pools, and paths fill the gardens. Tours and lectures are available. *39211 Woodward Avenue; 877-462-7262; wwwcranbrook.edu.*

■ TRAVEL BASICS

City Overview: Renovation and construction in Michigan's major urban center, the result of vigorous efforts to breathe fresh life into a downtown that fell victim to years of neglect, are ongoing, but there remain areas you'll still prefer to avoid. Check with your hotel or your hosts before heading out, and use normal caution when venturing away from well-lit beaten paths, whether in a car or on foot. Strolls downtown along the Riverwalk and around the Renaissance Center provide some fascinating vistas, and Detroit's museums are second to none. *www.visitdetroit.com.*
Getting Around: Outside Metro Detroit you'll need a car, but not downtown. Instead, take the People Mover—an elevated trolley that makes a 3-mile loop around the heart of the city, with stops at the RenCen, the Theater District, and Greektown, among others. Downtown is a maze of one-way streets, so pick up a good map or board one of the metro buses that resemble old-fashioned trolleys.

If you're driving, it's a good idea to learn the so-called "mile" roads that run east to west, beginning with 5 Mile Road, at that distance from the center of the city, and increasing with each mile up to 26 Mile, at the north end of the suburbs. The **Metropolitan Detroit International Airport,** 21 miles from downtown, is serviced mainly by limousines from the big hotels. *www.metroairport.com.*
Weather: Summers in Detroit are hot and humid, with temperatures averaging in the mid- to high 80s Fahrenheit; yes, it can rain, so bring your umbrella. Winters are not so much cold as they are wet and mushy, so be sure to bring your galoshes. Spring and fall tend to be balmy, inviting long walks along the Detroit River.

Because Detroit is a major metropolis, you can count on finding good restaurants and good hotels. *Refer to our list of suggested lodgings and restaurants beginning on page 274.*

S O U T H E A S T

Attracted by the flat terrain and rich soil, homesteaders began arriving in southeast Michigan in the early 1800s. They were soon followed by timbermen who, having exhausted the forests of the Northeast, were attracted to the vast tracts of Michigan white pine.

In 1835, as it sought statehood, Michigan claimed a piece of land on its southern border that Ohio (which had become a state in 1803) claimed as well. The bit of saber rattling that ensued revolved around an eight-mile-wide slice of land at the mouth of the Maumee River. Known as the Toledo Strip, this stretch of land formed the northern edge of the Black Swamp—a daunting, virtually impassable morass about 40 miles wide and 100 miles long (long since drained and built over). However, both Michigan and Ohio believed it would become the launching point for future inland development. (And they were right: today I-80, the nation's great bilateral highway, cuts right through the strip.)

A contemporary drawing allegedly depicting the River Raisin massacre in 1813.

"REMEMBER THE RIVER RAISIN"

During the War of 1812, the newly independent United States was pitted against its former master, Great Britain, which had allied itself with Tecumseh and his great Indian Confederation. The British held two strategic and critical forts: River Raisin, in Frenchtown (now Monroe), and Detroit. In January 1813 an American colonel, William Lewis, led 700 men, mostly Kentuckians, against the British at River Raisin. Crossing from Toledo under heavy fire over frozen Lake Erie, he captured the fort.

Fearing British reprisal, Lewis sent for reinforcements from his superior, Gen. James Winchester, who crossed over with 300 additional troops. Winchester, however, chose to billet them and himself across the river from the fort in order to stay in the comfortable house of a well-to-do Frenchman. So comfortable was he, in fact, that he failed to leave his warm lodgings after receiving word that the British were about to attack the fort. Before daylight on January 22 the British did so, and before Lewis's Kentuckians had time to form, they were set upon by the British and their Tecumseh-led Indian allies with devastating results. The tardy Winchester was turned back, many of his troops killed and scalped, and he himself captured. But the deadly fire of the Kentuckians from within the stockade forced the British to retreat.

It was a standoff, with many dead and wounded on both sides. The British commander, Col. Henry Proctor, convinced the Americans to surrender under the pretense that he could not prevent his Indian allies from wreaking havoc on civilians, even though Tecumseh was famous for his compassion toward prisoners and the wounded. Promised that the wounded would be protected by British soldiers and placed in the care of the Frenchtown civilians, Lewis capitulated, and Proctor marched his prisoners north toward Fort Malden in Canada. Early in the morning of January 23, however, about 200 whiskey-inflamed Indians—who historians believe were "opportunists" and not an integral part of Tecumseh's Confederation—swept through the village, murdering and scalping. Having found most of the wounded in two houses, they set the houses afire, hurling those who tried to escape back into the flames. The display of cruelty stunned the American forces, whose rallying cry "Remember the River Raisin" kept battlefield hatred for the British ablaze until the end of the war.

Seeking to resolve the conflict, Congress offered up a shotgun marriage—Michigan and Arkansas were to be admitted simultaneously into the Union on condition that Michigan recognize Ohio's claim to the Toledo Strip. To compensate Michigan for its loss, Congress tossed in the Upper Peninsula—then part of the Wisconsin Territory. Appalled and insulted by the offer, one Michigan senator scoffed that the Upper Peninsula "could furnish the people of Michigan with Indians for all time and now and then a little bear meat for delicacy." But the "U.P." would come to be seen as the most lucrative concession ever granted to an individual state.

The rush to statehood had been spurred by a congressional decree that all states admitted to the Union by January 1, 1837, would receive a launch grant of $400,000. While most Michigan politicians decried the proposal, a small group of Michigan delegates sneaked off to Ann Arbor and grudgingly acceded to it (illegally, some declared later)—in the nick of time to collect the bonus.

What Wisconsin thought of the loss of the Upper Peninsula, as colossal fortunes were reaped from its mineral riches, has not been recorded.

■ MONROE *map page 83, C-5*

In 1780 the French set up a trading post along the stream they named River Raisin after the heavy clusters of grapes that hung over the banks. A few French settlers built log cabins here, a community dubbed Frenchtown by the British. In 1835 Frenchtown changed its name to Monroe in anticipation of a visit by President James Monroe (1817–25). Today, alas, Monroe could be Any City, with its service turnoffs and strip malls. However, there are places of interest, and the downtown area is sprucing itself up with brick-paved streets and new shops.

Custer Statue and Museum
At the Monroe Street Bridge (which crosses over the Raisin in downtown Monroe) stands a bronze equestrian statue of Lt. Col. George Armstrong Custer of Little Big Horn fame. Monroe was Custer's home town, and the **Monroe County Historical Museum** contains ample quantities of Custer memorabilia. *126 South Monroe Street; 734-240-7780; www.co.monroe.mi.us/monroe.*

River Raisin Battlefield
In 1813, when the British were challenging the fledgling United States, a regiment of Kentuckians captured the British fort at River Raisin. The ensuing battle to retake the fort ended as a decisive defeat for the Americans and a massacre during which hundreds of them lost their lives. Two large wall maps on display at the

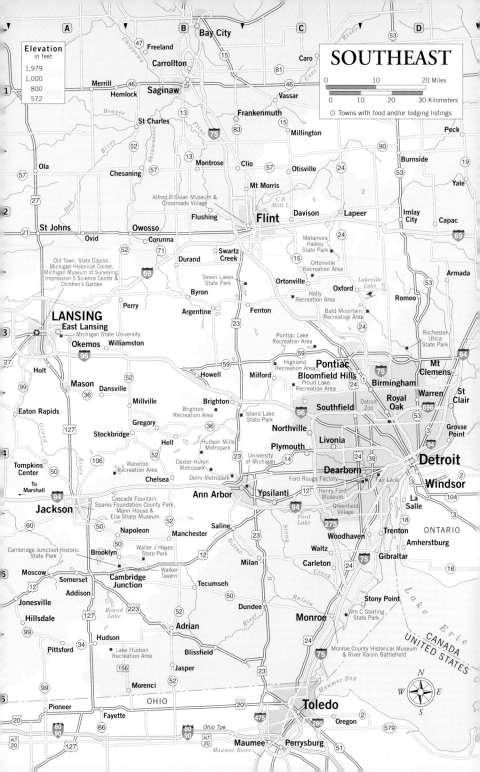

River Raisin Battlefield Visitor Center depict the ebb and flow of the battle. Recorded narrative and the clever use of fiber-optic lights embedded in the maps pinpoint the critical events that took place. Open weekends only, Memorial Day to Labor Day. *1403 East Elm Avenue; 734-243-7136.*

Shores of Lake Erie

The River Raisin is a twisting, turning river with reeds along its banks and low sand dunes where families picnic. Beyond the river, Lake Erie's gray-green waters beckon. Once declared dead, these waters have rebounded so successfully that they now provide some of the best walleye fishing in the country. "It's walleyes from May through July, then perch from mid-August through early November," explains Capt. J. M. Ulrich, owner of Trade Winds Sportfishing, a three-boat operation. *Erie Party Store and Dock; 6838 La Plaisance Road; 734-243-2319; www. tradewindscharter.com.*

Wm. C. Sterling State Park

After a recent $12 million renovation, the park now offers campgrounds along the lakeshore, upgraded fishing facilities, and many other improvements. Although smokestacks are visible both north and south, the marshes are splendid, especially when you're armed (and legged!) with bug repellent. Occasional lotus blossoms raise their snowy faces to the passersby, just as they did for the explorers who paddled past these sands 300 years ago. East from Exit 17 on Dixie Highway North and follow the signs. *2800 State Park Road; 734-289-2715; www.dnr.state. mi.us/parksandtrails.*

For information, contact: *Monroe County Convention & Visitors Bureau; 106 West Front Street; 800-252-3011; www.monroeinfo.com.*

■ STICKY MUD, PLANK ROADS, AND OAK OPENINGS

Settlers heading west from Monroe in the 1820s and 1830s faced more than 20 miles of tough going over the ancient beds of Lake Erie, which in earlier times had been as much as 230 feet higher than it is now but had retreated over the aeons, leaving behind an expanse of territory eroded into ridges and swales. Although not as bad as the Black Swamp around Toledo, Ohio, the route was full of wheel-shattering potholes and wagon-miring mud. Travelers formed small trains, affording them enough horse- and manpower to pull wagons out of the mud when they were trapped. Soon the trail was littered with household goods tossed aside to lighten their loads.

After such a struggle, the higher ground west of Adrian must have seemed a godsend to the settlers. Here, postglacial beach ridges had formed into flat regions called lakeplains, topped with mature oak trees whose limbs spread into canopied patterns shading the tallgrass prairie below. Light could not penetrate the canopies, so no undergrowth had developed to encumber travel—a blessing for the settlers compared with the swamplands around Toledo and parts of southern Michigan nearer the lake. These areas, called oak openings because of their stands of oaks, are part of a unique ecosystem of rare plants and animals that exists primarily in Michigan and Ohio and once covered millions of acres. When Michigan's first European settlers arrived, they covered about 20 percent of the territory that is now the state, but—threatened by modern farm practices and urbanization that alter the landscape and the high water table—just over 1,000 acres remain today, largely in southeast Michigan's Monroe, Wayne, and St. Clair counties.

Although some settlers stayed among the tall oaks, others journeyed farther west to the higher hills of northern hardwood forest around what is now Cambridge Junction, southeast of Jackson. This area reminded the Irish among them of their homeland, prompting them to call the hills the Irish Hills. Lush green in spring and ablaze with the red, bronze, and gold of autumn's glory in October, the Irish Hills are favored with the rich soil that marks the southern edge of the glacial drift from the last ice age.

■ **WALKER TAVERN** *map page 83, A-5*
At the junction of U.S. 12 and M-50 near Cambridge Junction stands the Walker Tavern, which was built in 1836 and served as a stagecoach stop along the Chicago Road until 1855. While the stage driver changed horses, travelers taking the five-day journey got out, enjoyed a meal, or spent a night in the two-story farmhouse. The Walker Tavern Historic Complex is open from June through August. *3220 M-50; 517-467-4401.*

■ **JACKSON** *map page 83, A-4*

In 1854, a much-ballyhooed new political party convened in Jackson with a fundamental goal: eliminating slavery in the territories. Several thousand men showed up (remember, this was 70 years before women's suffrage). The overflow crowd spilled into the street, and with temperatures skyrocketing in the meeting hall, the convention was hastily reconvened "under the oaks" at a place called Morgan's Forty just outside town. Before the sun had set, a party platform was drafted, a statewide slate of candidates was named, and the Republican party was born. Die-hard Republicans come to see the commemorative boulder and Michigan Historical Marker at what is now called Under the Oaks Park, and a museum is planned. *Second and Franklin Streets.*

■ **JACKSON AREA HIGHLIGHTS**

Cascade Fountain

The 465-acre Sparks Foundation County Park features the Cascade Fountain, a stair-step series of 18 waterfalls in six varying heights and

The Walker Tavern served as a rest stop for stagecoach passengers on the Chicago Road.

patterns built into the 500-foot hillside. It's especially attractive at night, when the fountain becomes a light show with a musical background. Open Memorial Day through Labor Day. *Follow brown Cascades Park signs; 517-788-4320.*

Ella Sharp Museum

With its pioneer-style log cabin, Victorian house and barn, and vintage carriages and sleighs, the Ella Sharp Museum is an evocative reminder of 19th-century farm life. The museum also houses three art galleries. *3225 Fourth Street; 517-787-2320; www.ellasharp.org.*

Mann House

Twelve miles west of Jackson on M-60, in the village of Concord is another historic farm. Daniel and Ellen Mann built this two-story, eight-room house in 1883 and furnished it with pieces dating from the 1840s. Visit the herb gardens and the restored Victorian Rose Garden. Open Wednesdays through Sundays, June through August. *205 Hanover Street; 517-524-8943.*

For more information: *Jackson Convention & Tourist Bureau; 6007 Ann Arbor Road; 517-764-4440; www.jackson-mich.org.*

■ **LANSING** *map page 83, A-3*

When visiting Lansing, look for the state capitol on the skyline, with its dome and spire rising 267 feet. Adjacent is East Lansing, home to Michigan State University. Together these two towns are beehives of state offices, restaurants, taverns, shops, and museums.

INTO THE WOODS

The region was, in one sense, wild, though it offered a picture that was not without some of the strongest and most pleasing features of civilization. The country was what is termed "rolling," from some fancied resemblance to the surface of the ocean, when it is just undulating with a long "ground-swell."

Although wooded, it was not, as the American forest is wont to grow, with tail straight trees towering toward the light, but with intervals between the low oaks that were scattered profusely over the view, and with much of that air of negligence that one is apt to see in grounds where art is made to assume the character of nature. The trees, with very few exceptions, were what is called the "burr- oak," a small variety of a very extensive genus; and the spaces between them, always irregular, and often of singular beauty, have obtained the name of "openings"; the two terms combined giving their appellation to this particular species of native forest, under the name of "Oak Openings."

—James Fenimore Cooper, *Oak Openings*, 1848

■ **LOOKING BACK**

From the beginning, Michigan politicians seem to have been cast from a different mold. When the Michigan Territory was formed in 1805, Lewis Cass was appointed governor. He got along well with the Indians (his whiskey barrel had no bottom), appointed capable men to conduct a state survey, spread the word to would-be settlers, and set Michigan on the way to settlement.

It was a time of several hot and divisive issues. For example, which city would be Michigan's capital? Since its beginnings, the capital of the Michigan Territory had been Detroit. But Detroit's distance from much of the state—as well as its proximity to the potentially hostile British and their Indian allies across the river in Canada—prompted legislators to seek a more central site. Such a wrangle! Almost every town and village from Calumet to Marshall vied for the honor, and probably Marshall tried the hardest. As legislators argued, Marshall's city fathers built mansions they believed fitting for a state capital—including some on wannabe Capitol Hill that are historic treasures today.

When Ingham County representative Joseph H. Kilborne proposed that the capital be sited in the Township of Lansing, legislators hooted at the idea. What was there? In 1837, a German tailor, Jacob Frederick Cooley, had claimed a plot of ground on the south bank of the Grand River. He liked the river, especially at the rapids, and had cleared some land and built a cabin for his family. A few other pioneers settled nearby, and they built a sawmill at the rapids to cut lumber for their homes. Ten years later, 88 souls were living in a 36-square-mile area around Cooley's cabin. That was Lansing.

Yet with the pressing deadline—a capital had to be declared by 1847—Lansing won the honor, largely because it was favored by no particular party.

State workers, politicians, lawyers, and storekeepers arrived together to construct the new town and hastily built a wooden statehouse. Legislators trudged to the capital amid stumps, fallen trees, and mud. They found lodging either with local residents or on the capitol floor. Within a few years, in 1855, Michigan Agricultural College (now Michigan State University) was founded. A brick capitol building replaced the wooden structure and was dedicated in 1879.

■ SEEING LANSING

Old Town
Somewhat off the beaten path in the north part of town, **Old Town** is a mix of art galleries, gift shops, and restaurants; festivals are held here during the summer months.

State Capitol
Restored in 1992, this dome- and wing-style building was constructed of slate, white pine, and copper. The rotunda rises three stories, with balconies on its perimeter. Woodwork in the Senate chamber gleams when sunbeams stream through the skylight. Now a national landmark, the building was one of the first state capitols to follow the design of the U.S. Capitol in Washington, D.C. *Capitol and Michigan Avenues; 517-373-2353; www.michigan.gov/hal.*

While in the area, visit the **Michigan Supreme Court Learning Center** for a hands-on introduction to the judicial branch of state government. *925 West Ottawa Street; 517-373-7729; www.courts.michigan.gov/plc.*

Six Horticultural Demonstration Gardens surround the Plant and Soil Sciences Building and its teaching greenhouses on the Michigan State University campus in East Lansing.

The Michigan State Capitol in winter.

Michigan Historical Center

This architecturally elegant complex houses the **Michigan Library,** the **Michigan Archives**, the **Michigan Historical Museum**, and the open-air **Rotunda,** with its three-story living white pine. The Historical Center features 26 permanent galleries on four levels, with interactive displays and dioramas portraying the state's history from early Native American times through the present. A meandering tour guides you through re-creations of an Upper Peninsula copper mine, 1920s village streets, and a lumber camp. *702 West Kalamazoo Street; 517-373-3559.*

Michigan Museum of Surveying

This fine small museum presents the history of Michigan's surveyors, who with a minimum of supplies spent months on end imposing order on the wilderness. They fought blackflies, deerflies, mosquitoes, and swarming no-see-ums whose bites stung like nettles. A favorite display is the famous "solar compass" invented by U.S. Deputy Surveyor William Austin Burt to circumvent the magnetic effect of the iron mountains of the Upper Peninsula. *220 South Museum Drive; 517-484-6605; www.surveyhistory.org.*

Impression 5 Science Center
Reminiscent of a mad scientist's lab, this museum offers more than 200 hands-on science exhibits. The century-old building with its original wood floors and brick walls is the perfect setting for kids of all ages to touch, feel, hear, smell, and watch to their hearts' content. *200 Museum Drive; 517-485-8116; www.impression5.org.*

Michigan State University
In 1855 the first land-grant college in the nation was created, with the stipulation that it be located within 10 miles of Lansing. Originally called the Michigan Agricultural College, the school had an enrollment during its first year of 81 students, who began classes in May 1857 and also worked four hours each day on the college farm. Today students at Michigan State University number more than 43,000, many of whom study hotel, restaurant, and institutional management. *U.S. 27 to East Lansing, take Trowbridge Road exit and proceed east on Trowbridge Road; 517-355-1855; www.msu.edu.*

On the university's campus are two museums. The **MSU Museum** (West Circle Drive; 517-353-9834; www.museum.msu.edu) is a quintessential university museum, housed in an ivy-draped building that seems right for the three floors of natural- and cultural-history exhibits found inside. Tours are available, or you can wander among the dinosaur skeletons and

A dormitory on the Michigan State University campus in springtime.

listen to the audiovisual presentations. In the Kresge Art Center, the **Kresge Art Museum** (Auditorium and Physics Roads; 517-353-9834; www.msu.edu/unit/kamuseum) mounts exhibits that span more than 5,000 years of art history, placing on view art objects from prehistoric times to the present.

Michigan 4-H Children's Garden

So the family has had its fill of museums and it's ready for a change! The kids are not the only ones who will enjoy the flowers, oversized nursery characters, and games at this institution. After a romp through the garden, drop in at the university's dairy store for the freshest of ice cream. *Corner of Wilson Road and Bogue Street; 517-353-6692; www.4hgarden.msu.edu.*

■ FLINT *map page 83, C-2*

In 1830, when John Todd found trader Jacob Smith living at the rapids where the Pontiac Trail intersects the Flint River, he was inspired to build a tavern and start a ferry for traffic crossing the river. With this meeting of two strangers, the city of Flint was born. In 1837, when Michigan became a state, a land office was added to the growing community, and more settlers moved in.

Flint, as photographed circa 1900, promoted itself as the "Vehicle City."

FLINT'S OUTSPOKEN SON—MICHAEL MOORE

In the mid-1950s, the civic leaders of Flint, Michigan, threw a fiftieth-birthday bash in honor of the city's largest employer, General Motors. The parade that marched through downtown Flint featured TV celebrities on floats, and its theme was "Promise for the Future."

In the mid-1980s, GM president Roger Smith announced the closing of Flint factories that employed almost 30,000 people—workers who were advised not to expect further prospects for employment by their former company.

For investigative journalist and Flint native Michael Moore, whose father had worked for GM for 33 years, the massive layoffs that devastated Flint's economy were a disgrace. "We enjoyed a prosperity that working people around the world had never seen before," Moore observes in his 1989 documentary, *Roger and Me,* "and the city was grateful to the company."

Not after the layoffs. Holding Roger Smith personally accountable, Moore set off to confront Smith face to face at GM's Detroit headquarters. His quest was ultimately unsuccessful—Smith was well insulated from those whom his executive decisions had outraged. The pursuit itself became the basis of *Roger and Me,* which made Moore's name virtually synonymous with mischievous, muckraking satire on behalf of working-class stiffs plowed under by corporate greed.

In Moore's book *Downsize This!* he writes: "I'm not talking about legitimate layoffs when a company is losing money and simply doesn't have the cash reserves to pay its workers. I'm talking about companies like GM, AT&T, and GE, which fire people at a time when the company is making record profits."

Parades still march down Flint's main drag, and the city carries on, but the factory closings of two decades ago appear to have dealt a mortal blow to the prosperity of this self-proclaimed "comeback city." Moore revisits his hometown in his later film *Fahrenheit 9/11,* in which military recruiters are shown targeting young African-Americans, offering a grimly tantalizing alternative to chronic unemployment: if there's no work for them in Flint, the United States Marine Corps will find a job for them—on the front lines.

—John Morrone

Crossroads Village and Huckleberry Railroad, circa 1900.

Lumbering was the area's first industry. Logs could be floated down the river from where they were harvested to the mills in Saginaw, but getting them from the forest across the boggy ground to the rivers was a problem. Thus ingenuity came into play, resulting in the invention of big-wheel, horse-pulled, log-hauling equipment capable of moving heavy logs overland. Flint was soon manufacturing big wheels, wagons, and road carts, and in 1868, as the lumber industry declined, turned toward the manufacture of carriages. Eighteen years later William ("Billy") C. Durant and partner J. Dallas Dort founded the Durant-Dort Carriage Company, the precursor to General Motors. GM would set Flint on the road to becoming the second-largest manufacturer of automobiles in the world, after Detroit.

Alfred P. Sloan Museum

This museum traces the history of Flint, with emphasis on regional history and the Buicks, Chevrolets, and other automobiles built in Flint's General Motors plants. More than 600 artifacts are displayed in addition to the many antique automobiles. *1221 East Kearsley Street; 810-237-3450; www.sloanmuseum.com.*

A MICHIGAN AUTOMOBILE TIMELINE

1890 A young Henry Ford builds a Silent Otto Engine from scratch.

1895 Ransom E. Olds patents a "gas or vapor engine" and changes the name of his father's Lansing carriage shop to the Olds Gasoline Engine Works.

1896 Henry Ford knocks out bricks to widen the door of his shop to make room for his "quadricycle," in which he toodles around his Detroit home.

1899 Ransom E. Olds establishes the Olds Motor Works in Lansing. Henry Ford finds investors and creates the Detroit Automobile Company. David Dunbar Buick invests the profits from the sale of his plumbing company in a new venture: the Buick Auto-Vim and Power Company in Flint.

1900 Ford collapses the Detroit Automobile Company, where he attempted to build one car at a time, blaming the failure on his investors, whose "main idea seemed to be to get money."
The Olds Motor Works relocates to Detroit and calls its products Oldsmobiles.

1901 The Olds Motor Works burns down, forcing Olds back to Lansing, where he employs subcontractors who, in turn, are later inspired to form their own companies to manufacture their own vehicles, among them Cadillac, Maxwell, and Dodge.

1903 Ford gathers other investors for his new enterprise: the Ford Motor Company.

1904 The first Buick leaves the plant in Flint. William C. Durant takes control of the company, leaving David Buick with one share of common stock. Ransom E. Olds sells his stock in the Olds Motor Works and founds Reo Motor Company, naming it after himself.

1905 Vincent Bryan and Gus Edwards compose the song "In My Merry Oldsmobile" in honor of the popular one-cylinder Curved Dash Runabout.

1908 Producing 1,400 cars per month, Buick's Flint plant is heralded as the world's largest.
William C. Durant sells the Buick Motor Company to his own new enterprise, the General Motors Company, then buys the Olds Motor Works and the Cadillac Motor Company.

1909 Henry Ford produces the Model T, the "Tin Lizzie" that puts America on wheels and ultimately changes the world forever.

1914 The first Dodge is manufactured by brothers John and Horace Dodge.

1924 Walter P. Chrysler creates the Chrysler Corporation and buys the Dodge Brothers Motor Company.

1937   Invoking "Unionism, Not Fordism," a 30-year-old Walter Reuther is assaulted by Ford-employed goons in full view of press photographers. The so-called Battle of the Overpass marks the birth of the United Auto Workers union.

1941   The Willys Jeep (short for GP, or General Purpose vehicle) is launched. Developed for war, it comes to stand for fun and adventure.

1949   The Volkswagen "beetle" arrives in America.

1952   A fiberglass-bodied Chevrolet Corvette prototype emerges unscathed from an accident during a test run. Fiberglass is chosen for the new sports car's body.

1954   The American Motors Corporation (AMC) is formed by combining the Nash Motor Company and the Hudson Motor Car Company.

1956   Ford launches the new mid-size car—and calls it the Edsel.

1959   Faced with near-total public rejection, Ford discontinues the Edsel.

1964   Pontiac releases the first "muscle car," the 389-cubic-inch, 325 hp V-8 GTO.

1964   Ford introduces the Mustang, and General Manager Lee A. Iacocca becomes a household name for backing the new concept of a compact sports car at affordable prices.

1965   Ralph Nader publishes *Unsafe at Any Speed,* targeting General Motors; soon afterward, Congress enacts new auto safety standards.

1973   The VW beetle becomes the most popular car ever produced, outselling Henry Ford's Model T.

1978   Lee A. Iacocca leaves the Ford Motor Company to become head of Chrysler.

1984   The Jeep Cherokee is introduced—the nation's first sport-utility vehicle (SUV).

1998   Daimler-Benz of Germany purchases Chrysler Corporation for $92 billion. Ford introduces the Lincoln Navigator SUV—5,470 lbs curbweight, measuring 75.2 inches high, 79.9 inches wide, and 204.8 inches long, and getting 12 mpg city, 20.7 mpg highway.
       The California Air Resources Board designates SUVs automobiles and requires that they be held to the same emission standards as cars.

2000   Amid record profits, GM admits that SUV sales have exceeded car sales but argues that Corporate Average Fuel Economy standards should remain frozen at 20.7 mpg for SUVs and 27.5 mpg for cars.

2001   GM Pontiac celebrates its 75th anniversary.

2002   Chevrolet's Corvette marks its 50th year, while Buick and Cadillac mark their 100th anniversary.

2003   Ford Motor Company celebrates a century of automobile production.

2004   The last Oldsmobile rolls off the assembly line in Lansing, after 107 years of production.

Mott Lake

Located on the shores of Mott Lake (named for the Mott family, General Motors' largest shareholders) just north of Flint are the 34 historic buildings and shops of the restored **Crossroads Village.** Wandering through here is like walking back to the 1860s. Michigan's oldest operating gristmill creaks and groans, and the steam-powered **Huckleberry Railroad** blasts its whistle at crossings as it winds through the village. The perfect way to conclude your visit is a lazy, water-slapping cruise of the lake on the *Genesee Belle,* a paddle-wheel riverboat that departs from the village. *6140 Bray Road; 800-648-7275; www.geneseecountyparks.org.*

For more information: *Flint Area Convention & Visitors Bureau, 316 Water Street; 800-253-5468; www.flint.org.*

■ TRAVEL BASICS

Area Overview: Monroe, Jackson, Lansing, and Flint are the main urban centers of southeast Michigan, each circled by small towns where citizens enjoy a relaxing Midwest suburban style of life. The state capital, Lansing, rests at the intersection of Interstates 96 and 69, in the middle of farmland and forest—a patchwork pattern that continues north and northeast to Bay City. The best time to visit is from late March to November.

Travel: The highways in this part of Michigan are a rough grid of interstates, with the long, lazy diagonal of U.S. 12 (the old Chicago Road) stretching from Michiana at the Indiana-Michigan border to downtown Detroit. Major airports are in Detroit, Flint, and Lansing.

Weather: Summers average between 85 and 90 degrees F and are humid and warm. Fall and spring are similar in temperature, ranging from 65 to 75 with lows in the 50s. Winters average in the upper 30s and drop to the 20s but rarely fall below zero, even on winter nights.

Food & Lodging: Cuisine in these parts is mostly fast food. However, many small-town diners and B&B breakfasts can be pleasantly surprising. *Refer to the listings beginning on page 274.*

A N N   A R B O R

by Dan Stivers

Ann Arbor, since 1837 the home of the University of Michigan, is a pleasant, sprawling city. Less than an hour west of Detroit along I-94, 30 minutes or so east of Jackson, and about a half hour north of Ohio along U.S. 23, "A-Squared" (or "A²"), as it's known to the locals, is seen by some Michigan residents as hip and energetic. Others see it as pretentious and galling. A head football coach at Michigan's other Big Ten school, East Lansing's Michigan State University (eternally battling an inferiority complex with regard to its sister to the south), once referred to University of Michigan adherents as "those arrogant asses."

Whatever others think, Ann Arborites—almost 115,000 of Washtenaw County's approximately 323,000 permanent residents—obviously enjoy living in one of Michigan's most comfortable, cosmopolitan, and intellectually stimulating environments. Money magazine consistently ranks Ann Arbor among the nation's most livable cities—although real-estate listings show it to be one of Michigan's priciest. Thanks in part to the think-tank atmosphere of the U of M, and in part to a recent growth spurt that pumped new energy into local businesses and manufacturing, Ann Arbor is one of the Midwest's leading centers of high technology and research.

Once an isolated world amid the cornfields of Michigan—and still seen that way by many—Ann Arbor has begun spreading its influence throughout neighboring small towns. Saline, Dexter, Chelsea, even the tiny Michigan town actually called Hell, are finding themselves little more than satellites to dynamic A².

Is this welcome? Feelings are divided. As a teenager growing up in Dexter, the first town northeast of Ann Arbor and home of the fearsome Dexter Dreadnaughts, I welcomed the film societies, student parties, and general sense of activity that prevailed just 8 miles up Dexter–Ann Arbor Road (named because it links Dexter and Ann Arbor; other imaginatively named roads leading out of Dexter are Dexter-Pinckney and Dexter-Chelsea—both honoring a local farmer because they really didn't lead much of anywhere).

Other residents, however, decry the "Ann Arborization" of such towns. As acre upon acre of farm fields leading to Ann Arbor becomes subdivisioned, and as auto

The Ann Arbor Art Fair on State Street.

parts stores in the hearts of small towns morph into quirky little galleries and coffeehouses, many longtime residents smell something noxious seeping under the door: progress, that very same devil they moved here to escape. And they don't like it one bit.

Should they? Many of these proud little towns trace their lineages back further than even Ann Arbor itself. Tractors pulling wagons of just-picked corn still creep down Main Street. Homecoming queens are still crowned at halftime. Weekly newspapers discuss whose sheds were broken into, and volunteer firemen risk their lives for their neighbors. So far, these small-town citizens remain reluctant to trade their laid-back Midwestern lifestyle for the rush of the mainstream "big daddy" next door.

■ HISTORY

In the fall of 1823, John Allen, a "well-proportioned and physically grand specimen of a man," rode out of Virginia with a herd of cattle and a hunger for fortune. Left behind were a new wife, Ann, and a pile of unpaid debts. No record of the cattle's fate survives, but Allen's ambitious wanderings over the next few months led him to Detroit. There, in January 1824, he met Elisha Rumsey, a New Englander and fellow fortune hunter.

(above) This lithograph shows the University of Michigan at Ann Arbor in 1874, about 30 years after it opened for classes. (opposite) The Huron River runs through Gallup Park.

Deciding that their best chance at wealth lay a few miles west of already-bustling Detroit, Allen and Rumsey rode a one-horse sleigh on a scouting trip deep into the newly minted county of Washtenaw. Little more than a month after shaking hands, the two entrepreneurs strode into the U.S. Land Office in Detroit, stomped the snow from their boots, and purchased 640 acres along the Huron River.

John Allen.

Luck appears to have been on their side, as territorial governor Lewis Cass quickly anointed their tract as the county seat. On May 25, 1824, the town plot was registered as Annarbour—in honor of Allen's and Rumsey's wives, both named Ann, who the men hoped would one day meet each other under a grape arbor.

The village grew quickly. In early June, Allen and Rumsey placed advertisements for their new town in Detroit's main newspaper. Before long several houses were under construction, two sawmills were operating, and a gristmill was on the drawing board. In autumn Ann Allen left her beloved Virginia behind and made the two-month journey to her namesake town, grudgingly moving with her husband into a two-room blockhouse.

As increasing numbers of settlers arrived, Ann Arbor's social, religious, political, and economic foundations developed around them. In 1825 John Allen built a crude log building at the northwest corner of Main and Ann streets and opened Ann Arbor's first school, funded by assessments paid only by parents who chose to have their children educated. Also in 1825, the civic-minded Allen—one can't help but wonder whether it was with Ann's blessing—opened his home for Methodist services held by itinerant clergyman John Boughman. This was followed in 1826 by a Presbyterian congregation whose organizers usurped the log schoolhouse. Thomas Simpson founded Ann Arbor's first newspaper, the *Western Emigrant,* in 1829, largely supported at first through notices placed by the village's doctors and lawyers.

By 1837, with John Allen's little village thriving and having been declared the county seat, Michigan's legislature named Ann Arbor the new home of the University of Michigan. A land company was formed, and the fledgling university was given 40 acres east of State Street. The university opened with five buildings in 1841, and its first graduates received their diplomas in 1845.

John Allen—and Ann Arbor—never looked back.

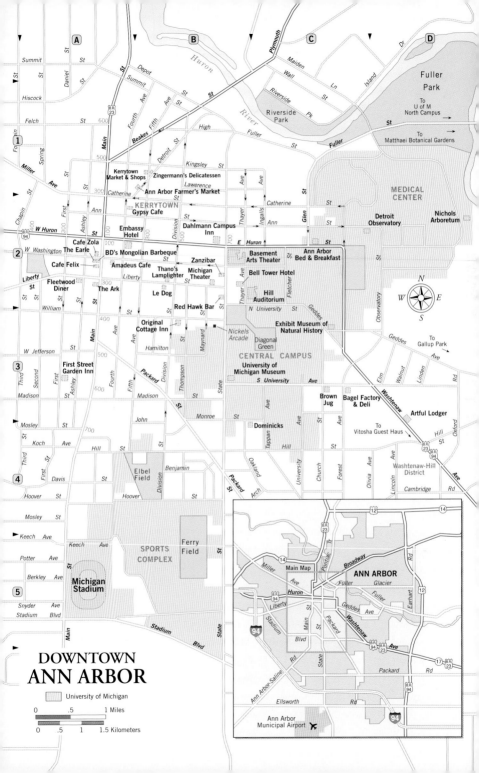

A   **B**   **C**   **D**

Summit St
Daniel St
Hiscock St
Felch St

Depot St
Summit St
Fourth Ave
Fifth Ave

Huron River

Plymouth Rd
Maiden Ln
Wall St
Riverside Pk
Island Dr

Fuller Park

To U of M
North Campus

To Matthaei Botanical Gardens

1

Fox
Spring St
Chapin St
Miller Ave
Main St
First St
Beakes St
Fifth St
Detroit St

High St
Fuller St
Kingsley St
Glen St

Fuller

MEDICAL CENTER

W Huron St

Kerrytown Market & Shops
Zingermann's Delicatessen
Ann Arbor Farmer's Market

Lawrence St
Catherine St

Detroit Observatory
Nichols Arboretum

KERRYTOWN
Gypsy Cafe

Thayer St
Ingalls St
Ann St
Catherine St

Embassy Hotel
Dahlmann Campus Inn

Division St

E Huron St

2

W Washington St
Cafe Zola
The Earle
BD's Mongolian Barbeque
Cafe Felix
Amadeus Cafe
Liberty St
Fleetwood Diner
The Ark
Thano's Lamplighter
Michigan Theater
Le Dog
Red Hawk Bar
William St

Basement Arts Theater
Zanzibar

Ann Arbor Bed & Breakfast

Bell Tower Hotel
Hill Auditorium
N University Ave
Fletcher St

Observatory St

Geddes

N
W E
S

Original Cottage Inn
Hamilton

Nickels Arcade
Diagonal Green
Exhibit Museum of Natural History

To Gallup Park

W Jefferson St

CENTRAL CAMPUS

Geddes Ave

3

First Street Garden Inn
Madison St
Third St
Second St
First St
Ashley St
Fourth Ave
Fifth Ave
Packard St
Division St
Thompson St
Madison St

University of Michigan Museum
S University Ave

State St

Brown Jug
Bagel Factory & Deli
Artful Lodger

Elm St
Walnut St
Linden St
Rd

Washtenaw Ave

John St
Monroe St
Dominicks
Tappan Ave
Hill St
University Ave
Church St
Forest Ave

To Vitosha Guest Haus

Washtenaw-Hill District

Oxford Rd
Hill St

4

Mosley St
Koch Ave
Third St
First St
Davis Ave
Hill St
Benjamin St
Elbel Field
Division St
Hoover St

Oakland Ave
Arch St

Olivia Ave
Lincoln Ave
Cambridge Rd

Hoover St

Mosley St
Keech Ave
Potter Ave
Berkley Ave

Keech Ave

SPORTS COMPLEX

Ferry Field

State St

5

Snyder Ave
Stadium Blvd

Michigan Stadium

Main St
Stadium Blvd

Packard Rd
State St

DOWNTOWN
ANN ARBOR

▨ University of Michigan

0   .5   1 Miles
0   .5   1   1.5 Kilometers

(inset map)

12
14
23
Main Map
Broadway
ANN ARBOR
Miller
Pontiac Tr
Ave
Fuller
Glacier
12
94
Huron
Liberty
Geddes Ave
Earhart Rd
94
Stadium Rd
Main St
Packard St
Washtenaw Ave
23
17 23
Blvd
23
94
Packard Rd
Ann Arbor-Saline Rd
State St
Ellsworth Rd
94
Ann Arbor Municipal Airport ✈

■ Ann Arbor Today

You can find virtually anything you want in or near Ann Arbor today—generally within a 20-minute drive. Are you looking for a cosmopolitan yet comfortable atmosphere? Ann Arbor's square mile or so of downtown, lazily meandering east until it dissolves into the University of Michigan's world-class campus, will fill that bill.

Theater? Any city that's cleared a space for the likes of U of M will, of course, have cleared space for theater. For traditional productions, try the **Performance Network** (120 East Huron Street; 734-663-0681) or the **Ann Arbor Civic Theatre** (322 West Ann Street; 734-971-0605), and for more experimental or innovative fare there's the student-run **U of M Basement Arts Theater** (105 South State Street; 734-764-6800).

Music? Leon Redbone cut his chops at the **Ark** (316 South Main Street; 734-761-1451; www.theark.org), a 1970s folk institution where Bob Seger banged out his first chords. Rock bars abound—this is, after all, a college town through and

ANN ARBOR ART FAIR

This annual fine-art free-for-all, held in a downtown that is closed to traffic, is Ann Arbor's biggest party. Spread over four days in mid-July, it is in fact huge: huge in reputation, huge in its throngs of art-loving attendees, huge in frustration and disappointment for those artists who watch streams of passersby glance at their works and quickly, wordlessly move on.

The event is actually four art fairs in one, each with its own sponsor. The original, juried **Ann Arbor Street Art Fair** (734-994-5260; www.artfair.org), begun in 1960 and one of the top-ranking arts festivals in the nation, takes place around the university's Burton Carillon Tower, on North University Avenue, Thayer Street, and East Washington Street. The **Ann Arbor Summer Art Fair** (734-662-3382; www.michiganguild.org), dating from 1970 and the largest of the fairs, runs along Main Street and a section of State Street. The **State Street Area Art Fair** (734-663-6511; www.a2state.com) runs along Liberty Street, and **Ann Arbor's South University Art Fair** (734-663-5300; www.a2southu.com/artfair.php), the newest event, dating from 2000, runs along South University Avenue. This annual ode to art covers about 25 city blocks and attracts more than 500,000 visitors. Street musicians abound, demonstrations of technique are given on every corner, and you are dared to leave without buying *something*.

Traffic snarl-ups in the area of the fair may have some drivers pounding the steering wheel and screaming bloody vengeance, but parking is still generally available for a price. Shuttles run from local mall parking lots, but you can always take your chances and drive straight in. Enduring—and enjoying—the madness of the art fair only to end the day waiting in line for a shuttle bus is never much fun, not when a $10 spot within easy walking distance might be found.

Expect crowds, expect "No Vacancy" signs, and expect to be overwhelmed.

through—where, for a small cover charge, you can listen to the raucous dreams of starry-eyed local kids.

Art? If you haven't heard of the **Ann Arbor Art Fair**, drop in around mid-July and fasten your seat belt.

Shopping? Downtown is thriving with art galleries, boutiques, thrift shops, clothing emporia, drive-through convenience stores, and other types of retail fun.

Let's take a closer look.

Main Street is lined with cafés and restaurants, many of which offer outdoor dining in warm-weather months.

■ **MAIN STREET** *map page 103, A-2*

The Main Street area (at most six blocks long) has few chain retailers and an abundance of art galleries and shops, many of them open well into the evening for the dining crowd.

The interesting pieces at **16 Hands** (216 South Main Street; 734-761-1110; www.16handsgallery.com) range from crafts to furniture to fine arts. **Gallery Von Glahn** (319 South Main Street; 734-663-7215; www.galleryvonglahn.com) is an upscale gallery showing original hand-signed serigraphs and lithographs by established artists, bronze sculptures, fine porcelain, and other decorative arts. **Overmyer's Gallery** (120 East Liberty Street; 734-213-3822) features lithographs, photographs, posters, and limited editions. Also worth a look are **Selo-Shevel Gallery** (301 South Main Street; 774-761-4620; www.seloshevelgallery.com), for imported folk art as well as the works of American artists, and the gallery and special exhibitions at the **Ann Arbor Art Center** (117 West Liberty Street; 734-994-8004; www.annarborartcenter.org).

At **Peaceable Kingdom,** a toy store with nary a GI Joe in sight, the highlight for many browsers is the middle aisle: bin after bin of cheap gewgaws, windup shuffling frogs, pencil sharpeners in the shape of a nose—guess where the pencil goes— and the like. *210 South Main Street; 734-668-7886.*

A trolley used to run down the middle of Main Street, as shown in this wintertime photo, taken around 1890.

The Ann Arbor Bicycle Club, circa 1887.

■ **KERRYTOWN** *map page 103, A/B-1/2*

Ann Arbor's hot **Kerrytown District** is just steps north of Huron and east of Main at the northwest corner of the University of Michigan. Only a few square blocks in total area, Kerrytown could well be a little city in itself. Along tree-lined streets of the original village of Ann Arbor, attractions include a museum, an art gallery, shops, restaurants, delis, the Kerrytown Concert House, and three historic brick and cobblestone buildings that make up **Kerrytown Market and Shops.** Connected by enclosed walkways, courtyards, and mini-parks, the market is a transformation of former warehouses dating back to 1874 that originally stored lumber, feed, and grain—all colorfully renovated.

In the **Kerrytown Market and Shops** it's almost as much fun to browse as to buy, with almost 20 shops from which to choose. Among the fine food markets are **Monahan's Seafood Market** and **Sparrow Meat Markets,** as well as **Partners in Wine and Cheese** and **Durham's Tracklements & Smokery.** Shoppers can obtain top-quality cookware at **Kitchen Port.** Cool kiddy delights you won't find at Toys-R-Us are featured at the fun, eclectic **Mudpuddles.** *407 North Fifth Avenue; 734-662-5008; www.kerrytown.com.*

The Tour De Kids bicycle race takes place annually in Ann Arbor.

The **Ann Arbor Farmer's Market** is the place that started all the excitement in Kerrytown. Farmers began selling produce here in 1900. The open markets sell everything from potatoes and onions to petunias and sunflowers on Saturdays and Wednesdays from May through December. On Sundays during those months, local artisans take over the space to peddle their own unique, affordable goods. *315 Detroit Street; 734-994-3276.*

If you're in the market for reusables and truly want to take home a memento of Ann Arbor, then choose something that's lived there for a while. Secondhand shops such as **Treasure Mart** (529 Detroit Street; 734-662-9887) and the **Tree** (419 Detroit Street; 734-663-2008) sell cast-off flotsam and jetsam, from used corduroys to ceramic mallards. When the Treasure Mart's fascinating warehouse-like space can't hold all the stuff the owners have collected, it spills out into the driveway. A place to relax after bargain hunting is **Gypsy Café** (214 North Fourth Avenue; 734-994-3940), which offers up art, poetry, coffee, and plenty of atmosphere.

Eating Out

Zingerman's Delicatessen is Ann Arbor's home of the stacked meat deli sandwich. Packed all day long, the place provides a taste of the New York deli experience—down to the Brooklyn Egg Cream that, explains the hand-lettered sign, "Contains

Neither Eggs nor Cream." Seating is haphazard and minimal (although the seating annex called Zingerman's Next Door offers additional options), so grab the first open table you see and hold on for dear life. *422 Detroit Street; 734-663-3354; www.zingermans.com.*

■ **STATE AND LIBERTY STREETS** *map page 103, B-2*

The area around Liberty and State streets, several blocks east of Main Street and south of Kerrytown, has a character all its own, shaped by its proximity to the U of M campus. There are new- and used-record stores aplenty. The original **Borders Books** (612 East Liberty Street; 734-668-7652), where today's national chain got its start, and secondhand- and rare-book havens such as **West Side Book Shop** (113 West Liberty Street; 734-995-1891), reward the curious browser. Pokémon addicts can feed their joneses and pick up a video or two at **Wizzywig Collectibles** (529 East Liberty Street; 734-213-1112).

The **Michigan Theater**—formerly the cavernous State Theater, now divided into two screens and restored to something like its original 1927 glory by the city—is the haunt of choice for local cinephiles. *233 South State Street; 734-761-8667.*

The Michigan Theater is Ann Arbor's most famous art-house cinema.

One especially interesting retail feature of this area is **Nickels Arcade**, a glass-covered passage between State and Maynard streets that offers a unique, hit-or-miss hodgepodge of shops.

Eating Spots
See Food & Lodging, page 274, for addresses, phone numbers, and additional options.
While numerous pizza places signal the proximity of students, you can't ignore the Original Cottage Inn. Don't be fooled by recent renovations—this is the same classic deep-dish pizza that Mom and Dad scarfed down in their undergrad days.

Thano's Lamplighter comes close to Cottage Inn's landmark status, serving a late-night menu that ranges from Greek specialties to, of course, deep-dish pizza. At **Red Hawk Bar & Grill,** half-pound burgers and varietal microbrews go great with the roasted red pepper bisque du jour, inexpensive enough for students yet satisfactory for just about anyone else. The two-story "pantropical bistro" **Zanzibar**—medium on the prices, high on the spices—blends Thai, African, Indian, and South American flavors into an eclectic mix.

And while **Le Dog** may be the only hot-dog stand this side of L.A. that serves bouillabaisse and lobster bisque alongside its franks, **Victors**—in the **Dahlmann Campus Inn**—offers up meat and potatoes, seafood, and other favorites, for the more traditional palate.

Lodging
See Food & Lodging, page 274, for addresses, phone numbers, and additional options.
The **Dahlmann Campus Inn** mentioned above vies with the **Bell Tower Hotel** as the most centrally located luxury hotel, and you'll pay upwards of $150 a night at either for the convenience. The Campus's outdoor pool will ease the pain during the summer months, though few parents of undergrads will be found lounging poolside. The Bell Tower has no pool but compensates with its warmth and charm. Among more moderate accommodations, the nearby Ann Arbor Bed & Breakfast is another worthwhile choice.

■ UNIVERSITY OF MICHIGAN CENTRAL CAMPUS *map page 103, C-3*

It's one of the nation's top ten universities, it's big, and its presence is pervasive throughout Ann Arbor, but so far you've just been skirting the U of M—which is a mistake, because its campus is a fine place to visit. Following the tree-shaded paths that wind through it will take you to world-class museums stocked with treasures from art to zoology. *734-764-4636; www.umich.edu.*

The wide-ranging permanent collection of the **University of Michigan Museum of Art,** at the corner of South State Street and South University Avenue, encompasses some 17,000 pieces of American, European, and African art, not to mention Asian art, in which the museum is especially strong. The special exhibitions alone are worth the price of admission—and would be even if admission weren't free. (Still, you should make a donation of at least a buck or two.) *525 South State Street; 734-764-0395; www.umma.umich.edu.*

The U of M **Exhibit Museum of Natural History** is essentially a smaller version of its Chicago counterpart, with massive displays of dinosaur and mastodon skeletons and special exhibits on Native American life. Again, it's *technically* free, but you should make a donation. *1109 Geddes Avenue; 734-764-0478; www.exhibits. lsa.umich.edu.*

My favorite stop is the **Detroit Observatory,** which has dominated a hilltop overlooking the northeast edge of the campus since 1854. Rope pulleys rotate the viewing dome, and original instruments still read the skies. In their time period, the refracting telescopes were among the largest in the world. *1398 East Ann Street; 734-763-2230; www.detroitobservatory.umich.edu.*

The main quad on the University of Michigan campus.

East of Central Campus you can hike to the hills or stay in the valleys at the 123-acre **Nichols Arboretum**. Both native Michigan plants and plants from around the world are cultivated at this peaceful escape, which is also a satisfying place for bird-watchers. *1610 Washington Heights; 734-998-9540; www.umich. edu/~wwwarb.*

In summer, a stroll through Ann Arbor's neighborhoods is a rewarding garden walk in itself, as tiny city lots are transformed by enterprising gardeners into sprays of color. But in bloom year-round is the good-sized indoor conservatory of the **Matthaei Botanical Gardens,** where the flora is divided according to climatic regions. Located about 8 miles northeast of downtown, the Matthaei's grounds feature 350 acres of woodlands, wetlands, ponds, and theme gardens. If quiet beauty is your thing, a few hours here are well spent. *1800 North Dixboro Road; 734-998-7061; www.lsa.umich.edu/mbg.*

■ **MICHIGAN STADIUM** *map page 103, A-5*
You wanna talk football? 'Scuse me, you wanna talk *football?* The U of M is known to play a mean game, and on a crisp, sunny autumn afternoon this is the place

The Asian collection at the University of Michigan Museum of Art.

where any "Go Blue" fan *has* to be. Built in 1927 to hold 72,000 fans, the nation's largest college-owned stadium now seats more than 107,000, from shy three-year-olds taking in the spectacle to lunatic, screaming face painters hoping to attract attention on national TV. Consistently sold out and leading the nation in attendance virtually every season, this place hasn't seen a crowd of fewer than 100,000 in at least 25 years. Deceptively small and looking like nothing more than still another college building with a stately, brick-facade exterior, the stadium becomes a sunken-bowl spectacle once you step through the gates. Surrounded by lawns and houses instead of asphalt, it is one of a kind. *Main Street and Stadium Boulevard.*

Eating Out

See Food & Lodging, page 274, for addresses, phone numbers, and additional options.
Since 1928 the **Brown Jug**, on South University Avenue, has been a favorite of students, faculty, townies, and anybody else looking for good food and drink. It's one of the few places where you can get a homemade hot turkey sandwich and coffee while your friend orders chili cheese fries and tequila. The walls are covered with decades of random snapshots.

Around the block is **Dominick's**, where outdoor seating has been raised to an art form. Whether you sit packed along the sidewalk or in the quieter, oddly charming courtyard complete with fountain constructed out of an unused (we hope) headstone, you'll have to admit that the time-honored sandwiches and pizza are just okay, and what keeps you coming back is the terrific atmosphere.

Lodging

See Food & Lodging, page 274, for addresses, phone numbers, and additional options.
Two distinctive establishments are within shouting distance of each other on busy Washtenaw Avenue. The **Vitosha Guest Haus** is a chalet-style home dating from 1917. Its 10 restored rooms offer private baths, fireplaces, and a healthy dose of Arts and Crafts charm. The **Artful Lodger** is a breathtaking 1859 Italianate Victorian home, topped with a cupola. Its four guest rooms come with private baths, off-street parking, and an eclectic theatrical decorating theme.

■ FAIRS AND FESTIVALS

Ann Arbor Antiques Market

From April through November, the third Sunday of the month brings more than 350 booths featuring every imaginable old thing, some priced quite reasonably, some quite ludicrously. It's fun to look and the food is good. *Washtenaw Farm Council Grounds, 5055 Ann Arbor Saline Road; 850-349-9766; www. annarborantiquesmarket.com.*

Ann Arbor Blues and Jazz Festival

Held after Labor Day, the Ann Arbor Blues and Jazz Festival is an outdoor affair that since 1969 has featured hundreds of world-class artists, among them Miles Davis, Muddy Waters, Ray Charles, and Bonnie Raitt. Events are held at various locations. *734-763-8587; www.a2.blues. jazzfest.org.*

Ann Arbor Book Festival

The Ann Arbor Book Festival (held at various locations) sponsors symposia, lectures, and authors' readings as part of its

Michigan Stadium is the largest college-owned stadium in the United States, able to seat more than 107,000 Wolverine fans.

drive to promote reading and call attention to literacy-related concerns. One significant element of the festival is the **Ann Arbor Antiquarian Book Fair** (530 South State Street). Since 1976 book dealers from throughout the Midwest have flocked to the event, which benefits the University of Michigan's William L. Clements Library. *734-662-7407; www.aabookfestival.org.*

Ann Arbor Film Festival

The Michigan Theater plays host to the annual Ann Arbor Film Festival, much of which is strictly for film buffs, although even the casual viewer can enjoy seeing independent or experimental films that won't turn up at the local multiplex. *734-995-5356; www.aafilmfest.org.*

Ann Arbor Folk Festival

This celebration of folk music benefits the nationally venerated Ark, Ann Arbor's nonprofit home for acoustic music, and generally brings out some big names. Emmylou Harris and Ralph Stanley headlined the 2004 show, held in comfortable Hill Auditorium in the heart of the campus. *734-761-1451; www.theark.org.*

■ YPSILANTI *map page 83, C-4*

No guide to Ann Arbor would be complete without mentioning Ypsilanti, its smaller sister city directly to the east. Often mispronounced *Yip*-silanti instead of the correct *Ip*-silanti, the city officially began its life as the settlement of Woodruff's Grove in 1823. Over the years, "Ypsi" (as it's affectionately called) became the home of Eastern Michigan University, the birthplace of S&H Green Stamps, and the spot selected by the Monahan brothers to open their first Domino's Pizza store. Victorian homes can be found throughout the city and especially along Geddes Road.

At the beginning of World War II, Henry Ford built a bomber plant just east of town at Willow Run. By the end of 1944 workers were rolling B-24 Liberators off the assembly lines at a rate of one per hour. Total production for the war years was 8,685. At war's end, the bomber factory and complex were sold to a succession of automobile manufacturers who produced Kaiser-Frazer products, Chevrolet Corvairs, and others. The complex, now called Willow Run Airport, is used for charter services, cargo, and general aviation.

Depot Town and Cross Street

Although the 1864 brick railroad depot alongside the tracks at Cross Street stands empty and neglected, it furnishes a name to charming Depot Town, which has streets lined with restored 19th- and early-20th-century buildings now occupied by shops and restaurants. Museums and summer parades of historic autos give reminders of the area's contribution to the aircraft and automobile industries. *www.depottown.org.*

Yankee Air Museum

Housed in a hangar at Willow Run Airport, formerly used by pilots flying out the World War II aircraft made in the factory here, the museum traces history with flyable craft and others under restoration. The massive B-52 Stratofortress is on display, along with a 5-105 Thunderchief that flew with the United States Air Force Thunderbirds, a Bell Huey UH-1 helicopter, and numerous others. From April through October you can book a flight on board a B-17G for a 40-minute area tour. Reservations are required. *2041 A Street, Belleville; 734-483-4030; www. yankeeairmuseum.org.*

Ypsilanti Automotive Heritage Museum

At the east end of Depot Town you can see antique cars, learn about Ypsi's role in the development of the auto industry, and discover more about the "other guys": Hudson, Tucker, Kaiser, and Frazer. Next door is Miller Motors Hudson, the world's last Hudson automobile dealership, with more antique cars. *100 East Cross Street; 734-482-5200; www.ypsiautoheritage.org.*

Cruise Night

Thursday night in Depot Town has become Cruise Night, a regular event sponsored by the Ypsilanti Automotive Heritage Museum, when dozens of sleek and shiny classic cars roll down Cross Street for ogling and general camaraderie. On any given night, cars pulling in for the "show-and-tell" can include a customized 1934 Ford coupe or a late-1940s Kaiser-Frazer that was made right here at Willow Run.

Silver Spoon Antiques (27 East Cross Street; 734-484-9960) is filled with antique furniture, glassware, and other unusual old things, while **Apple Annie's Vintage Clothing** (29 West Crossing Street; 734-481-0555) concentrates on apparel and jewelry.

Eating Out

See Food & Lodging, page 312, for addresses, phone numbers, and additional options.
Aubree's Saloon is great for sandwiches and Mexican food, as well as a mean shepherd's pie on St. Patrick's Day. In **Sticks,** the pool hall above Aubree's, you can work up a hunger or have an "Ypsi aperitif" (take your pick from more than 100 beers on the menu). The nearby memorabilia-filled **Cady's Grill** is a bit more Ann Arborish, serving up fish and pasta. Good burgers can be had at the **Sidetrack Bar & Grill**—legendary home of Frog Island Beer.

Cruise Night takes place on Thursday nights in Ypsilanti's Depot Town.

■ **DAY TRIPS**

On a nice spring or summer day, take Main Street north out of Ann Arbor, veer left on Huron River Drive just before you climb onto the M-14 expressway, and settle in for a winding, slow-speed, extraordinarily pretty drive. Watch for bicyclists who seem emboldened by the beauty, riding three abreast and risking life and limb in their private pursuit of washboard abs.

■ **HURON-CLINTON METROPARKS: DELHI, DEXTER-HURON, AND HUDSON MILLS** *map page 83, B-4*

The parks themselves are clean and open if you feel like being mellow and tossing a Frisbee, but the main reason to be here is to canoe. Check at the front gate for instructions, but you should be able to rent a canoe inexpensively and spend the afternoon ambling down the leisurely Huron River.

Trips begin either from the Dexter-Huron Park for the (too) short trip or from Hudson Mills for the longer (about right) trip. If you start upriver at Hudson Mills, stop at the Mast Road bridge just short of Dexter-Huron and walk over to the party store for a cupcake and a cold one. Either way, you'll end up at Delhi, where Skip the canoe man or one of his kids will haul you back to get your car. Easy and painless. *www.metroparks.com.*

If lazy canoeing seems too heavenly, who in his or her right mind would turn down the chance to ride a horse in Hell?

■ **HELL, MICHIGAN** *map page 83, B-4*

About a half hour out of Ann Arbor, southwest of Pinckney, sits lovely Hell, Michigan, at the corner of Patterson Lake Road and Silver Hill Road.

Visitors to Hell can drink with bikers at "the hottest spot in Hell," the **Dam Site Inn** (4045 Patterson Lake Road; 734-878-9300), then sidle next door to the party store to buy every imaginable kind of play-on-words trinket and send postcards to anyone they think should go to Hell too.

The other local industry seems to be **Hell Creek Ranch.** With a couple of days' notice, a riding hand from Hell—though he or she probably lives in Gregory, which is nowhere near as much fun to say—will show you the finer points of riding and squire you around the ranch. *10866 Cedar Lake Road; 734-878-3632; www.hellcreekranch.allhell.com.*

■ TRAVEL BASICS

City Overview: In Ann Arbor, a textbook example of a college town, the University of Michigan extends outward from the campus hub in all directions to embrace different neighborhoods. The university's touch is gentle, even exciting, and the neighborhoods are resilient, charming, and authentic. All in all, this is one of the nicer American cities to get lost in. *734-995-7281 or 800-888-9487; www. annarbor.org.*

Getting Around: Parking can be difficult during the school term, but there are many convenient parking structures. Although it has no subway, Ann Arbor does have an impressive bus system that stretches to neighboring small towns such as Dexter and Chelsea. **Metropolitan Detroit International Airport** is about 20 miles east of Ann Arbor on I-94 and is easy to navigate, and the customary rental car, taxicab, and limousine services are available. Ann Arbor Municipal Airport and Ypsilanti's Willow Run Airport have no major commercial passenger services. The Amtrak station is just north of downtown Ann Arbor. The train makes for an enjoyable way to get to Ann Arbor by way of small-town main streets and everyone else's backyard and is highly recommended.

Weather: Summer is a mixed bag. Could be sunny and more perfect than anything this side of San Diego; could be cold, wet, and absolutely wretched, with life-threatening lightning storms, tornadoes, or heat waves. Likewise, winters can cheerily live up to Michigan's former "Water Winter Wonderland" motto or be marked by week after week of single-digit temperatures and howling winds—a sunless horror, devoid of joy or hope. Halloween night can greet trick-or-treaters with anything from 60 degrees F to 20 degrees, maybe even the winter's first blizzard. TV weathermen out of Lansing or Detroit, who should understand Michigan's weather as well as anyone, are generally no more accurate or informed than a chimp flipping a coin.

Food & Lodging: Ann Arbor offers more lively bars, trendy nightclubs, and sophisticated restaurants than most other college-related environments. And given the large number of students, parents, friends, and faculty and the frequent turnover, lodging options are plentiful, from the relatively inexpensive to the deluxe. *For some suggestions, see the listings beginning on page 274.*

THE THUMB

The "Thumb" of Michigan's "mitten" is dominated by farmland and small towns. Highway M-25, which edges Lake Huron's shore from Port Huron to Bay City, traces the eastern outline of the Thumb, while M-46 bisects its middle like a rifle shot from Port Sanilac to Saginaw. Rimmed with blue water and scattered green forests, the land is comparatively flat, a bucolic countryside with weathered barns and cows peering placidly over fences at passersby. It is the "closer up north"—the countryside resembling "up north," only "closer" to the urban areas in the southern part of the state. With few tourists, entertainment is for the locals: farm festivals, fishing tournaments, auctions, parks, and main streets where folks jaywalk against traffic lights. It's where farms offer "U-pick" orchards and vegetable and berry patches in summertime, fields full of pumpkins in the fall.

As you look north across Lake Huron from the head of the St. Clair River, it's easy to see why early explorers called the lake La Mer Douce—the Sweet Sea. The lake and its shore are the source of endless entertainment—swimming, boating, fishing, scuba diving, and sightseeing. A walk along the beach provides an interlude for contemplation, for listening to the sea's sweet song.

Weather, however, can transform that song into a howl with unexpected suddenness. Two underwater preserves mark graveyards for the ships that met their fate on La Mer Douce: the Thumb Area Great Lakes State Bottomland Preserve at Port Hope, and Sanilac Shores Underwater Preserve off Port Sanilac and Lexington.

■ HISTORY

In 1686, to stymie the English traders who were trying to reach the upper lakes, Jacques René de Bresay de Denonville, governor of New France, ordered Daniel Greysolon, Sieur Du Luth, to build a fort between Lake Huron and Lake Erie. Du Luth did so at what is now the north end of Port Huron and named it Fort St. Joseph. Governor Denonville (who in 1689 built another Fort St. Joseph at present-day Niles) planned an all-out war against the Iroquois to punish them for leading the English into French territory. Fort St. Joseph was the mobilization center, bringing together about 200 *coureurs de bois* (woods runners, Frenchmen illegally trading in furs with American Indians) and nearly 500 Indians—Chippewas,

A dairy farm along Highway M-25, near Harbor Beach.

Hurons, Menominees, Winnebagos, Potawatomis, Illinois, Fox, Kickapoos, and Mascoutens. The campaign fizzled, but the force gathered demonstrated that a large body of Frenchmen and Indians could be quickly assembled to defend the French fur trade. Two years later Du Luth's replacement, Louis Armand de Lom d'Arce, Baron de Lahontan, an ardent sportsman, excellent wit, and articulate observer of New France, anticipating a winter of intolerable boredom, burned the fort to the ground and returned to the relative civility of Fort Michilimackinac. Regional authority was shifted to Fort Ponchartrain du Detroit, which became the focal point of conflict among the French, British, and Americans in Michigan.

■ LUMBER INDUSTRY

The Thumb was once a magnificent and seemingly limitless forest of white pine and hardwood, with trees so tall and a canopy so dense that sunlight seldom reached the forest floor. As a prime source of white pine, the Thumb was where lumbering really took off after Detroit was destroyed by fire in 1805 and sawmills on the St. Clair River were set whirling to rebuild it. Thus began Michigan's initial industrial boom, laying the pattern for what was to come. In 1834 the first steam sawmill was erected on the Saginaw River, and by 1854 there were 558 mills in operation. In 1876, with the timber business entering a decline, a sawmill between Harbor Beach and Bad Axe sent a plank to the World's Fair in Philadelphia. Cut from a single tree and measuring 16 feet long by 4 feet wide, it became known as the Centennial Plank and symbolized the rapidly vanishing grandeur of Michigan's forest treasure.

■ THE FIRST PLANK ROAD

Fort Gratiot, set where Lake Huron empties into the St. Clair River, immediately north of what is now the city of Port Huron, was built by the Americans as a supply post during the War of 1812. In 1829 funding was provided to build the Fort Gratiot Turnpike, connecting Fort Gratiot to Detroit. This turnpike—made of heavy timbers laid wagon-wide over soft muddy ground to form a passable route— was Michigan's first "plank road." It, along with the St. Clair River and later the Erie Canal, channeled settlers into Michigan from Canada and the eastern United States. Some homesteaders continued westward; others settled around Port Huron to engage in shipbuilding. Still others moved up the Thumb to grub out small farms on the logged-over "stumpland."

■ FOREST FIRES

Fires in the Thumb were always a hazard, as they were throughout Michigan. In the early days before logging, the settlers had simply burned the "useless" logs that piled up as they cleared the land. Sometimes fires would be deliberately set—in order, it was claimed, to increase the harvest of blueberries. However, in 1871 and 1881, two great fires changed the ecology of the Thumb forever. Fueled by heaps of slash from reckless logging, these fires roared across the Thumb, destroying cities and obliterating the landscape.

While both fires were disastrous, the 1881 fire was the more devastating of the two. All through August of that year, small wildfires burned out of control, hopping and skipping across the countryside, changing direction unpredictably with each shift of the wind. Then on September 3 an extraordinary weather phenomenon occurred. Darkness covered the land. By noon housewives were lighting lamps. By 3 P.M., lanterns were lit along village streets throughout the Thumb. Newspapers recorded the bizarre event as "an Egyptian darkness like the darkness

Michigan lumbermen often entertained themselves by seeing how many massive old-growth logs they could stack on a single sled. Above is a winning load, stacked and photographed for posterity in 1890.

of an eclipse." Wind increased to a gale, howling and coursing through the Thumb at tornado force. The small fires converged. It was, by all accounts, the perfect firestorm. Around 4 P.M. fireballs began soaring through the sky like meteors, dropping down to explode and devour everything in their paths. Then picking up oxygen created by their own draft, they would shoot back into the air again. Sergeant William O. Bailey, with the Michigan Department of Conservation, later reported that "even the earth sometimes took fire." People sought refuge in Lake Huron; others crawled into wells, where many suffocated.

The fire raged for 48 hours. At its conclusion 282 lives were reported lost, 15,000 people had been rendered homeless, and more than 3,400 buildings had been destroyed. Perhaps the only positive thing to emerge from the 1881 fire was the first relief effort undertaken by Clara Barton and her newly formed American Red Cross.

Long beaches on the Thumb, such as those at Albert Sleeper State Park on Saginaw Bay, are favorite vacation spots for many Michiganians.

■ THE THUMB TODAY

After the "endless" forest was reduced to sawdust and ashes, the land beneath it was plowed, and farming became a major factor in the economy of the Thumb, as it still is today. In some places the replanting of trees has enabled a small resurgence in the timber industry, but the largest sector of the Thumb's economy is tourism. With its long lakefront beaches, hidden lagoons, canoeable rivers, fishing, and hunting, the Thumb remains (as it has been for more than a century) the favored vacationland for working folks from Detroit, Toledo, and other cities nearby.

Alas, farmland in the southern part of the Thumb and along I-75 is rapidly being gobbled up by suburbs. Writer Tom Carney has lived his life in what he terms the "bottom knuckle of the Thumb" around Shelby Township, now Greater Pontiac. Whenever he drives north on M-53, which cuts through the middle of the Thumb, he says he never feels that he's in farm country "until I'm north of Imlay City and I can see, sometimes smell, the rich, dark loam on either side."

■ UP THE ST. CLAIR RIVER AND THE THUMB

Interstate 94, having split from I-90 at Billings, Montana, charts a high, arching path across the high plains. It then travels down through Wisconsin to Chicago and loops around the bottom of Lake Michigan before crossing Michigan diagonally to Detroit, finally coming to rest at Port Huron. It's definitely the fastest way from Detroit to Port Huron. The slower, prettier state highway M-29 skirts the international waterway shared with Canada and saunters through the quaint little river towns of Algonac, Marine City, and St. Clair (with its 1,500-foot-long river boardwalk). Car ferries here can shuttle you from St. Clair to Ontario, Canada. Ontario Highway 33 hugs the river from Fort Lambton to the south edge of Sarnia and makes for an appealing drive that passes through several small towns. Parks along the way open to the river, affording great views of ships moving upriver and down.

■ PORT HURON *map page 126, D-4*

Port Huron can claim its own Great Lake, a river, a lighthouse, a trolley, the twin spans of an 8,021-foot-long bridge, an international neighbor, and a history as one of the oldest settlements in the state. Old-timers call Port Huron the sailor's nursery: young lads come here to watch the big ships on the river, dreaming of faraway places, and later learn to throw ships' lines instead of lassos. In 1679 French explorer La Salle's ill-fated *Griffin* became stuck here, and 12 crewmen had to haul her across the shallow rapids into Lake Huron.

Thomas Edison Drive

From M-25, access Thomas Edison Drive and follow it north along the St. Clair. When you see the Blue Water Bridge, pull into the parking area next to the statue of a young Thomas Alva Edison. This is where Alva, as his family called him, spent his boyhood and conducted his first experiments.

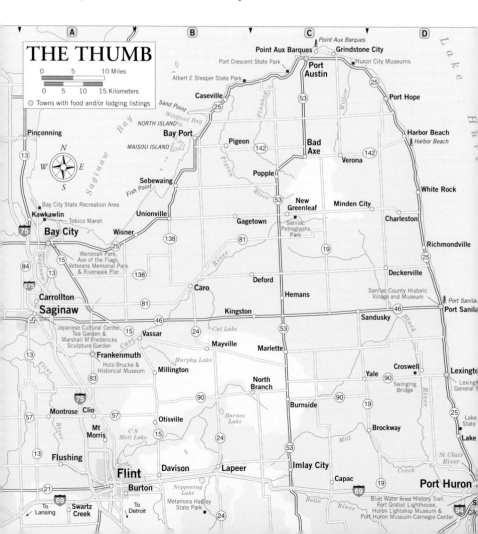

THE THUMB

0   5   10 Miles
0   5   10   15 Kilometers
○ Towns with food and/or lodging listings

Point Aux Barques
Point Aux Barques   Grindstone City
Port Crescent State Park
Albert E Sleeper State Park   Port Austin
Caseville   Port Hope
Sand Point   Wildfowl Bay   Huron City Museums

Pinconning   Bay Port   Harbor Beach
Harbor Beach
NORTH ISLAND   Pigeon   Bad Axe
MAISOU ISLAND   Verona   White Rock
Popple
Sebewaing   New Greenleaf   Minden City
Bay City State Recreation Area   Charleston
Kawkawlin   Unionville   Gagetown   Sanilac Petroglyphs Park
Tobico Marsh   Richmondville
Bay City   Wisner   Deckerville
Wenonah Park,   Deford   Port Sanilac
Ave of the Flags,   Hemans   Sanilac County Historic
Veterans Memorial Park   Caro   Village and Museum
& Riverwalk Pier   Kingston   Sandusky   Port Sanilac
Carrollton   Black
Saginaw   Japanese Cultural Center,   Cat Lake
Tea Garden &   Vassar   Marlette
Marshall M Fredericks   Mayville   Croswell   Lexington
Sculpture Garden   Frankenmuth   Yale   Lexington General
Holz-Brucke &   Millington   North Branch   Swinging Bridge
Historical Museum   Burnside   Brockway   Lake State
Montrose   Clio   Otisville   Barnes Lake   Lake
Mt Morris   C S Mott Lake
Flushing   Davison   Lapeer   Imlay City   St Clair River
Flint   Capac   Port Huron
Burton   Nepessing Lake   Belle River   Blue Water Area History Trail,
To Lansing   Swartz Creek   To Detroit   Metamora Hadley State Park   Fort Gratiot Lighthouse, Huron Lightship Museum & Port Huron Museum-Carnegie Center

Blue Water Area History Trail

One of the nicest things to do in Port Huron is to stroll along the Blue Water Area History Trail, which begins under the Blue Water Bridge and follows the St. Clair River south, parallel with the Thomas Edison Parkway. Historic markers are posted along the way. The twin spans of the Blue Water Bridge (connecting to Sarnia, Ontario) rise 152 feet to afford passage to the 1,000-foot-long "salties," huge sea-going freighters hauling cargo from and to ports around the world.

An ore freighter enters the St. Clair River at Port Huron.

Fort Gratiot Lighthouse

At Lighthouse Park and U.S. Coast Guard Station, guarding the junction of the St. Clair River and Lake Huron, is the 86-foot-high white brick Fort Gratiot Lighthouse. Built in 1825, it is accompanied by a light keeper's home dating from 1874. *Omar and Garfield Streets north of the Blue Water Bridge; 810-982-0891; www.phmuseum.org.*

Huron Lightship Museum

Downriver, the Huron Lightship is moored permanently in Pine Grove Park. Now a museum, the 97-foot ship with its 52-foot lantern mast was the last lightship on the Great Lakes, guiding ships through shallows and treacherous shoals. Closed from January through March. *810-982-0891; www.phmuseum.org.*

Port Huron Museum-Carnegie Center
Another worthwhile stop on the waterfront is this museum, which includes displays of Indian artifacts, exhibits on maritime history, and Thomas Edison memorabilia. *1115 Sixth Street; 810-982-0891; www.phmuseum.org.*

Port Huron to Mackinac Race
Banners fly along the waterfront in preparation for the annual Port Huron to Mackinac yacht race in mid-July. The highlight is the Mardi Gras–style water parade of nearly 300 racing craft down the Black River, up the St. Clair, under the Blue Water Bridge, and into Lake Huron to reach the starting line near the Fort Gratiot Lighthouse. Then, 259 unpredictable miles later, competitors lay anchor in the Mackinac Island Marina, and the winner is declared. For pre-race viewing, check out the yachts docked along the Black River in downtown Port Huron. On race day, my favorite spot is along the St. Clair River.

For more information: *Blue Water Area Convention & Visitors Bureau; 520 Thomas Edison Parkway; 800-852-4242; www.bluewater.org.*

(above) The Blue Water Bridge forms a backdrop for the Huron Lightship.
(opposite) Visitors tour the Huron Lightship Museum.

■ Towns and Sights along the Huron Shore

Lakeside towns ring the Thumb like small beads on a string. Their short main streets line M-25, with side streets leading to Lake Huron.

■ LEXINGTON *map page 126, D-3*

The village of Lexington preserves a touch of New England in its architecture, with steepled churches and a tidy downtown of Victorian-style storefronts on the slope above the marina. The 134-year-old **Lexington General Store,** replete with creaky floors and glass bins filled with penny candy, offers a cornucopia of country wares. *7272 Huron Avenue; 810-359-8900.*

■ CROSWELL *map page 126, D-3*

Detour 5 miles west on M-90 to Croswell to reach the fruit and berry farms. At harvest, **Croswell Berry Farm** bakes "Berry-Berry-Cherry" pies, a juicy mix of the farm's own black and red raspberries with cherries. *33 Black River Road; 810-679-3273; www.croswellberryfarm.com.*

Walk off the calories at the "Be Good to Your Mother-in-Law Bridge." The 139-foot swinging bridge over the Black River was built in 1905 without railings or handrails. Safety rails were installed later, but the name stuck.

■ PORT SANILAC *map page 126, D-3*

Eleven miles north of Lexington, M-25 reaches Port Sanilac, another shore village and one with an 1886 brick lighthouse. The lighthouse is on private property, but there are great views of it from the marina. When Port Sanilac's first settlers arrived in 1844, the only sign of settlement was a shack thrown together by tanners who distilled tannin from the evergreen trees. To spread news around the area, the postmaster and storekeeper in the growing community laid a pile of newsprint on the general-store counter along with a stack of pencils. Whoever had news to print wrote his or her own. Called the *Bark Shanty Times,* this was the only newspaper in Michigan without editors, reporters, or a printing press. Most everybody stopped in to read the news.

The town's 1875 **Loop Mansion,** one of seven buildings that make up the **Sanilac County Historic Village and Museum,** is staffed by ladies in hoopskirts and wide picture hats who will lead you through exhibits spanning three centuries. The members of builder Dr. Joseph Loop's family were avid collectors, and the museum's exhibits draw from maritime antiques, souvenirs of four wars, and natural history objects. Dr. Loop's own medicines are still on the shelves. The building is part of a reconstituted village that includes a pioneer log cabin, a country store, a one-room schoolhouse, a dairy museum, and the Barn Theater. Open June–September. *228 South Ridge Road (M-25); 810-622-9946; www.sanilacmuseum. com.*

■ **WHITE ROCK** *map page 126, D-2*
Nineteen miles north of Port Sanilac on M-25, a road sign indicates the location of White Rock. During 1835–36, when the Michigan Territory was clamoring for statehood, banking laws fell lax and land speculation ran wild. When the first land office opened in Detroit, the city became a beehive of shysters pushing bogus real estate. It all looked fine on paper: supposed cities complete with streets lined by hotels, stores, and homes. Alas, most buyers found only wilderness or swamp. White Rock was a classic scam, named for a boulder at the mouth of a river on Lake Huron; its alleged "virtues" were touted in broadsides posted in Detroit's hotel lobbies and on barroom walls. Naturally, there was nothing at all in the "town" of White Rock, and today it remains merely a curiosity along the road.

The Port Sanilac Marina at dawn.

■ **HARBOR BEACH** *map page 126, D-1*

During Prohibition, the fishing and tourist town of Harbor Beach was used as point of entry for illegal liquor smuggled across the lake from Canada. Local historian Leonard DeFrain relates a singular confrontation between bootleggers and G-men when a boat loaded with 24,000 bottles of beer and wine was headed for Port Hope, 8 miles north of Harbor Beach, where trucks were ready to speed the goods to Chicago. Word spread that federal agents were waiting for them, so the boat pulled into Harbor Beach instead. But the agents, who had been tipped off about the change of plan, surprised the smugglers and tried to set the boat afire. As flames licked at the wooden deck, the bottles started exploding, but because of their low alcohol content the beer and wine spewing from the bottles doused the flames as fast as the agents could start them. The G-men finally gave up, resorting to axes to scuttle the offending craft.

About a mile south of Harbor Beach, Crane Point juts from a woodland into Lake Huron. The point was named after an amiable hermit who admitted to a farmer neighbor that he was coining and engraving illegal currency, including Mexican, Canadian, and German banknotes, a skill he had learned while working at the U.S. Mint. He hid his presses in shanties scattered through the forest in order to evade federal agents.

■ **HURON CITY MUSEUMS** *map page 126, C-1*

On M-25 at the northeast tip of the Thumb sits the ghost town of Huron City, preserved as a 19th-century museum town. Among other buildings, it has a visitors center, an inn, a lifesaving station, a church, a general store, and the 16-room House of Seven Gables, built by lumberman Langdon Hubbard in 1881, when the lumber industry in the Thumb was at its peak. Later, the Gables became the summer home of Hubbard's son-in-law William Lyon Phelps, one of the nation's most popular professors and syndicated columnists. His remarkable Sunday services in the little white church regularly drew overflow crowds that stood outside in the dirt street to listen to his inspiring sermons. Open from Memorial Day to Labor Day and on weekends in September. *On M-25, between Port Austin and Port Hope; 989-428-4123; www.huroncitymuseums.org.*

■ **PORT AUSTIN** *map page 126, C-1*

Set at the tip of the Thumb, Port Austin is a friendly town with wide streets. Residents and visitors gather along the half-mile breakwall to observe the first blush of morning streak across Lake Huron. They return in the evening as the sun-

(above) Huron City is a Victorian-era ghost town with many architecturally significant structures under preservation, such as this log cabin. (following pages) Sunset over Port Austin.

set casts long purple shadows over Charity and Little Charity islands in Saginaw Bay.

The red **Garfield Inn** bed-and-breakfast is rich in stories of the nation's 19th president, James A. Garfield, and the raven-haired wife of a Michigan lumber baron. The president met Maria Learned when she and her husband, Charles Learned, lived in New York. In 1857, Learned followed the harvest of tall timber to Michigan and purchased a stately home and carriage house in the Thumb. Garfield was a regular visitor, and in 1868 he delivered a stirring political speech from the Learneds' third-floor balcony—now in the inn that bears his name.

Some time later, word reached Garfield in Washington that Maria was gravely ill. He caught a train and headed back to Michigan. In a swaying railroad car, he penned these words in his diary: "As I drew near . . . my heart began to ache afresh. All my hopes, fears, doubts, concerning Maria came into my heart afresh. The thought that in a few moments I might hear 'she's dead' or 'she's dying' was so terrible that it seemed as though I could not meet it."

Maria recovered, but in 1881 she and Garfield died within months of each other, Maria of tuberculosis and the president by an assassin's bullet. *8544 Lake Street; 800-373-5254; www.garfieldinn.com.*

Fishing off the city pier in Port Austin.

■ SAGINAW BAY NATURAL AREAS

From Port Austin Highway, M-25 follows the west side of the Thumb along the shore of Saginaw Bay. Lakeside cottages stand back modestly from shore; sandbars reach long fingers into the bay; idle watercraft sway in stilted boat hoists where the water is too shallow for shore landings. The area is dotted with marshes and wetlands that attract ducks, geese, and hunters.

■ PORT CRESCENT STATE PARK   *map page 126, C-1*

■ ALBERT E. SLEEPER STATE PARK   *map page 126, B-1*

Four miles southwest of Port Austin are the twin state parks of Port Crescent and Albert E. Sleeper, separated by **Rush Lake State Game Area**. Boardwalks lead across the dunes to decks fine for picnicking. Children take to the low dunes with relish, building sandcastles or leapfrogging into Mother Nature's sandbox, while adults loll about in the sun or dash into the water for a cooling plunge before returning to their chosen park's campground. Virtually the whole western shoreline of the Thumb is parkland. South of Alfred E. Sleeper are two extraordinary sites for viewing waterfowl: **Wildfowl Bay State Wildlife Area** (989-872-5300) and

Fish Point State Wildlife Area (989-674-2511), both of which allow hunting. *Port Crescent State Park; 989-738-8663. Albert E. Sleeper State Park; 989-856-4411; www.dnr.state.mi.us/parksandtrails.*

■ **BAY PORT** *map page 126, B-1*

Slow down, or you'll miss this fishing village in the curve of Wildfowl Bay. Fifty years ago the city was home to the largest freshwater fishing fleet in the world. During those busy days when fleets docked here, fish were so big and plentiful that they threatened to break the nets. Overfishing and pollution exhausted the resource, and today only the **Bay Port Fish Company,** founded in 1895, remains in operation. Stop by to watch the fishing boats pull in with their latest catch, or check out the market for the freshest of fish. *1008 First Street; 989-656-2121.*

■ **BAY CITY** *map page 126, A-2*

Bay City is a thriving city of 39,000 straddling the Saginaw River about 10 miles upstream from where the river empties into Saginaw Bay at the crook of Michigan's Thumb and Mitten.

Pointe aux Barque's lighthouse rests on the tip of the Thumb.

An elevated boardwalk crosses through Port Crescent State Park.

■ HISTORY OF BAY CITY AND SAGINAW

Between 1850 and 1900 Bay City and Saginaw were brawling twin lumbertowns, literally and figuratively duking it out over which town was number one in timber production. At the climax of the white pine craze in 1882, sawmills lined the banks from town to town, noisily slicing their way through the logs. Other mills sawed up some of the best oak in the world, the bulk of which went to build ships, adding to the ever-growing fleet of timber ships that ferried the pine along Lake Huron, down the Detroit River, and across Lake Erie to Buffalo. Many a captain claimed he could steer his ship up the Saginaw River by sawdust smell alone.

By 1900 the timber was gone, and the once-roaring mills lining the banks of the Saginaw had fallen silent, rusting monuments to greed surrounded by acres of sawdust and leftover cuts of lumber. Saginaw moved on beyond the timber era. Bay City hung on briefly as a shipping supply and repair yard, but by 1908 that activity too had followed the trail of the tall pines and beautiful oaks. All that remained of this furious enterprise were the barons' mansions and elegant churches that stand today, still the most graceful elements of Bay City.

■ VISITING BAY CITY

Parks and river walks line the banks; restaurants provide dockside service; marinas offer boat rentals and launches. The river teems with pleasure craft and huge ocean-going freighters: Bay City is the second-busiest Michigan port on Lake Huron.

The city's heart beats in **Wenonah Park**, a riverside park named for the mother of Hiawatha. The Avenue of Flags represents the ships from around the world that regularly call here. The path through the flags leads to a fountain and the World Friendship Arts Shell, where summer concerts and performances are held. I always find time to claim a bench in Wenonah Park to sit and watch the river traffic and families out for a stroll.

Across the Saginaw River, **Veterans Memorial Park** includes picnic areas, tennis courts, a music pavilion, a boat launch, and a marina. Hikers and bicyclists take the path along the waterfront on the way to the 700-foot **Riverwalk Pier,** another personal favorite. This is not just a straight shot into the river. It's a zigzag with balconies where fishermen can cast their lines and a gazebo where wanderers can pause to gaze at the islands upriver.

Fascinating trolley-bus tours of Bay City's old mansions, or

A sign for the Bay Port Fish Company, founded by Henry Engehardt, who claimed that his fish stand offered the state's first (and best) fast food.

"painted ladies," begin each Saturday at 2 P.M. at the **Historical Museum of Bay County.** *321 Washington Avenue; 989-893-5733.*

Next door, the 1894 Romanesque-style City Hall features a dramatic freestanding staircase with wrought-iron railings winding from the foyer to the fourth floor. Woven in 1977 by local artist Monika Chmielewska, a 31-foot tapestry depicting Bay City's history hangs in the council chambers. *301 Washington Avenue; 989-894-8147.*

For a fishing charter, Capt. Dave DeGrow is always ready with his 27-foot SeaRay Amberjack, named ***Beaner.*** *989-692-0255; www.degrow.com/dave.*

The 65-foot topsail schooner ***Appledore*** (901 Saginaw Street; 888-229-8696) is a striking feature on the waters of Saginaw Bay. It sails from Wenonah Park on Fridays, Saturdays, and Sundays, June through September. For more weekend sailing, board the ***Princess Wenonah*** or the ***Islander.*** Bookings from June through September are handled by the Bay City Antiques Center (1010 North Water Street; 989-891-2628).

For more information: *Bay Area Convention & Visitors Bureau; 901 Saginaw Street; 989-893-1222 or 888-229-8696; www.tourbaycitymi.org.*

A red-bellied woodpecker.

Swans migrating from the far north stop to rest in Michigan's lakes.

■ **BAY CITY STATE RECREATION AREA**

Walk to the observation tower over the wetland and marsh of Tobico Lagoon, a favorite perch from which to follow the comings and goings of hundreds of birds. The adjacent 1,700-acre Tobico Marsh refuge attracts more than 100 species of migratory waterfowl and other birds. *Three miles north of Bay City at 3582 State Park Drive; 989-667-0717.*

■ **SAGINAW** *map page 126, A-3*

■ **SAGINAW AND ITS INDIAN HISTORY**

The Cass, Flint, Bad, Shiawassee, and Tittabawassee rivers all cut across wide marshes before draining into the short, deep Saginaw River, which then flows into Saginaw Bay. In 1819 the U.S. government in Washington forwarded $10,000 to Michigan's territorial governor, Lewis Cass, with instructions to negotiate a treaty with the Indians for a pie-shaped portion of Michigan along Lake Huron. Cass sent word to the Ottawa and Chippewas occupying the land to meet at the junction of the rivers flowing into the Saginaw River during the full moon of

September. Two ships were loaded and dispatched from Detroit with supplies and liquor to be distributed at the proper time.

Since fur trader Louis Campau had a reputation of getting along well with the Indians, he was instructed to build a council house for the meeting. Cass arrived on September 10, flanked by assistants and instructors. Cass was a good negotiator. Indians called him "Big Belly" for his portly figure. Over the next two weeks up to 4,000 Indians wandered in and out of the encampment. The area specified in the proposed treaty encompassed one-sixth of Michigan's total land area from the tip of the Thumb, deeper south beyond the Saginaw Valley, and north to Thunder Bay up the Lake Huron shore. When the treaty seemed stalled, Cass suspected it was the subversive work of trapper Jacob Smith. Cass offered Smith a buyout of 11 sections of land and $3,000 in silver coins. Smith accepted, and the Indians swung their vote to accept the trade.

Campau was furious, claiming part of the silver was rightly his, to pay off the past debt the Indians already owed his post. To celebrate the signing, Cass ordered whiskey to be distributed among the Indians. In the book *Michigan*, Willis F. Dunbar and George S. May give the following account:

> Campau now had his revenge. He opened ten barrels of his own whiskey, and began passing it out. The Indians became roaring drunk, and their violence alarmed Cass. "Louis! Louis!" he cried. "Stop the liquor." Campau replied, "General, you commenced it; you let Smith plunder me and rob me." But after another plea, Campau restrained the Indians, saying, "I lost my money; I lost my fight; I lost my liquor; but I got good satisfaction."

■ TIMBERING AND TAILORING IN THE SAGINAW VALLEY

The Saginaw Valley held dense forests of some of the finest timber: white pine that was strong and durable, did not warp, crack, shrink, or splinter, and floated like a cork. Soon a line of sawmills stood on the river from Saginaw to Bay City.

With the April thaw, the swaggering "red-sash brigade" was on: French-Canadian lumberjacks with red sashes tied at their waists, bright mackinaws, and tasseled caps worn at a jaunty angle. Add to that a mix of many ethnicities, and the men from the woods presented a dramatic picture. All winter they worked hard, and when spring came they played even harder, drinking and carousing on an epic scale.

Lumbering towns pushed to outboast each other with tall tales of their orgies, and most were true. Saginaw's Potter Street offered 32 saloons within nine blocks. The town hired its own Wyatt Earp, ex-cavalryman Marshall Charles Meyer. When fighting turned mean, Meyer rode his horse into the barroom and clubbed away in all directions with his nightstick.

Little Joe "Jake" Seligman, a diminutive 4-foot-11-inch haberdasher, counted on his size, or lack thereof, to pocket his share of lumberjack cash. Having established a reputation for outlandish self-promotion in Pontiac, he moved to Saginaw and established a store, Little Jake's. Popular with the lumberjacks, who appreciated his sense of humor, Jake became a huge success. Among his many stunts was the construction of a large tower atop which he mounted a giant copper statue of himself, thereby proving his motto: "The largest retail clothier in Michigan."

One fondly recounted legend has him tossing vests from his store's second-story window to a crowd of lumberjacks, promising a free coat and trousers to every man who caught one. Most of the time the vests were torn to shreds before they made it back through the door. But Jake was allegedly as good as his word: the victor received a new $12 suit for free—but had to remunerate Jake $12 for the ruined vest.

A Saginaw Valley logging scene. Railroads first began to be used to haul logs out of the Michigan forest in the 1870s.

■ SAGINAW SIGHTS

Japanese Cultural Center

The Japanese Cultural Center, a gift from Saginaw's sister city, Tokushima, Japan, is surrounded by paths winding through sculptured gardens, symbolizing the binding together of two cities half a world apart. A footpath along the Flint River cuts through a tree-shaded garden, with bridges over small streams, to the sculptured garden surrounding the Tea Garden. On the second Saturday afternoon of each month you can witness the mesmerizing formal Japanese tea ceremony. *527 Ezra Rust Drive and South Washington Avenue; 989-759-1648.*

Shiawassee National Wildlife Refuge

This 9,000-acre refuge includes wetlands that spread along creeks and bayous cut by dikes. Will Hufton operates his **Johnny Panther Quests** (810-653-3859)— three- to five-hour treks into what he calls Michigan's Everglades, maneuvering his 16-foot flat-bottom motorized boat in and out of creeks and bayous he's prowled since childhood. "This has been my playground since I came here with my father when I was three," Hufton says. *6975 Mower Road; 989-777-5930; midwest.fws.gov/shiawassee.*

Marshall M. Fredericks Sculpture Museum

Here you can wander among the outdoor and indoor displays of monumental sculpture (models, casts, and

At the Marshall M. Fredericks Sculpture Museum, a plaster and fiberglass cast of the monumental bronze Fredericks made for the 1964 World's Fair.

finished pieces) by Michigan artist Marshall M. Fredericks, whose works grace many civic venues in the state and who also cast a monumental bronze, *Freedom of the Human Spirit,* for the 1964 World's Fair in Flushing Meadows, New York. *Exit 160, then left on M-84. Follow the signs to Saginaw Valley State University; 7400 Bay Road, University Center; 989-964-4000; www.svsu.edu.mfsm.*

■ **U-PICK FARMS**
Throughout Saginaw County numerous small towns have attractions worthy of a stop. Around the villages of Freeland, Hemlock, and Merrill are nine or more "U-pick" farms offering strawberries, raspberries, and blueberries in season. At **Bayne's Apple Valley Farm,** northwest of Freeland, aromas are tantalizing in the autumn air, with fresh juice squeezed at the cider mill and the spicy smells of apple cookies, muffins, and homemade pies wafting out from the bakery. I certainly can't resist coming away with a bushel of fresh fruit and a caramel apple in hand. Open August through January. *North on Midland Road (M-47) to 5395 Midland Road; 989-695-9139.*

For more information: *Saginaw County Convention & Visitors Bureau; 800-444-9979; www.visitsaginawcounty.com.*

■ **FRANKENMUTH** *map page 126, A-3*

One August day in 1845, with four grueling months of travel behind them, a small group of Bavarian colonists loaded their belongings and two church bells brought from their homeland onto an oxcart at Saginaw and pushed their way 12 miles southeast, through dense wilderness and swamps, to carve out a settlement at the Cass River. Impassioned by a new beginning and zeal to convert the resident Indians, by Christmas Day they had built their St. Lorenz Church and mission, and the church bells were ready to ring. The Indians quickly headed west while the group, soon joined by other family members and neighbors, established themselves as Bavarian Lutherans, a heritage that is preserved today. A replica of the old log church stands near the present St. Lorenz with the original bells displayed nearby.

Frankenmuth is known for its Bavarian style of architecture, glockenspiel towers, and festivals with plenty of sausages, beer, and polka music. The 239-foot-long **Holz-Brucke** (wooden bridge), a 1980 replica of a 19th-century covered bridge, spans the lazy Cass River. The **Frankenmuth Historical Museum** (613 South Main Street; 989-652-9701) highlights the area's German ancestry with permanent and changing exhibits.

The Frankenmuth Bavarian Inn Restaurant.

The 1856 Exchange Hotel evolved into **Zehnder's Restaurant** (730 South Main Street; 989-652-0450 or 800-863-7999). Across the street, the 1880 Fischer Hotel evolved into the **Frankenmuth Bavarian Inn Restaurant** (713 South Main Street; 989-652-9941 or 800-228-2742). Both restaurants are famous for their all-you-can-eat chicken dinners, a family-style tradition that attracts more than 1,000 people a day.

Bronner's Christmas Wonderland, the world's largest Christmas store, might best be described as four football fields of glittering baubles, with sparkling garlands chasing rings around the Christmas trees. Wally Bronner opened the fairyland holiday store in 1945; he still stands at the door wearing his contagious grin 361 days of the year. *25 Christmas Lane; 989-652-9931 or 800-255-9327; www. bronners.com.*

For more information: *Frankenmuth Convention and Visitors Bureau; 635 South Main Street; 800-386-8696; www.frankenmuth.org.*

■ Travel Basics

Area Overview: Farmlands, small towns, long and leisurely drives past the beaches, harbors, lighthouses, and wetlands along Lake Huron's shore—this is the Thumb. Not heavily populated and not thronging with tourists, even in summer, this is Michigan's nearest faraway place. The best time to visit is from Memorial Day through October. From mid-June to Labor Day the beaches along Saginaw Bay and the small lakeside towns on the eastern side beckon weary city dwellers. Bird-watchers and hunters return in autumn when migratory fowl visit the wetlands.

Weather: Summer temperatures are in the 80s, and all along Lake Huron the beaches are at their most inviting. Fall brings daytime highs of 65 degrees F. Winter days usually stay above freezing; nights drop into the high 20s—enough to keep about 3 inches of snow on the ground through February. Spring and fall bring rain, so don't forget your umbrella.

Food & Lodging: This is not great restaurant country, but the small-town cafés and diners offer a lot in the way of personality. Some of the B&Bs are wonderful. *See listings beginning on page 274.*

S U N R I S E   S I D E

First comes a soft morning glow across the eastern sky. Then dawn leaps out of Lake Huron, spreading glitter on the waves and casting the lighthouses guarding the shore in sharp silhouette. So begins the day on Michigan's "Sunrise Side," where the flatlands of the south roll into the hills of the north, creased with rivers that invite canoeing, kayaking, tubing, and fishing.

U.S. 23 hugs the shoreline as it follows the Circle Lake Huron signs from Bay City to Mackinaw City at the top of Michigan's mitten. Interstate 75 marks the western boundary of this section, while between the two highways M-33 zigzags through the forested heartland from the village of Alger (on I-75 between Standish and West Branch) north to Cheboygan. I savor driving these Sunrise Side high-

This painting by George Catlin depicts the expedition of René-Robert Cavelier, Sieur de La Salle, leaving Fort Frontenac in 1679.

ways, whether on a 90-degree summer day with car windows down and wind blowing free or on an icy February morning when snowflakes speckle my windshield and Lake Huron claws at the beach over my shoulder. Along the way are 19th-century lumbering and fishing towns, small villages such as Wooden Shoe and Red Oak, as well as the major towns of Bay City and Alpena.

Other than on I-75, traffic moves slowly, without horns or squealing brakes. There are no shopping malls or crowded tourist attractions. "We can fancy up, but plain just suits us better," says longtime Rogers City resident Harry Whiteley. Inland, folks tend to work hard through the week, eat out on Friday night, attend church on Sunday, and line up for parades on holidays; on weekends they'll likely tow their boats out to one of the myriad lakes for a day of fishing, picnicking, and swimming.

■ HISTORY

The first European to trace the length of the Sunrise Side in a craft larger than a canoe was French explorer René-Robert Cavelier, Sieur de La Salle. In 1679 he built a 45-ton schooner, the *Griffin,* above Niagara Falls and sailed her across Lake Erie, up the Detroit River, and into Lake Huron.

After his ship nearly capsized in rough seas, he dropped anchor at St. Ignace for a few days' rest before sailing on to Green Bay. There he loaded the *Griffin* with furs and ordered her back to Niagara for more supplies. She never made it. (The remains of this long-lost craft are believed to lie on the floor of Lake Huron near Tobermory, Ontario.) It would be 100 years before a ship the likes of the *Griffin* would again hoist sails on the lower Great Lakes.

During the 1700s, eastern Michigan was largely ignored by settlers. Small Indian villages, each with approximately 30 inhabitants, clustered around the river mouths. Occasionally a fur trapper or lone fisherman built a crude shelter and stayed awhile. Surrounding these villages, a great forest of white pine and hardwood covered the land, the canopy of intertwining branches so dense it blocked the sun from reaching the forest floor. Lakes and rivers teemed with whitefish, sturgeon, and the trout-like grayling.

Then came timber fever. After loggers had leveled the forests around Saginaw and the Thumb, they turned north for yet more timber. They followed the harvest from the Rifle River to the Au Sable and Black rivers, working their way farther north to Thunder Bay and Cheboygan and leaving in their wake the rubble and slash of clear-cut forests and decimated spawning grounds. Towns such as Tawas City, Oscoda, Harrisville, Ossineke, Alpena, Rogers City, and Cheboygan were suddenly forced to figure out new ways to survive.

By the end of the 19th century the white pine on the morning side of Michigan had been felled, their canopies pulled down, their whisper silenced. Fishermen came for the grayling with the same zeal as the lumberjacks had for timber—with the same results. It has taken nearly 50 years of careful management to restore a significant timber harvest, but the grayling, like the blue pike, is now extinct and no longer brightens the Au Sable. Pioneers scratched farms from the poor soils of the cutover land, and new industries slowly evolved as best they could. Today, a century after the timber fever burned its way across the land, the economy of eastern Michigan is based on a carefully resuscitated timber industry, light industry, limited farming, and tourism—for it remains a beautiful place to come to restore one's depleted spirits.

■ UP THE SUNRISE SIDE

■ RIFLE RIVER RECREATION AREA *map page 152, C-6*
The meandering Rifle River, which empties into Saginaw Bay near the village of Omer on U.S. 23 east of Standish, is the core of the 4,300-acre **Rifle River Recreation Area**. To begin a 90-mile canoe float trip from RRRA headquarters at Devoe Lake, take I-75 north to Alger, drive north on M-33 to Rose City, then east on Rose City Road, following the RRRA signs. Rustic campgrounds, coveted by fishermen, are scattered along this slow-moving, sparkling river. *989-473-2258; www.dnr.state.mi.us/parksandtrails.*

If a 90-mile canoe trek seems a tad daunting, stop off in Sterling and put in along a very pleasant mile of maintained river. **River View Campground and**

Canoe Livery will set you up with the canoe or kayak of your choice. *5755 Towline Road, Sterling; 989-654-2447; www.riverviewcampground.com.*

From the Rifle River at Omer, follow U.S. 23 northeast along the coast for 29 miles to the twin cities of Tawas City and East Tawas, which hug the wide sweep of Lake Huron's Tawas Bay. (The name "Tawas" comes up a lot while visiting here.) The main street, Newman Street, is lined with shops, and on lazy afternoons folks stroll the marina boardwalk licking ice-cream cones.

Curving like a comma into Lake Huron, **Tawas Point State Park** offers a few campsites directly on the powdery sand and another 200 sites only steps from the water's edge. In the evenings, as if on cue, campers by the dozens gather on the bay beach to watch the sun reflecting on the water before it drops behind the distant hills.

Within the park, the **Sandy Hook Nature Trail** is a fine place to look for shorebirds along the water's edge and to listen for the musical *o-kaleee!* song of red-winged blackbirds atop the cattails. In spring and fall Tawas is a regular migratory stop for numerous songbirds; in mid-August monarch butterflies stop here for brief rests before fluttering on. The trail leads past the **Tawas Point Lighthouse,** a 70-foot conical tower of white brick built in 1876, next to its redbrick keeper's quarters. Still a working lighthouse, it's open to the public from May 15 through October 15 on Saturdays, Sundays, and holidays. Tours can be arranged. *686 Tawas Beach Road; 989-362-5041; www.dnr.state.mi.us/parksandtrails.*

For more information: *Tawas Bay Tourist & Convention Bureau; 402 Lake Street (U.S. 23); 800-558-2927; www.tawasbay.com.*

■ **AU SABLE AND OSCODA** *map page 152, D-5*

When you arrive at the Au Sable Bridge in the small town of Au Sable, you know you're in paddling country: the canoes are stacked high along the banks of the Au Sable River, a designated State Natural River. The spiderweb headwaters of this shallow, fast-flowing waterway converge to become one of Michigan's favorite canoeing and trout fishing streams about 70 miles west of here (as the crow flies), at the mid-Michigan town of Grayling. Then the river twists and turns for 120 miles before reaching Au Sable and its twin town of Oscoda on the Lake Huron shore. En route, deeper waters lie in "ponds" (actually small lakes) created by power dams. During the last weekend of July, the demanding course of the annual **Au Sable River Canoe Marathon** challenges would-be world champions with at

SUNRISE SIDE

0   10   20 Miles

0   10   20   30 Kilometers

◯ Towns with food and/or lodging listings

Elevation
in feet

2,675
2,500
2,000
1,500
1,000
500
Sea Level

A **B** **C** **D**

CANADA
UNITED STATES

Mackinac Bridge
Round Island Light
Mackinaw City
Historic Mill Creek State Park
Pt Aux Pins
BOIS BLANC ISLAND
Carp Lake
To St Ignace
River Range Front Light
Cheboygan State Park
Ninemile Pt
Levering
Cheboygan
Opera House, City Straits Park & Cheboygan Crib Light
Cheboygan River
Forty Mile Pt Light
Forty Mile Pt
Brutus
Mullett Lake
Aloha State Park
Black Lake
Onaway State Park
Hoeft State Park
Rogers City
Alanson
Burt L
Topinabee
Adams Pt
Afton
Tower
Onaway
Ocqueoc Falls
New Presque Isle Light
Old Presque Isle Light
PRESQUE ISLE
Presque Isle
Burt Lake State Park
Wolverine
Posen
Grand Lake
Presque Isle Township Cemetery
Black Bear
Vanderbilt
Clear Lake State Park
Elk Ridge
North
Branch
Long Lake
Middle Island Light
MIDDLE ISLAND
Thunder Bay Island Light
Gaylord Country Club
The Classic
Treetops
Hillman
Lachine
Alpena
Alpena Light
Thunder Bay
North Pt
Gaylord
The Loon
The Natural
Johannesburg
Atlanta
John A Lau Saloon & Jesse Besser Museum
SULPHUR ISLAND
Otsego Lake
The Lake
The Lake
Lewiston
Fletcher Lake
Devils Lake
Thunder Bay National Marine Sanctuary and Underwater Preserve
Otsego Lake State Park
Otsego Lake
Black Forest
Garland
Comins
Hubbard Lake
Negwegon State Park
Frederic
Hartwick Pines State Park
Fairview
Hubbard Lake
Black River
Au Sable
Curran
Sturgeon Pt Light
Grayling
River
Harrisville
Sturgeon Pt Lighthouse and Museum
Fox Run
Luzerne
Pine
Harrisville State Park
North Higgins Lake State Park
Glennie
Greenbush
Roscommon
Lumberman's Monument
Foote Pond
Oscoda
Higgins Lake
Iargo Springs
Foote Site Village
Au Sable
South Higgins Lake State Park
Lake St Helen
Devoe Lake
Devoe Lake to Omer Canoe Trip
Au Sable Pt
Houghton Lake
Rose City
Rifle River Recreation Area
Hale
Tawas Lake
Houghton Lake
Prudenville
West Branch
East Tawas
Tawas Point State Park
Tawas City
Tawas Pt Light
Tawas Pt
Whittemore
Tawas Bay
Alabaster
Skeels
Alger
White Stone Pt
Harrison
Wilson State Park
Omer
Big Cr
Au Gres Pt Lookout
CHARITY ISLANDS
Port Crescent State Park
White Star
Arenac
Albert E Sleeper State Park
Beaverton
Standish
Au Gres
Pt Au Gres
Caseville
To Bay City & Saginaw
Wixom Lake
To Bay City & Saginaw
Pinconning
Sand Point
NORTH ISLAND
Bay Port
Pigeon
Clare
Curtis
Edenville
MAISOU ISLAND
Saginaw Bay

Lake Huron

least 14 hours of full-bore paddling, and leg-straining portages over the river dam support banks that reach higher than a three-story building. Crowds come to cheer on participants.

For more information: *Oscoda Area Convention & Visitors Bureau; 4440 North U.S. 23; 800-235-4625; www.oscoda.com.*

Before the arrival of the marathoners and power dams, these waters served as a transportation trail for Chippewas and other Great Lakes tribes. When lumber barons along the Saginaw River saw their supply of white pine dwindling, they found along the Au Sable high-quality red pine that floated like a fish bobber. Soon the Au Sable reverberated with sounds of falling timber, the vibrating ping of the blacksmith's anvil, and the clang of the camp dinner bell. By 1836 Oscoda was a sawmill town, with rows of taverns, Saturday-night brawls after payday, and "shady ladies" along the back streets.

Now that its use as a log highway is over, the Au Sable has reverted to less intrusive business. Charter captains like Dennis Bidigare at **Bidigare's Charter Service** (989-739-1342) in Oscoda and Ron Horton with his **Bluebird Charters** (989-876-6469) in Au Gres join other boats heading for the waters of Lake Huron in pursuit of whitefish, perch, and, when they're running, salmon and steelhead.

Canoeing the Au Sable River.

THE LUMBERJACK CODE

Mythic hero of Michigan's ancient forests, the lumberjack captured the American imagination in almost as grand a fashion as the cowboy. Paul Bunyan with his blue ox, Babe, was deliberately drawn larger than life, but beneath that legend lay a reality of derring-do and mind-boggling excess. The pioneering folk-life historian Richard Dorson sought to capture many of the tales and as much of the lore of that era as he could before it disappeared completely. This excerpt describes the inconsistent and highly contradictory code of that now-vanished way of life.

The white pine lumberjack has grown into legend, the legend of a swashbuckling, ferocious, tenderhearted superman. . . . The life of the jacks followed an unwritten creed, and he who violated its articles suffered dishonor and dismissal from a proud fraternity. . . . More surely than any union contract, the lumberjack code extracted from the woodsmen unslacking, prodigious toil. "They worked all day from the first light until deep into the night; they'd work their heart out for you," Moonlight Schmidt said. To be the Number One jack in a camp was a coveted honor; to haul the most board feet of logs into camp was an incentive that spurred rival teamsters; to belong to the best camp was a proud assertion backed up with flying fists.

Skill and superstamina being taken for granted, the code next stressed the ability to brawl and the necessity to get insensibly drunk. The lumberjacks have been aptly styled "whiskey-fighting men." Every spring when camp would break, a jack must leave the woods where he has lived in monastic seclusion for six or seven months, hike to the nearest town and blow his entire stake of four or five hundred dollars on rotgut whiskey. . . . Many jacks never escaped the woods because they blew every stake they made for liquor. . . . Just why the jack had to spend all his earnings thus futilely none of the old woodsmen can quite explain, all accepting the matter as fundamentalist doctrine quite beyond inquiry.

—Richard M. Dorson, *Blood-Stoppers and Bear-Walkers: Folk Tales of Immigrants,*
Lumberjacks and Indians, 1952

■ **HURON NATIONAL FOREST** *map page 152, C-5*
The 22-mile-long **River Road National Scenic Byway** follows M-65 from Oscoda west along the south bank of the Au Sable through the Huron National Forest to Rollway, at Loud Pond. Outside Oscoda, a special area planted with jack pine provides critical habitat for the tiny Kirtland's warbler. This and other wooded areas developed within the Huron are the only nesting sites for this endangered gray-and-yellow songbird, which winters in the Bahamas. *USDA Forest Service; 5761 North Skeel Road, Oscoda; 989-739-0728.*

About 10 miles up the Scenic Byway is **Foote Site Village**, a mecca for steelhead and salmon anglers. Forgot your gear? All you'll need can be bought at Karen Usler's and Robert Lammi's **The Dam Store** (1879 River Road; 989-739-9979).

One quarter mile farther west, on the shores of Foote Pond, a 7-mile-long waterway created by the Foote Dam, the white ***Au Sable River Queen*** paddle-wheel riverboat is available for leisurely cruises. *1775 West River Road; 989-739-7351; www.ausableriverqueen.com.*

About 10 miles from Foote Pond is **Cooke Pond**, another lake created by a power dam. On a bluff overlooking the pond is the famous **Lumberman's Monument**. It was erected to honor the woodsmen who surveyed and harvested the trees, skidded logs to the rollways and into the

The Lumberman's Monument.

streams, who watered down the ice roads and drove the teams of horses. Displays include an interpretive visitors center, logging wagons, big wheels, and other equipment from the early years.

A few miles farther along the Au Sable you reach a turnout. This is **Iargo Springs**. Some 294 steps descend a steep wooded hillside where a walkway spans a boggy glen under pines and spruce so tall one feels the need to speak in whispers. According to legend, Chippewas came to Iargo Springs to partake of its "mystical" waters, which seep from springs at the bottom of the hillside. Here are low waterfalls and water plants greening in the seeps and the shallows of Cooke Pond, where visitors toss coins to gleam among forgotten logs.

■ HARRISVILLE *map page 152, D-4*

North of Oscoda, U.S. 23 is lined with modest vacation cottages and year-round homes fronting on Lake Huron. A half-mile south of Harrisville at **Harrisville State Park** (989-724-5126), campsites are set among groves of pines and aromatic cedars.

Four miles north of Harrisville is the **Sturgeon Point Lighthouse and Museum**, a designated state Scenic Site. Of Michigan's 117 lighthouse museums, this one is

Sturgeon Point Lighthouse was built in 1869.

Scenic U.S. 23, shown here in autumn colors, follows the shoreline of Lake Huron.

my favorite, built in 1869 and still actively warning boaters of the deadly reef just offshore. Its fiery-red window trim and doors contrast dramatically with the white of the keeper's quarters and connecting 70-foot conical tower. The tower is off-limits, but you're invited to tour the keeper's quarters, now a museum. Furnishings in the first-floor rooms (kitchen, bedroom, and library) date from the early 1900s, down to the pince-nez glasses resting on an open Bible. The walls are painted the same shade of green as they were when the keeper's family lived here in 1913. A room on the museum's second floor holds displays of the lifesaving station that once stood along the shore. Outdoor displays include the rudder from the ship *Marine City*, a wooden steamer that caught fire in August 1880 and sank two miles north with 100 passengers and a crew of 41 on board (most of whom were rescued, you'll be glad to know). *Off U.S. 23 to Lakeshore Drive and Point Road; 989-724-5126.*

■ **HUBBARD LAKE** *map page 152, C/D-3/4*
Michigan's third-largest inland lake—rated third cleanest, and second in clarity by Michigan's Department of Natural Resources—the spring-fed **Hubbard Lake** offers 30 miles of shoreline. It's been a popular vacation destination for more than 100 years, and was also a favorite of Great Lakes Indians who considered a very

large boulder at the head of the lake a holy place. In 1881 lumbering brought settlement to the area, and the tall, straight pines from around the lake were logged and shipped to the Atlantic seaboard as masts for oceangoing vessels.

Today the woods along the shoreline are interrupted by 1950s-vintage resorts, small restaurants, ice-cream and sandwich shops, marinas, and the occasional market. The community of South Shore is crowded with small private summer cottages and is as jam-packed as a third-grader's sleepover party. Boats and water toys are stacked along the shore, but because the lake is so large, it rarely seems overpopulated.

"If I saw 12 boats at one time, I would say the lake was crowded," says Don Geib, owner of **Churchill Pointe Inn** on the east shore. Hedged in greenery with banks of flowers circling the walkways, the 1927 inn and restaurant is a favorite with visitors and locals alike. From the long lakeside deck shaded by giant oaks, boaters can order dockside dining served on board. Open from May through October. *5700 Bennett Road; 989-727-2020; www.churchillpointeinn.com.*

The Brown Trout Festival in Alpena takes place in the fall.

■ ALPENA *map page 152, D-3*

Alpena, the largest city on the Sunrise Side, hugs the northern shore of Lake Huron's Thunder Bay. Approaching from the south on U.S. 23, you pass through the marshlands of Squaw Bay, where waterbirds flit among the reeds, from mergansers in the shallows and plovers in the grasses to great blue herons circling overhead.

Old Town

Electric streetlights first illuminated Alpena in 1883, two years after their invention, and telephones began ringing here one year after their invention. Old Town itself comprises three blocks of Second Avenue along which the brick streets and storefronts have been restored to their late-1800s appearance.

John A. Lau Saloon

The 1893 John A. Lau Saloon stands on the site of the original, where lumberjacks came on payday—hell-bent on hell-raising. Lau kept three bartenders on hand—a German, a Frenchman, and a Pole—so that the language of most any lumberjack who bellied up to the bar could be understood. More sedate today, the saloon serves tasty barbecued ribs. *414 North Second Avenue; 989-354-6898.*

Thunder Bay National Marine Sanctuary and Underwater Preserve

This preserve, one of at least 11 diving parks in Michigan, protects an estimated 116 historically significant shipwrecks within a 448-square-mile area, the heaviest concentration of shipwrecks per square mile in the Great Lakes. The Michigan Nature Association manages 17 islands scattered in the bay, all key habitats for migrating waterfowl. *145 Water Street; 989-356-8805; www.thunderbay.noaa.gov.*

Jesse Besser Museum

This museum features a re-created 19th-century Avenue of Shops, a general store, a harness shop, a post office, and clapboard houses with oil lamps and lace curtains at the windows—all allowing a marvelous peek into bygone times. The museum's Gallery of Early Man displays 20,000 artifacts dating back 7,000 years, drawn primarily from a collection by the museum's historian and curator, Robert Haltiner, and his father, Gerald. *491 Johnson Street; 989-356-2202; www.bessermuseum.org.*

Duck Park and Island Park

At the corner of U.S. 23 North and Long Rapids Road, a gaggle of geese and ducks is sure to greet you at the first of these parks, Duck Park, along the Thunder Bay River, even before you follow the trails to the footbridge that crosses to the second, neighboring **Island Park,** with more trails and fishing platforms. Both parks are in the 600-acre Alpena Wildlife Sanctuary, which teems with ducks, swans, a wide variety of songbirds, and occasionally a barred or great horned owl.

■ PRESQUE ISLE LIGHTHOUSES *map page 152, D-2*

When the first lighthouse was built in the 1840s at Presque Isle Harbor, 19 miles north of Alpena, somebody goofed—it was built on the north side of a small cove, and the 38-foot-tall light could not be seen by southbound boats. Nevertheless, the old tower kept watch over the scene for 30 years, until finally, in 1870, another lighthouse was built a mile north. At 113 feet, the newer light tower is the tallest on the Great Lakes.

Besser State Natural Area, on the shores of Lake Huron, lies across False Presque Isle Harbor from Presque Isle.

Ocqueoc Falls, one of the few waterfalls in Michigan's Lower Peninsula, is about 15 miles west of Rogers City.

The **Old Presque Isle Lighthouse & Museum** features a spiral staircase with hand-chiseled stone steps that wind to the top. The English-style whitewashed-brick light keeper's cottage reflects the mid-1800s with displays of nautical instruments, foghorns, anchors, a windlass, a ship's wheel, and Fresnel lenses. One mile north, the **New Presque Isle Lighthouse,** still a working light, can also be climbed (130 steps). Next door, the former keeper's house, the 1905 House, has been restored as a small museum. The new lighthouse also has a gift shop. *Old Presque Isle Lighthouse Museum, 5324 East Grand Lake Road; 989-595-6979; New Lighthouse Museum, 4500 East Grand Lake Road; 989-595-9917.*

Along the road to the lighthouses, stop at the **Presque Isle Township Cemetery** and the graves of Bill Green, Fred Piepkorn, and Charlie Priest. During the Depression, when liquor was hard to come by, these three pals usually found more than their share. In a toast to their friendship, they pledged that as each pal passed on, the others would raise their bottles and pour a drink on their buddy's grave. In each cement slab is drilled a hole above the dearly departed buddy, waiting for his drink. Which buddy was the last to go? You'll have to check that out on your own. (Bring a flask!)

Michigan Brown Trout Festival
In mid-July, fishermen head to Alpena for the state's oldest and, at 10 days' duration, longest fishing tournament, which also includes the state's largest ladies' class event. Since 1975 the Michigan Brown Trout Festival has set the pace for similar tournaments statewide. Festival headquarters at the City of Alpena Marina buzz with activities that include boat shows, food, and entertainment, while fishermen take to the surrounding waters. *www.alpenami-browntrout.com.*

For more information: *Alpena Convention & Visitors Bureau; 235 West Chisholm; 800-425-7362.*

■ HILLMAN *map page 152, C-3*

The tiny town of Hillman lies 22 miles due west of Alpena on M-32. In the warm and breezy summertime, the fields along the road are planted with sunflowers that raise their broad yellow faces eastward. In spring, delectable morel mushrooms grow in the forest, and in autumn, trees blaze red and gold.

Wintertime, after a good snowfall, is my favorite time to visit Hillman, because that is when I can view the elk at the **Thunder Bay Golf & RV Resort** from a horse-drawn sleigh on the way to a five-course gourmet meal at Jack and Jan Matthias's **Elk Antler Log Cabin.** The wagon ride is offered throughout the year, but nothing beats a winter sleigh drawn by draft horses, their breath puffing visibly in the icy air. Return in summer for golf and fishing. *27800 M-32; call for directions: 989-742-4875 or 800-729-9375; www.thunderbaygolf.com.*

■ ROGERS CITY *map page 152, C-2*

Twenty-nine miles north of Alpena is Rogers City. The **Quarry View** platform reveals the workings in the 3-mile-long by 2-mile-wide open limestone quarry, the largest such quarry in the world.

■ CHEBOYGAN *map page 152, A-1*

Long ago, the combination of lakes and rivers along the Cheboygan River formed the dividing line between the Ottawa Nation on the west side and the Chippewas to the east. Indian tribes planted summer gardens along the river banks. In the 1800s it became an important lumbering center. Today quiet Cheboygan retains little of the rough-and-ready atmosphere that prevailed 90 years ago, when eight sawmills whined and screamed along the river day and night. They spit so much sawdust that it floated in the air, settled underfoot and over the town, eventually accumulating in a pile covering 12 acres and towering "higher than the tall masts of a schooner." In 1960 the mound still stretched 1,000 feet along the river.

At the **Opera House**, built in 1877 and now restored to Victorian elegance, the-atrical performances are staged throughout the season. The vaulted ceiling is sup-ported by five ornate arches decorated with scrolls and garlands of pink and red roses highlighted in gold. *403 North Huron Street; 231-627-5432; www. theoperahouse.org.*

At the mouth of the Cheboygan River the **City Straits Park** walkway leads over the sand to the **Cheboygan Crib Light.** Here you'll find a beach, a playground, and picnic facilities. A raised boardwalk overlooks Michigan's largest cattail marsh, a nesting site for 54 bird species.

The river is home port for the U.S. Coast Guard cutter *Mackinaw,* the largest of the Great Lakes icebreakers. Visitors are welcome aboard when the cutter is in port (231-627-3181). Car ferries make runs from the river to Pointe Aux Pins, a small village on the southern shore of Bois Blanc, a picturesque island in Lake Huron and a mecca for sportsmen.

Just upriver from the Cheboygan's mouth, the 1869 **Cheboygan Lock** raises boats 15 feet onto the Inland Waterway, which connects Lake Huron to Crooked Lake. The waterway covers 38 miles, flowing from Lake Huron to the Cheboygan River, through Mullett Lake to the Indian River, through Burt Lake to Crooked River, and then into Crooked Lake. The Great Lakes Indians called it the "shortcut to nowhere," for after a relatively easy canoe trip west to Crooked Lake they still faced an 8-mile overland portage to Lake Michigan. Nevertheless, Indians and then fur trappers preferred it to the treacherous waters and long paddle through the Straits of Mackinac. Now boaters enjoy the scenic route with stops in small towns along the way. *www.cheboygan.com/waterways.php.*

For more information: *Cheboygan Area Tourist Bureau, 847 South Main Street; 800-968-3302; www.cheboygan.com.*

■ TRAVEL BASICS

Area Overview: The rolling hills along Michigan's Lake Huron shore are dotted with small towns that beckon tourists, campers, boaters, and picnickers, most of whom dutifully travel along the newly designated Sunrise Side Coastal Highway Heritage Route (U.S. 23) as it curves gently northward following the lakeshore from Bay City to the top of Michigan's mitten at Mackinaw City. Several highways cut across the section to connect with the major north–south trucker highway, I-75, and many of them offer marvelous side trips redolent of Michigan's past and its special beauty.

Weather: As in the rest of Michigan, water tempers the climate along the lakeshore throughout the year. Alpena, in particular, profits from its lake position, enjoying some of the mildest temperatures in the state. Summer is T-shirt-and-shorts weather. Daytime temperatures average in the 80s, dropping into the 60s at night for good sleeping. Spring and fall temperatures drop to 60, and the nights are cool. Winters are sometimes the coldest in the Lower Peninsula, creating ideal weather for ice fishing and snowmobiling. However, winter days can climb into the 40s.

Food & Lodging: Small cafés and local favorite restaurants can be surprisingly good; B&Bs abound and lakeside cottages can often be rented, but be sure to plan ahead! *See listings beginning on page 274.*

A tugboat sits idly at an inland waterway lock in Cheboygan.

S O U T H W E S T
& W E S T C E N T R A L

Fort St. Joseph, on the St. Joseph River near the present city of Niles, was the center of the fur trade for the Illinois country and southwest Michigan. Strategically placed, the fort has flown the flags of France, Spain (for one day!), England, and finally the United States. In the early 1800s, with the decline of the fur trade and the displacement of the indigenous tribes, a strong military presence was no longer needed. Troops were withdrawn and the fort deteriorated. Swampy and difficult to traverse, the area remained wilderness.

Although a few settlers began arriving in the St. Joseph River valley in the 1820s, the region did not attract the interest of most settlers until the mid-1830s, after the completion of the Erie Canal and the construction of the Chicago Road (later renamed the Red Arrow Highway, then designated U.S. 12). A plank road that connected Chicago with Fort Detroit, the Chicago Road followed the Old Sauk Trail that the Indians had used for centuries.

With the draining of "the Great Swamp," as the area was known, settlers uncovered rich, black earth in which crops would flourish. Today the only reminders of Fort St. Joseph are the excellent historical exhibits at the Fort St. Joseph Museum in Niles.

■ MICHIGAN'S FRUIT BASKET

Southwest Michigan abounds in small towns with colorful names such as Sodus, Cassopolis, Dowagiac, and Paw Paw. There are sleepy lakeside villages with streetside markets selling homegrown herbs, flowers, and vegetables. Out in the country, roadsides are dotted with fruit and vegetable stands, vineyards, and "U-pick" farms. In 1939, the authors of the WPA guide to Michigan wrote: "Johnny Appleseed, the almost legendary eccentric who planted nurseries of apple trees in the Ohio River Valley and distributed the trees to the Indians, is generally credited with being the founder of southwestern Michigan's extensive fruit culture."

■ TREE-MENDUS FRUIT FARM *map page 171, B-5*

The big event out here is the **International Cherry Pit Spitting Contest,** held the first Saturday in July at the **Tree-Mendus Fruit Farm** at Eau Claire, 7 miles west of Dowagiac. As Herb Teichman, the farm's owner, candidly states, "I started the contest in 1974 when I was looking for something to do." The pit-spitting rules are strict (*see page 169*). When the contestant is ready, he or she carefully selects a freshly picked cherry, chews, and swallows. Keeping the pit rolling inside the cheek as the seconds tick away, the contestant arches back, gives a mighty forward thrust with the entire torso, and lets 'er fly.

"It's a wonder they don't get hernias," one spectator observed.

The record pit spit is 93 feet, 6.5 inches, set by Brian "Young Gun" Krause of Lansing in 2003, topping his own previous record. With three Krause family members former winners, father Rick "Pellet Gun" Krause of Arizona, a 12-time winner, and Marlene Tuffy Krause, a four-time winner in the women's division, Teichman calls them the "first family of spitting." For would-be contestants who feel they need a bit of practice, Teichman sells Cherry Pit Spit Training Kits. *9351 East Eureka Road, Eau Claire; 269-782-7101 or 877-863-3276; www.tree-mendus.com.*

■ **WICKS' APPLE HOUSE** *map page 171, B-5*
Aromas of fresh fruit and vegetables mingle with the cinnamony fragrance of apple pies and other desserts as they pass from the see-through bakery window to the Orchard View dining room. There is also a cider mill and gift shop. Open Memorial Day to Halloween. *52281 Indian Lake Road, Dowagiac; 269-782-7306; www.wicksapplehouse.com.*

Lake Michigan's moderating effect on the climate in Michigan allows cherries to grow as far north as the Leelanau Peninsula.

■ **WINERIES**

Southwestern Michigan is proud of its winemakers. **Tabor Hill Winery** (185 Mount Tabor Road; 800-283-3363; www.taborhill.com) at Buchanan, for example, gets high marks for its demi-sec sparkling white wine—it was served at the White House for the inauguration of Gerald Ford. Tours are available, and the winery's restaurant serves eight-course "winemaker's dinners." Tabor Hill also has tasting rooms at Saugatuck and Ann Arbor. The **Lemon Creek Fruit Farm and Winery** (533 East Lemon Creek Road, Berrien Springs; 269-471-1321; www. lemoncreekwinery.com), family operated since 1855, produces 26 blends from its 300 acres of varietals. Our favorites? The seyval blanc, the cabernet sauvignon, and the riesling.

At Paw Paw, stop in at the **St. Julian Winery** (716 South Kalamazoo Street; 269-657-5568; www.stjulian.com). The guided winery tour ends in the tasting room where the merlot and chardonnay are most drinkable. Nearby, choose a table in the wine-garden restaurant at **Warner Vineyards** (706 South Kalamazoo Street; 269-657-3165 or 800-756-5357; www.warnerwines.com) and watch the Paw Paw River flow past.

A commercial vineyard in the Paw Paw–Lawton area, Michigan's prime grape-growing region.

International Cherry Pit Spit Competition Rules

1. The contest is open to everyone regardless of age or sex.
2. All contestants must register in qualifying court prior to spitting, unless spitter is awarded a special exemption by the official tournament judge. Registration deadline is 12:00 noon on day of Championship.
3. No foreign objects may be held in the mouth which would give an advantage in spitting the pit. Denture racks will be provided for those wishing to remove their teeth.
4. The contestant's foul line will be determined on a handicap basis according to height, in order to remove any advantage to taller contestants. The handicap will consist of a two-inch withdrawal from the base foul line for each one-inch of contestant height over four feet. Any contestant four feet tall or less will stand at the base foul line. The decision of the tournament line judge is final.
5. Contestants must select three cherries from the regulation variety (Montmorency) supplied by the tournament committee. Cherries must be washed and chilled to 55-60 degrees F pit temperature.
6. Each cherry must be inserted in the mouth whole, all solids eaten prior to spitting of the pit. No part of the cherry may be removed from the mouth after insertion.
7. Each contestant must spit his/her pit within 60 seconds of the time he/she is called to the line by the tournament judge. Three spits are allowed. The longest of the three is recorded. If the pit is swallowed, that spit is forfeited.
8. Contestants' hands must remain below the shoulders (to avoid popping one's cheeks).
9. Contestants' feet may not touch or cross the foul line.
10. Spitters must stand flat on the ground—or ground-level platform—to spit. Spitters are prohibited from using any kind of mechanical or other device to improve body thrust or spit length (including hydraulic hoists, wall support, etc.).
11. The pit-spitting range will be available for practice spitting from 10:00 A.M. until noon on the contest day. Practicing spitters will be allowed three spits.
12. Qualifying rounds for the Championship contest will be held Friday, the day before the Championship, at 11 a.m. and 3 p.m., and on Saturday, day of the Championship, starting at 10 a.m. Deadline for reporting to qualifying court is noon on contest day. (All times listed are EDT.)

This pictograph, drawn by the great Lakota chief Sitting Bull, is on exhibit at the Fort St. Joseph Museum.

■ **NILES** *map page 171, B-6*

In 1691 the French built Fort St. Joseph at a point where the old Sauk Trail (now U.S. 12) intersected the St. Joseph River, just south of the present city of Niles. (This was the second Fort St. Joseph, the first—at Port Huron—having been razed to the ground by its commandant prior to his return to Fort Michilimackinac.) With it, Niles became the first settlement in western Michigan. The **Fort St. Joseph Museum** contains the best collection of 17th-century French and Indian artifacts in Michigan, including a fascinating set of pictographs made by the great Lakota chief Sitting Bull. *508 East Main Street; 269-683-4702.*

■ **FERNWOOD BOTANICAL GARDENS AND NATURE PRESERVE**
Fernwood is a 105-acre preserve that nurtures more than 2,000 species of exotic plants and ferns. Colors throughout the garden change with the seasons, building to an autumn peak in the arboretum with its wide variety of trees and shrubs. Plan for lunch in the café, and make time to browse through the gift shop. *Northwest from Niles off I-31, 13988 Range Line Road; 269-695-6491; www.fernwoodbotanical.org.*

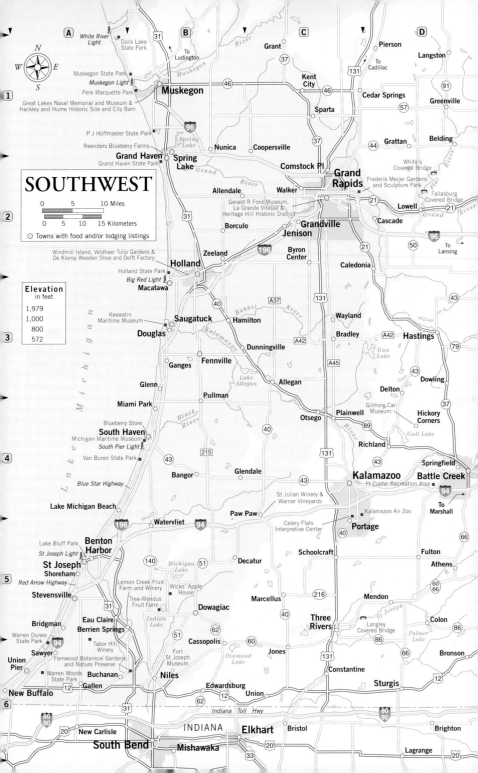

Tower Hill, at Warren Dunes State Park, is a popular launching spot for hang gliders and thrill seekers with their own equipment.

■ RED ARROW HIGHWAY

From Niles you can reach the Lake Michigan shoreline via U.S. 31. If you're coming from Paw Paw, you can take truck-crowded I-94 or you can pick up the Red Arrow Highway, which runs parallel to I-94, at Warner Vineyards. This is a leisurely drive through a bucolic countryside, past Maple Lake and through Hartford to St. Joseph and Benton Harbor.

■ ST. JOSEPH AND BENTON HARBOR *map page 171, A-5*

These two towns are on opposite sides of the St. Joseph River, with St. Joseph to the south and Benton Harbor to the north. St. Joseph traces its history back to 1679, when French explorer René-Robert Cavelier, Sieur de La Salle arrived at the mouth of the St. Joseph (then Miami) River with 14 men in four canoes. On a bluff overlooking the lake they built stockaded Fort Miami, the first such outpost in Lower Michigan. One trading post or mission faded into another until 1831, when enough people moved in to make up the community that would become St. Joseph.

Thirty-five years later, Benton Harbor across the river became the area's lake port, and 60 years ago Benton Harbor was the rising star of the two. In 1941 the Michigan WPA guide observed that the two cities were "so homogeneous that only residents can be perfectly sure of the boundary lines, and the existence of any marked difference, apart from size, is scarcely discernible even by them." In 1968 race riots gutted much of Benton Harbor's downtown, leaving physical and emotional scars from which it has not fully recovered. However, times are changing. Today downtown buildings are finally being restored, and an art gallery district features galleries, shops, and restaurants.

Along St. Joseph's bluff, **Lake Bluff Park** marks the site of old Fort Miami, with paths stretching from **Maids of the Mist Fountain** to **Pioneer Watch**. Sculptures and monuments line the park's walking path, and steep steps descend to old the town, where what were once fishermen's cottages are now tidy, trendy homes.

The **Blossomtime Festival,** the state's oldest (since 1906) multicommunity festival, celebrated throughout southwestern Michigan in late April and early May, figures prominently in the events calendar of these two towns. Each spring, apricot blossoms are the first to burst forth, followed by plum, pear, the wild pink of crab apples, cherries, peaches, and the wide sweep of apple blossoms as fresh and white as a bridal gown. After a week of festivities in surrounding communities, including Blessing of the Blossoms, pageants, and games, crowds show up for the festival's two-hour-long Grand Floral Parade, which begins in St. Joseph and concludes in Benton Harbor. *269-026-7397; www.blossomtimefestival.org.*

For more information: *Southwestern Michigan Tourist Council, 2300 Pipestone Road, Benton Harbor; 269-925-6301; www.swmichigan.org.*

Once I'm ready to leave town, I have to make a choice: south to Warren Dunes State Park or north on the Blue Star Highway along the Lake Michigan shore? It's not an easy decision! We're now smack in the middle of the longest continuous stretch of freshwater beach in the world, and either direction offers unique pleasures. Today, I head south, still on the Red Arrow Highway as it continues to parallel I-94, meandering through shore villages and past elegant hotels and grand homes (many now B&Bs) that date from the coast's halcyon years in the early 1900s.

Just south of St. Joseph–Benton Harbor, in Stevensville, are several popular restaurants. **Tosi's Restaurant** (4337 Ridge Road, 269-429-3689; www.tosis.com) features northern Italian cuisine and pastries from **Bit of Swiss Bakery**, located directly behind the restaurant. Seafood is a specialty at **Grande Mere Inn** (5800 Red Arrow Highway; 269-429-3591), open for dinner only, Tuesdays through Saturdays.

■ **Warren Dunes State Park** *map page 171, A-6*

At Sawyer the Red Arrow Highway passes through forest that gradually gives way to a succession of dunes and **Warren Dunes State Park**—2 miles of light, granular sand piled into 240-foot dunes. When the wind is favorable, hang gliders take to the air from the summit of Tower Hill. There is also camping, picnicking, fishing, and swimming. *Exit 16 off I-94; 269-426-4013; www.michigandnr.com/parksandtrails.*

For more information: *Southwestern Michigan Tourist Council, 2300 Pipestone Road, Benton Harbor; 269-925-6301; www.swmichigan.org.*

■ **South Haven** *map page 171, A-4*

North from St. Joseph–Benton Harbor along the Blue Star Highway, South Haven is like a toy village, with shops stacked down the slope to the Black River. More shops and boutiques are tucked into **Old Harbor Village** on the riverbank.

At the north end of the drawbridge that spans the river, the **Michigan Maritime Museum** recounts the area's water-travel history from Potawatomi Indians in birchbark canoes to the era of hulking lake steamers. The museum sponsors boatbuilding programs in the boathouse. Stop by and watch boats in the making. *260 Dyckman Avenue; 269-637-8078; www.michiganmaritimemuseum.org.*

This is blueberry country. In August the area stages a four-day **National Blueberry Festival** in Riverfront Park, with blueberry pizzas, blueberry sausages, blueberry shakes, blueberry popcorn, and a 5-foot-wide community blueberry pie. After eating enough pie to "sink a ship," walk the 500-foot boardwalk along the river to the beach and the **South Haven South Pier Light,** a photogenic 1903-vintage structure.

At the **Blueberry Store** (the one with the electric-blue awnings you can't miss) delicious aromas waft forth all year: blueberry candles, soaps, teas, and much more. Girls in blueberry-colored shirts help you select blueberry jams, jellies, books, and souvenirs. *525 Phoenix Street; 269-637-6322.*

For more information: *South Haven Visitors Bureau; 546 Phoenix Street; 269-637-5252 or 800-764-2836; www.southhaven.org.*

■ **Kalamazoo** *map page 171, C-4*

Titus Bronson is recognized as the first settler of "Kazoo," as it is called by those who know it best, and his original 1830 log cabin stands in downtown Bronson Park. But Kazoo's main claim to fame, besides being the home of Western

The rolling farmland in Cass County southwest of Kalamazoo.

Michigan University, was the invention in 1885 of a dissolvable sugar coating used by Dr. William E. Upjohn to sweeten his pills. The rest, as they say, is pharmaceutical history.

Another claim to fame was celery, which flourished in the rich black muck of the marshlands along the Kalamazoo River and Portage Creek. Eventually, urban sprawl overtook the celery farms, but a Michigan Historical Marker at the intersection of Crosstown Parkway, Balch, and Park streets relates this early triumph:

> A Scotsman named Taylor grew the first celery in Kalamazoo in 1856. Diners at the Burdick Hotel regarded it with curiosity. Cornelius De Bruyn, a gardener, who came here from the Netherlands in 1866, developed the modern type of celery from the earlier soup celery. J. S. Dunkley sold medicines and condiments made of celery. Soon Kalamazoo celery was known the nation over. Michigan has been a leading producer ever since.

I had not expected entertainment from celery, so I was amusingly surprised at **Celery Flats Interpretive Center**, with its early history of hawkers meeting the

trains to peddle their "new" product to passengers as proudly as if it were ice cream. Along with the museum exhibits, there are a working farm, a one-room mid-19th-century schoolhouse, a playground, and venues for summer festivals and other entertainment. *7335 Garden Lane, Portage; 269-329-4522.*

The **Kalamazoo Air Zoo** houses legendary vintage aircraft such as the Grumman Tigercat, Bearcat, and Hellcat, names that prompted museum supporters to dub the former Kalamazoo Aviation History Museum the Air Zoo. Museum or zoo, it has permanent and changing exhibits that increase the pulse beat of anyone who's ever dreamed of flying, with more than 80 vintage aircraft on display. The zoo is also the new home of the National Guadalcanal Memorial Museum and the Michigan Aviation Hall of Fame. There are rides, theaters, flight simulators, and more. *6151 Portage Road; 269-382-6555 or 866-524-6555; www.airzoo.org.*

At **Hickory Corners**, 18 miles northeast of Kalamazoo, vintage automobiles are parked on 90 acres of rolling lawns at the **Gilmore Car Museum,** teasers for nearly 200 antique and collector cars in the eight restored Michigan-red barns in the

(opposite) A quiet spot in Kalamazoo's rural hinterland. (above) A replica of a 1930s Shell station displayed at the Gilmore Car Museum, northeast of Kalamazoo.

museum park. Displays range from an 1899 Locomobile and the ever-popular Model T to the replica of a 1930s Shell filling station, with full-size service bay and grease pit. *6865 Hickory Road; 269-671-5089; www.gilmorecarmuseum.org.*

Did I say my car brakes for lighthouses? Well, it most definitely goes out of its way for covered bridges. And the **Langley Covered Bridge,** southeast of Kalamazoo, is a great one. At 282 feet, the bridge, built over the St. Joseph River in 1887, is Michigan's longest covered bridge. *U.S. 131 south for 20 miles to Three Rivers, then 6 miles east on M-86 to Centreville and north 3 miles on Covered Bridge Road.*

For more information: *Kalamazoo Convention & Visitors Bureau; 346 West Michigan Avenue; 800-530-9192; www.discoverkalamazoo.com.*

■ BATTLE CREEK *map page 171, D-4*

Say "Battle Creek" to most Americans, and breakfast-cereal commercials will likely come to mind. In 1894, while searching for a grain-based food to serve in their health sanatorium, brothers Dr. John Harvey Kellogg and William Keith Kellogg started a morning dietary revolution when they created flaked cereal. Meanwhile,

The Langley Covered Bridge, built in 1887, is Michigan's longest covered bridge.

Dr. John Harvey Kellogg.

client and patient Charles W. Post conducted similar experiments in a nearby barn and came up with the hot beverage Postum. Today Battle Creek is dubbed Cereal Capital of the World. Visiting kids get to shake hands with Tony the Tiger at **Kellogg's Cereal City USA**, a large entertainment center along the downtown riverfront that features a cereal assembly line and the Red Onion Grill, modeled after a 1930s diner. You can order a Fruit Loops sundae at the ice-cream parlor. *171 West Michigan Avenue; 269-962-6230; www.kelloggscerealcity.com.*

Each June the **World's Longest Breakfast Table** is set up downtown. Bowls of cereal are dished up to more than 60,000 people. In July the city's skies come alive with brightly hued balloons during the **Team U.S. Nationals Hot Air Balloon Championship and Air Show.**

In the mid-19th century Battle Creek was a major stop on the Underground Railroad, the loose network of safe houses that allowed slaves from Southern states to reach freedom in the North. In **Monument Park,** a 12-foot bronze sculpture stands in tribute to the outspoken, 6-foot-tall former slave **Sojourner Truth,** who carried her rally for freedom all the way to President Lincoln and called Battle Creek home for the last 27 years of her long, trailblazing life. Days before her death in 1883, she told her family, "I isn't goin' to die, honey, I'se goin' home like a shootin' star." In the park is also the nation's largest monument to freedom, the **Underground Railroad Movement,** depicting local abolitionists leading a group of runaway slaves to safety. **Heritage Battle Creek** (171 West Michigan Avenue; 269-965-2613) conducts tours of Monument Park and other Battle Creek sites of the Underground Railroad. *Intersection of Division Drive (M-66) and Hamblin Avenue.*

The 430-acre **Binder Park Zoo** is renowned for its safari-style elevated boardwalk, which winds through the "savanna" of its "African National Park." Open April–October. *Exit 100 off I-94, 7400 Division Drive; 269-979-1351; www.binderparkzoo.org.*

For more information: *Battle Creek/Calhoun County Visitor & Convention Bureau; 77 East Michigan Avenue; 800-397-2240; www.battlecreekvisitors.org.*

■ MARSHALL

map page 171, D-4

With big plans to lure the state capital their way during Michigan's early years, the town of Marshall built a governor's mansion and enticed political leaders into building showy estates of their own. When the new capital went to Lansing, Marshall was left with a legacy of well-preserved Greek Revival, Gothic Revival, Queen Anne, Italianate, and other architectural delights. Downtown, ornate storefronts house cafés, specialty shops, boutiques, and antiques stores. It's no wonder that Marshall's historic district is designated a National Historic Landmark.

The Sweetheart of the Corn began to appear in Kellogg's advertising in 1907, and if you took the plant tour (discontinued in the mid-1980s), she was your guide.

Once a stagecoach stop along today's I-94, the 1835 **National House Inn** is a two-story redbrick inn with 15 guest rooms; rough planks cover the lobby floor, and hand-hewn timbers frame the oversize hearth. *102 South Parkview; 269-781-7374; www.nationalhouseinn.com.*

After serving as U.S. consul to the Sandwich Islands (later Hawaii), Michigan Supreme Court judge Abner Pratt returned home to Marshall, but he couldn't leave the islands behind. In 1860 he built **Honolulu House,** with liberal uses of teak and ebony, tall ceilings, wide doorways, and wall murals of tropical plants and animals. The judge even adopted the island style of tropical dress, a habit that contributed to his death. On a freezing-cold drive home from Lansing he caught pneumonia and later died. *107 North Kalamazoo Avenue; 269-781-8544; www. marshallhistoricalsociety.org.*

For more information: *Marshall Chamber of Commerce; 424 East Michigan Avenue; 800-877-5163; www.marshallmi.org.*

■ GRAND RAPIDS *map page 171, C-2*

Michigan's second-largest city after Detroit, Grand Rapids straddles the Grand River at the junction of highways I-96, I-196, and U.S. 131. Art and industry both flourish in this city. World-famous sculpture, world-class manufacturing plants, scenic river walks, elegant showrooms of style-setting furniture, the Heritage Hill Historic District, the wild lupine along the highways, and friendly, down-to-earth residents all combine to make Grand Rapids a lovely city to visit.

The Grand Rapids of today is a far cry from the Indian fishing encampments that Detroit fur trader Louis Campau found along the rapids of the Grand River in 1826. Before moving to west Michigan, Campau, called the Fox by the Indians, had already platted the new town of Saginaw and had assisted Gov. Lewis Cass in negotiating the Treaty of Saginaw with the Ottawas and Chippewas. At Grand Rapids the trader purchased a 72-acre tract and built a cabin, trading post, and blacksmith shop in what would later be the heart of the city, slyly blocking the adjacent property's access to the river—property owned by rival surveyor and Michigan Territory delegate Lucius Lyon. The unfortunate legacy of this ploy is a frustrating jumble of dead-end streets in the heart of downtown.

In 1838 Commissioner of Indian Affairs Henry

Honolulu House in Marshall.

Rowe Schoolcraft visited Grand Rapids and wrote:

> The fall of Grand River here creates an ample water power; the surrounding country is one of the most beautiful and fertile imaginable, and its rise to wealth and populousness must be a mere question of time, and that time hurried on by a speed that is astonishing. This generation will hardly be in their graves before it will have the growth and improvement which in other countries are the result of centuries.

It was an apt prediction. As the fur trade declined and the timber industry flourished, lumberjacks floated logs down the Grand River to the falls that had been harnessed to power sawmills. Attracted by the quality and low cost of the hardwoods here, cabinetmaker William Haldane moved to Grand Rapids and set up shop. By 1837 he had established a reputation for quality furniture that continues to this day.

This 1856 panoramic painting by Grand Rapids artist Sarah Nelson shows her town. At far right is St. Mark's Episcopal Church, built in 1848 and still standing today.

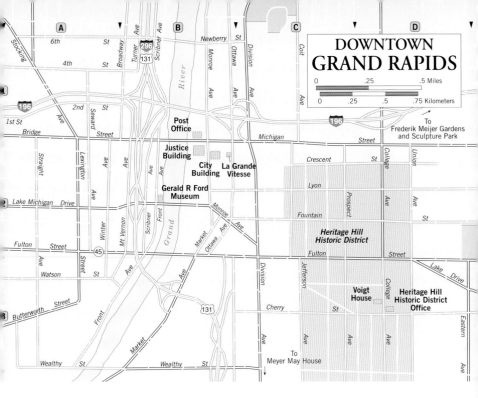

The Grand River Trail from Chicago was surveyed in 1842, and a plank road (now I-96) was laid down to Kalamazoo. Mark Twain took this road once and commented that the ride would have been enjoyable had not "some unconscionable scoundrel now and then dropped a plank across the road."

■ GERALD R. FORD MUSEUM *map page 183, B-2*

Across the steel-gray river from where Campau's trading post once stood is the museum honoring native son and 38th president of the United States Gerald R. Ford. Among the many interesting objects on display are the burglary tools used to break into the offices of the Democratic National Committee at the Watergate Apartments during Richard Nixon's 1972 reelection campaign. *303 Pearl Street NW; 616-451-9263; www.geraldrfordmuseum.org.*

Sculpture

Grand Rapids is also home to one of the world's great sculptures, Alexander Calder's 40-foot red ***La Grande Vitesse***. This American classic is dramatically installed adjacent to the black Kent County Building on Ottawa Avenue between Michigan and Lyon streets.

However, the huge **Frederik Meijer Gardens and Sculpture Park** now features a rival: a 24-foot bronze statue of a horse, a re-creation of one designed by Leonardo da Vinci. In 1476 da Vinci was commissioned by Ludovico Sforza, the Duke of Milan, to create the world's largest equine sculpture, but the necessary bronze got used up making cannons during Milan's defense against France, leaving only a clay model and da Vinci's drawings to indicate its form and scale. Some 500 years later, American artist Nina Akamu was tapped to cast the great horse. A duplicate casting resides in Milan.

Numerous other sculptures are scattered throughout the park, by artists ranging from Auguste Rodin to Henry Moore to Keith Haring. Inside the gardens' five-story glass conservatory, paths meander across bridges and along pebbled streams that are surrounded by more than 300 tropical plants gathered from five continents. True, the orchids are extraordinary, but my favorite spot is a small brook that cascades down a 14-foot waterfall before burbling off through the garden. *Take East Beltline from I-96 West; 1000 East Beltline Avenue NE; 616-957-1580; www.meijergardens.org.*

■ **HERITAGE HILL HISTORIC DISTRICT** *map page 183, C/D-2/3*
Adjacent to downtown Grand Rapids, this extensive historic district contains some 1,300 vintage homes dating from 1848 through the 1920s. Here turreted mansions share the same street with prim Victorian cottages. Most are private homes that are usually closed to the public, with two major exceptions: Voigt House and Meyer May House. **Voigt House** (115 College Avenue SE; 616-456-4600; www.grmuseum.org/voigt), dating from 1895, features a wraparound porch and all the original furnishings of Carl G. A. Voigt and his family. A set of period china is set out upon the dining room table as if, at any minute, the whole family were about to arrive for dinner. The **Meyer May House** (450 Madison Street SE; 616-246-4821) has been completely restored and refurbished by its owner, the Steelcase Corporation. Both its interior and exterior now appear as originally designed by Frank Lloyd Wright in 1908.

The district is bounded by Crescent Street on the north, Pleasant Street on the south, Union Avenue on the east, and Lafayette and Jefferson avenues on the west. You can pick up a free map of three self-guided tours at the Heritage Hill office. *126 College Avenue SE; 616-459-8950; www.heritagehillweb.org.*

For more information: *Grand Rapids/Kent County Convention & Visitors Bureau; 171 Monroe Avenue NW; 800-678-9859; www.visitgrandrapids.org.*

Entitled The American Horse, *this 24-foot bronze statue in the Frederik Meijer Gardens and Sculpture Park is a replica of a horse designed by Leonardo da Vinci.*

■ MUSKETAWA AND WHITE PINE TRAIL

The 26-mile-long **Musketawa Trail** is a "rails to trails" park following the Marne to Muskegon railroad corridor of the old Muskegon, Grand Rapids and Indiana Railroad, which began operation in 1886. No trains have run this way since 1989, and the 12-foot-wide, asphalt-paved trail is now alive with bicyclists, joggers, and in-line skaters, who give way to snowmobilers and cross-country skiers in winter. *Off I-96 about 10 miles northwest of Grand Rapids; 231-853-5476; www. musketawatrail.com.*

The **White Pine Trail State Park** is another "rails to trails" park that traces a 92-mile path from Belmont to Cadillac through forests, bucolic farmlands, and quaint rural towns. *231-832-0794; www.michiweb.com/cadillac/wptrail.*

■ FLAT RIVER'S COVERED BRIDGES

Fifteen miles east of Grand Rapids is Lowell, and about 4 miles northeast of Lowell the **Fallasburg Covered Bridge** spans the Flat River at the south end of **Fallasburg Park.** The 100-foot-long latticework truss bridge, built of white pine in 1871, still bears a sign that reads thus: "$5 Fine for Riding or Driving on this Bridge Faster Than a Walk." *M-21 to Lowell, then north on Fallasburg Park Drive to the park.*

Farther upriver the weathered, narrow 1867 **White's Covered Bridge** is fastened with wooden pegs and handmade square iron nails and is topped by a gabled roof. Jared N. Brasee of Ada, who built both bridges, used hand-hewn trusses sheeted over with rough pine boards. *From the Fallasburg Covered Bridge, drive north on Covered Bridge Road, turn east onto Potters Road, then north onto White's Bridge Road; www.wmta.org/coveredbridges.*

■ SAUGATUCK-DOUGLAS *map page 171, B-3*

The natural beauty of the Kalamazoo River delights the eye as it flows between the towns of Saugatuck and Douglas, then widens into Kalamazoo Harbor before arcing into a wide oxbow and emptying into Lake Michigan.

The oxbow harbors an intriguing Michigan legend: the "lost city" of Singapore. Early in the 19th century a sawmill town named Singapore thrived around the oxbow. It had sprung up in 1831 when Horace H. Comstock established a trading post for settlers moving inland. Over time the outpost grew into a company mill town with a bank, three sawmills, boarding houses, two hotels, two general stores, and a lighthouse on the Lake Michigan shore. Its glory, however, was short-lived.

SINGAPORE BANKING

My favorite story of Singapore, Michigan, has to do with the wildcat banking practices that once were rampant in the state. In 1837 the legislature passed a law that authorized any 12 landowners to form a banking association with capital stock of no less than $50,000, with 30 percent in specie (preferably gold) to support their paper currency. Banks sprang up all across southern Michigan. Since few of the banks actually had the gold, one bank would prop up the next when the inspectors came around every three months.

When the Allegan bank about 20 miles downstream on the Kalamazoo River from Singapore heard that the inspector was on his way, it borrowed gold coins from two neighbors to pass the inspection. With Singapore the next stop, the Allegan banker handed off the bag of gold to a certain Maksaube, a friendly Ottawa Indian. He dashed out the back door, jumped into his canoe, and paddled up the Kalamazoo well ahead of the banker who was making his way on horseback.

Four miles short of Singapore, Maksaube's canoe hit a snag and tipped, and the bag of gold splashed overboard into the deepest part of the river. While the banker summoned blacksmith James Harris to pound out a hook to drag the river, a runner was dispatched to the village of Richmond 6 miles downstream where the inspector was to cross the river. Obliging folks at Richmond's new tavern detained the inspector with a lively reception until word reached them that the Singapore team had indeed struck pay dirt. Oblivious of the to-do, the unwitting inspector continued on to Singapore to count the same gold over again.

By 1875 all the timber had been logged out and the last sawmill dismantled and loaded onto a ship bound for the tree country up the coast. Citizens moved on to areas with jobs, and the abandoned town was left to the drifting dunes.

Today dunes are piled high above the site, but, alas, there is no city buried beneath them. Most of the buildings were salvaged for the new town of Saugatuck on Kalamazoo Harbor about 4 miles inland; the others, including the Singapore Bank Bookstore (now located at 317 Butler Street in Saugatuck), were slid out on logs and hauled down a frozen Kalamazoo River. "Sometimes I find handmade nails, old glass, or a dish or two," says local historian Kit Lane of Douglas. "It's the only evidence that the town was ever there."

The village of Saugatuck fared better. Soon after Singapore vanished, artists discovered this delightful small town in the fork of the river behind the dunes. By

1910 the Art Institute of Chicago had established a summer camp in the nearby oxbow with programs that drew artists from all over the world. The summer school, **Ox-bow** (simply called "O"), still conducts programs in painting, drawing, performing arts, and writing. It also offers permanent galleries and crafts boutiques. *3435 Rupprecht Way; 269-857-5811 June–August, 312-899-7408 year-round; www.ox-bow.org.*

Saugatuck-Douglas, the self-proclaimed Art Coast of Michigan, may well have more galleries, studios, and B&Bs than any other location in Michigan. Adding to the fun is the 1838 **Saugatuck Chain Ferry,** a pedestrian-only connection across the channel that cuts between Saugatuck and the dunes. Ring the bell, and the operator hand-cranks the Victorian-style ferry along a 280-foot chain. It's absolutely the best dollar ride in the state, and the only such ferry remaining along the Great Lakes. Once across, climb up the 282-foot dune, Mount Baldhead—so named before it was planted with trees—and enjoy the view, especially at sunset.

Saugatuck is known for its art galleries, crafts boutiques, and shops.

Seasonal only.

Moored next to the Saugatuck-Douglas Bridge (Blue Star Highway and Union Street) is the 350-foot SS *Keewatin,* a coal-burning overnight steamer that operated on the Great Lakes from 1907 until 1965—the last of the Great Lakes passenger steamers—and is now doing the honors as the **Keewatin Maritime Museum.** Wander through the many staterooms, the elegant ballroom with its chandeliers and finely carved mahogany bar, the captain's suite, the huge galley, and the ornate two-deck-high lounge with hand-painted skylights. There are shades of *Titanic*-inspired luxury, but thankfully no Irish bagpipes to put it over the

The Kalamazoo River and Saugatuck town as seen from Mount Baldhead.

top. Open from Memorial Day to Labor Day. *On the Douglas side of the Kalamazoo River waterfront; 269-857-2464; www.keewatinmaritimemuseum.com.*

Good fun also can be had, from May through October, cruising the river and lake aboard the 67-foot stern-wheeler *Star of Saugatuck* (716 Water Street; 269-857-4261; www.saugatuckboatcruises.com). Other recommended adventures include sailing, kayak tours, dune rides, sportfishing charters, golf, and a ride on the Harbor Duck water taxi.

For more information: *Saugatuck-Douglas Convention & Visitors Bureau; 269-857-1701; www.artcoast.com.*

■ HOLLAND *map page 171, B-2*

When Rev. Albertus C. Van Raalte led a group of 53 Dutch settlers to the sandy shores of Lake Michigan in 1847, they brought along memories of windmills and wooden shoes. Choosing a site on Lake Macatawa, which connected to Lake Michigan via a shallow outlet, Van Raalte called his new town Holland. Its early years were hard: mosquitoes, no-see-ums, and smallpox plagued these pioneers, who were ill equipped for the rigors of the new land.

When the government refused to dredge the outlet to Lake Michigan less than half a mile away, townsfolk picked up their shovels and dug it themselves, thus opening Holland to trade; the town soon became famous for its fine woodwork.

Holland Tulip Time Festival

No matter what your ancestry, you can pretend to be Dutch during this May festival. A clanging brass bell signals the beginning: "Hear ye! Hear ye! The streets are dirty and they must be scrubbed," the town crier calls in Dutch, then English. With splashes from wooden water buckets, swishes of brooms, and clacks of the *klompen* (wooden clogs) echoing along the streets, 10 days of parades and festival begin. Young men in baggy pants dance with lovely girls in billowy skirts. Children march in tulip-shaped hats. Bands play. *800-822-2770; www.tuliptime.org.*

Windmill Island

At Seventh Street and Lincoln Avenue a drawbridge leads to a 36-acre miniature Dutch town in the midst of which is **DeZwann**—a 1780s windmill given to the city of Holland by the city of Amsterdam. Lazily turning in the wind, it powers a flour mill. *616-355-1030; www.windmillisland.org.*

Veldheer Tulip Gardens

I discovered a little bit of everything Dutch here. A maze of windmills, canals, and drawbridges, these gardens are abloom in spring with more than 100 varieties of tulips, followed by late-spring and summer annuals. On the grounds is the **DeKlomp Wooden Shoe and Delft Factory,** which not only makes shoes but is the only factory in the nation producing the distinctive hand-painted blue-and-white delftware porcelain. *12755 Quincy Street; 616-399-1900.*

Dutch Village

This theme park off U.S. 31 North replicates an old-world village, featuring rides suitable for all ages and shops selling Dutch chocolates, cheeses, and other imported specialties. Order a Dutch-style sandwich from Hungry Dutchman Café and enjoy it on the outside patio. Shops operate year-round; the theme park is open from late April to early October *12350 James Street; 616-396-1475 or 800-285-7177; www.dutchvillage.com.*

Big Red

This Holland Harbor lighthouse at the end of South Shore Drive is not open to the public, but it's a great place for a stroll or a picnic. Or create a water memory

The Veldheer Tulip Gardens in Holland.

cruising on the 65-foot Victorian paddle-wheeler **Holland Princess,** from mid-June through September. *Dunton Park, 290 Howard Avenue; 616-393-7799; www. hollandprincess.com.*

For more information: *Holland Area Convention & Visitors Bureau; 76 East Eighth Street; 800-506-1299; www.holland.org.*

■ GRAND HAVEN *map page 171, B-1/2*

Approaching Grand Haven from the south on U.S. 31, watch for **Reenders Blueberry Farms.** Pick your own or select a ready-to-go basket filled with delicious marble-size berries. *9981 U.S. 31; 616-842-5238.*

The mouth of the Grand River was the site for several presettlement dramas, none more fascinating than that observed by the American Fur Company's fur trader Gurdon Hubbard. In his autobiography Hubbard relates how in 1819 he and his men were invited to observe a "Feast of the Dead," an annual memorial celebration carried out by the Indians in honor of the departed members of their tribe and also a day of reckoning for past offenses. Assembled on a high dune over-

Grand Haven Beach and State Park is a favorite weekend spot on hot summer days.

Grand Haven Lighthouse.

looking Lake Michigan, a chief and his family awaited the return of an Indian condemned for killing the chief's son. On that day he was to pay for his crime with a ransom of furs or with his life. After trapping throughout the hard winter with poor results, the condemned man returned with his family to the dune and stood empty-handed before the chief. With his family watching, the proud Indian stood without flinching while the chief's remaining son thrust a knife into his chest and killed him.

Like most other Michigan port cities, Grand Haven began as a sawmill town. It got a boost in 1855 when the railroad from Detroit was completed. Later, the line was called the Emigrant Route, as pioneers rode the trains to Grand Haven and then boarded steamers to cross Lake Michigan to settle in Wisconsin.

Grand Haven's nightly spectacle is the **Musical Fountain**, the largest fountain in the world, with waterspouts and colored lights synchronized to perform "duets" with the music. View from Waterfront Stadium. *1 North Harbor Drive; 616-842-2550; www.grandhaven.com/fountain.*

For more information: *Grand Haven/Spring Lake Area Visitors Bureau; 1 South Harbor Drive; 800-303-4096; www.grandhavenchamber.org.*

■ MUSKEGON *map page 197, A-6*

In the 1880s, when it became known as Lumber Queen of the World, Muskegon could brag that it had 40 lumber millionaires, as well as 47 sawmills buzzing along the Muskegon River. The side-by-side Victorian mansions of Thomas Hume and philanthropist Charles H. Hackley, along with the stables where their horses and carriage drivers lived, are now museums of that era, the **Hackley and Hume Historic Site and City Barn.** Both houses are in the late-19th-century Queen Anne style, but the furnishings of the Hackley house approximate its 1890 appearance, whereas those of the Hume house hark back to its look in 1915. *West Webster at Sixth Street; 888-843-5661; www.muskegonmuseum.org.*

During summer, a bright red double-decker trolley (231-724-6420) makes its rounds downtown past Victorian storefronts and alongside modern department stores, office buildings, city parks, and beaches. The schedule is casual. A sign reads "So Don't Be Upset If We Are a Little Late—or a Little Early. Just Flag Us Down." If you drive here, bring a map: it's easy to get lost in the maze of downtown streets.

From **Rafferty's Dockside Restaurant** you can enjoy a view of Muskegon Lake while you're eating dinner (they serve pretzel-crumbed walleye). Or pull your boat up to the dock and dine on board. *701 Terrace Point Boulevard; 231-722-4461.*

At **Pere Marquette Park,** the beach comes alive with volleyball tournaments in summer while pleasure boats parade up and down the river, out past the cherry-red lighthouse, and into Lake Michigan. Nearby, on the south side of the channel wall near Lake Michigan, the **Great Lakes Naval Memorial and Museum** displays two historic ships. The USS *Silversides* was commissioned on December 15, 1941, only eight days after the Japanese attacked Pearl Harbor. This 312-foot submarine sank 23 ships in World War II, ranking third highest in total tonnage sunk. During the tourist season visitors squeeze their way along the cramped passageways and listen for the resounding klaxon that sounded the "Dive!" command during the sub's many attacks. Next to *Silversides,* tour the U.S. Coast Guard cutter *McLane,* commissioned in 1927 and destined to search-and-rescue assignment; then participate in a simulation of WWII hazardous-patrol duty. *1346 Bluff Street; 231-755-1230; www.silversides.org.*

The big nautical news in these parts is the new *Lake Express,* a high-speed 250-passenger car ferry that makes daily runs across Lake Michigan between Muskegon

The mansions built by Hackley (foreground) and by Hume (background) in Muskegon are fine examples of Victorian fantasy homes.

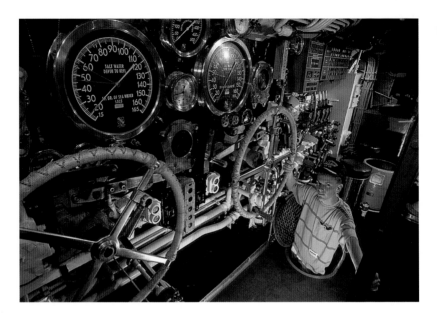

The control room of the USS Silversides *submarine.*

and Milwaukee, Wisconsin, during the June–September tourist season. *Great Lakes Marina, 1920 Lakeshore Drive; 231-755-0308; www.milwaukee-muskegon.com.*

At the city's Pontaluna Road, follow the signs west to the 1,000-acre **P. J. Hoffmaster State Park,** in the heart of towering sand dunes and long stretches of white-sand beaches. Campgrounds, picnicking, hiking, and swimming are available. The glass-fronted **Gillette Sand Dune Visitor Center** is one of the best of its kind, with hands-on exhibits that explain how dunes are formed and serve as habitats for animals and vegetation. *6585 Lake Harbor Road; 231-798-3711; www.dnr. state.mi.us/parksandtrails.*

For more information: *Muskegon County Convention & Visitors Bureau; 610 West Western Avenue; 800-250-9283; www.visitmuskegon.org.*

■ LUDINGTON *map page 197, A-3*

On the Lake Michigan shore, behind a strip of barrier dunes, lies the safe deepwater harbor of Pere Marquette Lake, long an important shipping center. The M-10 terminates its east-west crossing of "the mitten" at Ludington, becoming wide Ludington Avenue, which runs through the town all the way to the lakeshore.

The story of Ludington could easily be the story of any other lumber town, but it's not. Originally called Marquette in honor of Father Jacques Marquette, the missionary-explorer who is presumed to have died here in 1675, the town was renamed by well-heeled Chicago businessman James Ludington, who bought up lumber mills and property—basically the whole town. Nothing untoward here, given the egotism characteristic of tycoons, except that he required that all the property deeds stipulate that no liquor would be sold on the premises, stating: "So long as I can control the matter I will not allow a liquor saloon to live in the village that bears my name." Ludington, unique among lumber towns, was dry.

Historic White Pine Village, on the southern outskirts of Ludington, is a cluster of 22 historic buildings, including the cabin built by French trapper William Quevillon about 1850. The village stages festivals and special events throughout the year. *1687 South Lakeshore Drive; 231-843-4808; www.historicwhitepinevillage.org.*

In summer take the 4,200-ton **SS *Badger*** car ferry on one of its daily 60-mile round-trips across Lake Michigan to Manitowoc, Wisconsin. During the four-hour crossing, the renovated Great Lakes steamer offers its 620 passengers two restaurants, movies, games, shopping in the Badger Boutique, an interesting maritime historical exhibit, and even an overnight stay in a *Badger* stateroom. Or just loll about on deck enjoying the cooling breeze and gazing out at the lake. Reservations recommended. Mid-May through early October. *701 Maritime Drive; 888-337-7948; www.carferries.net.*

North of town, beautiful **Ludington State Park** arcs around Lake Hamlin, popular with canoeists and fishermen. The park offers excellent hiking, swimming, camping, and all the requisites for goofing off pleasantly. A 2-mile route leading to **Big Sable Point Lighthouse** (231-845-7343; www/bigsablepointlighthouse.org) is among the hiking trails. This is a very popular park, especially with its long stretch of Lake Michigan's sandy shore and many outdoor activities. *Eight miles north of Ludington on M-116, 231-843-2423.*

For more information: *Ludington Area Convention & Visitors Bureau; 5300 West U.S. 10, 877-420-6618; www.ludingtoncvb.com.*

■ **MANISTEE** *map page 197, A-2*

If Ludington was dry, not so Manistee. "At Manistee," writes Milo M. Quaife of the little town 20 miles north, "open barrels of whiskey were placed in the streets, into which passersby who were reluctant to imbibe were sometimes thrust head first by the merry loggers"—"merry," of course, being a euphemism for rip-roaring hammered.

Nowadays, Manistee primly wears the title Victorian Port City. Restored Victorian "painted ladies," resplendent in their gingerbread trim and fanciful gables, are found around most every corner, and downtown is listed on the National Register of Historic Places. Residents here take their Victoriana seriously; the Manistee Victorian Christmas features a Sleighbell Parade with horse-drawn floats and a Victorian Santa waving from his sleigh. Even the conductors in the bright-red tour trolley wear period costumes. The 1889 fire-engine-red brick fire-house, a Romanesque Revival–style hall with a copper dome, remains Michigan's oldest continuously operating fire station.

■ Manistee National Forest

After decades of replanting, a lot of it by the Civilian Conservation Corps during the 1930s, a mixed forest of pine and hardwood now stands thick and tall across northwestern Michigan, especially in the Manistee National Forest, which stretches east from Manistee to Cadillac and south almost to Muskegon, encompassing more than 500,000 acres. In the springtime people come for mushrooming and fishing, in winter snowmobiling and cross-country skiing.

Inland from Manistee are three National Wild and Scenic Rivers: Pere Marquette (emptying into Pere Marquette Lake at Ludington), Pine, and Manistee. The Little Manistee, Big Sable, and their tributaries also provide opportunities for recreation. For generations people have come to these exquisite rivers to fish, canoe, and camp. *800-821-6263.*

For more information: *Manistee County Convention & Visitors Bureau; 50 Filer Street; 800-288-2286; www.manistee.com.*

■ Cadillac *map page 197, D-2*

Forty-eight miles east of Manistee on M-55 lies Cadillac, surrounding Lake Cadillac, which is itself connected by a narrow inlet to larger Lake Mitchell. Little wonder that water sports are the main summer attraction. When winter covers the hills with snow, recreation shifts to skiing and snowmobiling. We Michiganians love our snow and being out in it bundled up against the cold, and we relish the adrenaline rush of a downhill ski plunge or cross-country trail.

Five cross-country ski trails wind through dense forests here; some are even lit for night skiing. In addition, a network of 200 miles of groomed snowmobile trails connects with other marked trails throughout northern Michigan. The big event of the year is the **North American Snowmobile Festival,** which in early February brings up to 10,000 snowmobilers to ice-capped Lake Cadillac with races, outdoor picnics, sleigh rides, and fireworks.

For more information: *Cadillac Area Visitors Bureau; 222 Lake Street; 800-225-2537; www.cadillacmichigan.com.*

■ HOUGHTON LAKE *map page 152, A-5*

Thirty miles east of Cadillac, M-55 connects with U.S. 27 and then with I-75 some 18 miles north. Inside the triangle formed by these converging highways are Houghton and Higgins lakes. Houghton Lake, 10 miles long, 8 miles wide, with a 72-mile shoreline, is Michigan's largest inland lake. Although camping and fishing are popular year-round, nothing on any of Michigan's lakes creates more excitement than the annual **Tip-Up Town U.S.A.,** held on the third and fourth weekends of January. While fishermen gather to drill holes in the ice on Houghton Lake and set their fishing gear for "tip-ups" that signal that a fish is on the line, the carnival on ice goes into full swing. One highlight is the polar bear dive through a hole in the ice. After you!

For more information: *Roscommon County-Houghton Lake Area Tourism & Convention Bureau; 1625 West Houghton Lake Drive; 800-676-5330; www. roscommoncounty.com.*

■ TRAVEL BASICS

Area Overview: Most of southwest and west-central Michigan is pretty flat, and stays that way until you're around Manistee and Cadillac. The major population and commercial centers are around Grand Rapids and Kalamazoo, but wide expanses of farmland, orchards, sandy Lake Michigan beaches, and vineyards beckon off the main highways, as do small, intriguing towns and villages that make this part of Michigan so interesting.

Travel: The two main east–west arteries are I-94 (filled with commuters and semis between Battle Creek and Kalamazoo) and I-96 (the less heavily traveled rocketway between Detroit and Muskegon). The main north–south route through the area is

Manistee's new Riverwalk runs more than a mile from downtown Manistee to Lake Michigan.

U.S. 131, which runs from the Indiana border north through Kalamazoo, Grand Rapids, and beyond. Scenic routes include the two-lane Red Arrow Highway from the Indiana border north to Benton Harbor, where it becomes the Blue Star Highway north to Holland. Air service is available from Grand Rapids and Kalamazoo-Battle Creek. Amtrak makes runs from Chicago to Grand Rapids, Pontiac, Port Huron, and other stops along the way. Lake Express out of Muskegon provides daily car-ferry service to Milwaukee, Wisconsin, during the main tourist season.

Weather: Summer temperatures average around 85 degrees F and above, with balmy 60-degree nights. Fall and spring temps average in the low 70s with nights in the 50s. There's rarely any snow before December, but the west side can receive heavy lake-effect snows.

Food & Lodging: Fine dining can be enjoyed in any of the major cities. The many B&Bs and small-town lodgings often offer great food *and* great prices. *See listings beginning on page 274.*

N O R T H W E S T
& M A C K I N A C I S L A N D

The Straits of Mackinac mark the transition between Lake Huron to the east and Lake Michigan to the west—a kind of Great Lakes Cape Horn. Fearsome gales and treacherous waves can make it exceedingly dangerous to cross, and because the Straits link two great bodies of water, Indian tribes and European nations sought to control the area and keep others out.

In the 1680s, under the orders of the governor of New France, Louis de Buade, the French became the first Europeans to establish a fort north of the Straits of Mackinac, at what is now St. Ignace. The Straits area was already known by its Chippewa name, *Michilimackinac* (pronounced Mich-ele-*mack*-a-naw), meaning Land of the Great Turtle and referring to the 3.5-mile-long nearby Straits island (Mackinac Island) that from an approaching canoe can indeed resemble the back of a great turtle. Fort de Buade thus became better known as Fort Michilimackinac, the first of three forts in the Straits to bear this name.

The first fort was abandoned in 1697 when its commander, Antoine de la Mothe Cadillac, left with his troops to take command of a new fort at what would become Detroit. By 1715, however, the French were back in the area, with a new fort south of the Straits at the present Mackinaw City—the *second* Fort Michilimackinac. In 1760, during the French and Indian War, the British won control of this fort, and in 1763 Ojibwa warriors took it over and massacred its occupants, having gained entrance using the ruse of a game of baggataway, similar to lacrosse. Under new command, the British regrouped and moved back in.

When British lieutenant governor Patrick Sinclair assumed command of Fort Michilimackinac in 1779, fearing an American invasion after the Revolutionary War, he searched for a more strategic location. Finding it atop the limestone cliffs of Mackinac Island, he dismantled the fort to salvage usable parts and moved across the frozen Straits. What remained of the old fort was burned to the ground. The island fort, the *third* Fort Michilimackinac (later shortened to Fort Mackinac), remained in a seesaw of control between the British and Americans for a while, with the American troops taking over in 1796 and the British seizing it during the War of 1812. Three years later American troops returned to Mackinac Island by treaty.

Until 1813 and the death of the legendary Shawnee chief Tecumseh, the entirety of Michigan, as well as most of Indiana, Ohio, and Kentucky, was figuratively and literally dominated by his Confederation of Algonquian-speaking tribes: Ojibwas, Ottawas, Wyandots, Potawatomis, Miamis, Shawnees, Kickapoos, Fox, Iowas, Winnebagos, Senecas, and Osages. Even the Seminoles in Florida felt his influence. Tecumseh's death all but ended indigenous resistance to the unrelenting flood of settlement sweeping westward through the Ohio Valley and onto the Great Plains. Andrew Jackson's Indian Removal Act (famous for the Cherokee Trail of Tears) was the final step of the "ethnic cleansing" of the Ohio Valley.

Throughout most of Michigan, settlement in the early 1800s revolved around the fur trade controlled by John Jacob Astor's American Fur Company on Mackinac Island. After the passing of the beaver-hat fad in Europe had killed the fur trade, lumbermen moved in to log the state from south to north, and farmers moved in behind them to till the opened land. At the north end of the peninsula,

This 1842 lithograph depicts Fort Michilimackinac when it stood on Mackinac Island; Round Island is in the background.

soil was not as rich as in the southwest, and they began planting orchards, finding that apples and cherries were especially suited to the climate. These days it's tourism that powers the economies of Traverse City, Bay Harbor, Petoskey, Mackinaw City, and Mackinac Island. So, what's to see?

■ FRANKFORT *map page 205, A-6*

Heading to the Lake Michigan shoreline, we follow M-115 to the charming small town of Frankfort, south of Crystal Lake. Aptly named, the 10-mile-long lake sends sparkles of sunlight dancing across its surface. Tucked between a hill and Lake Michigan, Frankfort boasts a deep-water recreational harbor on Betsie Lake with an outlet to Lake Michigan.

Some believe that the Jesuit missionary and explorer Father Jacques Marquette died here in 1675—a wooden cross marks the supposed spot—but conventional wisdom has it that the priest died farther south in Ludington. Whether it was in Frankfort or Ludington, the intrepid priest's faithful Indian friends returned the following year and carried his remains north to St. Ignace for final burial.

The **Point Betsie Lighthouse**, a favorite of mine, lies just off M-22 about 5 miles north of Frankfort. Thanks at least in part to its backdrop—rolling dunes, sandy beach, driftwood, green lawn—the white brick tower, built in 1858, is one of the most photographed lighthouses in Michigan. *231-352-4915; www.pointbetsie.org.*

Seventeen miles east of Frankfort and the Lake Michigan shore, the landscape climbs sharply into hilly terrain that Midwesterners like to classify as "mountains," such as those found at the family-oriented **Crystal Mountain Resort** in Thompsonville. Snow bunnies romp over 45 downhill slopes and 40-plus kilometers (about 25 miles) of Nordic trails. There's golfing at the resort in summer. *12500 Crystal Mountain Drive, Thompsonville; 231-378-2000 or 800-968-7686; www.crystalmountain.com.*

For more information: *Benzie County Chamber of Commerce; 826 Michigan Avenue; 231-882-5801; www.benzie.org.*

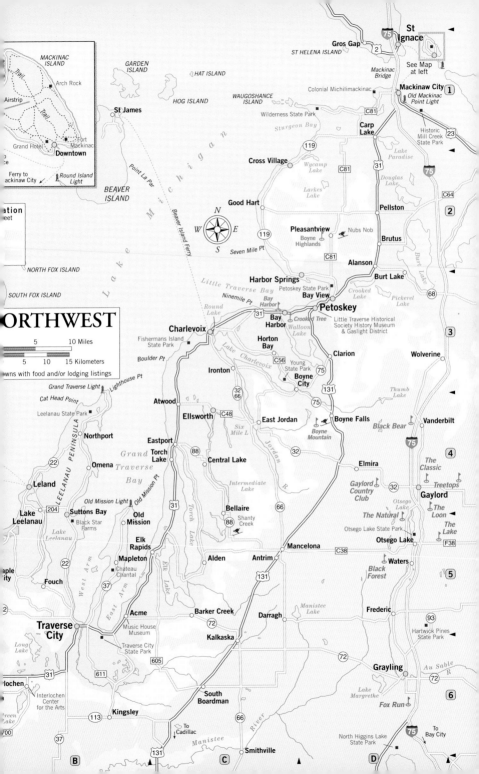

MACKINAC ISLAND (inset map)

Arch Rock
Airstrip
Trail
Fort Mackinac
Grand Hotel
Downtown
Ferry to Mackinaw City
Round Island Light

St James

BEAVER ISLAND

NORTH FOX ISLAND

SOUTH FOX ISLAND

ORTHWEST

5   10 Miles
5   10   15 Kilometers

wns with food and/or lodging listings

GARDEN ISLAND
HAT ISLAND
HOG ISLAND
WAUGOSHANCE ISLAND
St Helena Island
Gros Gap
St Ignace
See Map at left
75
2
Mackinac Bridge
Colonial Michilimackinac
Mackinaw City
Old Mackinac Point Light
1
Historic Mill Creek State Park
23
Wilderness State Park
Sturgeon Bay
C81
Carp Lake
Lake Paradise
31
Douglas Lake
75
C64

119
Cross Village
Wycamp Lake
C81
Larkes Lake
Pellston
2

Good Hart
Pleasantview
Boyne Highlands
Nubs Nob
Brutus
C81
Alanson
68

119
Seven Mile Pt
Nubs Nob
Burt Lake
Burt Lake

Point La Par
Beaver Island Ferry

Harbor Springs
Petoskey State Park
Crooked Lake
Pickerel Lake
Little Traverse Bay
Ninemile Pt
Bay View
Crooked River
3
Round Lake
Bay Harbor
Petoskey
Little Traverse Historical Society History Museum & Gaslight District
31
Bay Harbor
Crooked Tree
Walloon Lake

Charlevoix
Fishermans Island State Park
Lake Charlevoix
Horton Bay
Clarion
Wolverine
Boulder Pt
C56
Young State Park
75
Thumb Lake

Lighthouse Pt
Ironton
Boyne City
131
Grand Traverse Light
32
66

Cat Head Point
Atwood
75
Black Bear
Vanderbilt
Leelanau State Park
Ellsworth
C48
Six Mile L
East Jordan
Boyne Mountain
Boyne Falls
75

Northport
Eastport
88
Elmira
The Classic
Treetops
4
22
Torch Lake
Central Lake
32
Omena
Grand Traverse Bay
Intermediate Lake
Jordan R
Gaylord Country Club
Gaylord
The Loon

Leland
Old Mission Light
Old Mission Pt
Bellaire
88
66
The Natural
Otsego Lake
The Lake
204
Shanty Creek
Otsego Lake State Park
F38
Lake Leelanau
Suttons Bay
Black Star Farms
Old Mission
31
Torch Lake
Otsego Lake

Lake Leelanau
Elk Rapids
Elk Lake
Mancelona
C38
Waters
5
22
Mapleton
Chateau Chantal
Alden
Antrim
Black Forest

Fouch
37
West Arm
East Arm
131
Frederic

aple ty
Acme
Barker Creek
Darragh
Manistee Lake
93
2
Music House Museum
72
Hartwick Pines State Park
Traverse City
Kalkaska
Grayling
Au Sable R
72
Traverse City State Park
605
72
Long Lake
611
Lake Margrethe
6
31
Fox Run
South Boardman
75
lochen
Interlochen Center for the Arts
Kingsley
113
66
Smithville
To Cadillac
To Bay City
North Higgins Lake State Park
37
131
Manistee River
700

B   C   D

Point Betsie Lighthouse in summer.

■ SLEEPING BEAR DUNES NATIONAL LAKESHORE
map page 205, A-5

The hilly dunes of the 71,000-acre Sleeping Bear Dunes National Lakeshore stretch for 35 miles along Lake Michigan. Maple and beech forests encircle the inland lakes and climb the hills nearby. Beautifully juxtaposed are pale and powdery dunes, which roll from forested inland valleys all the way to the blue waters of Lake Michigan, in some places reaching heights of 460 feet—making them the highest sand dunes outside the Sahara Desert.

Pick up a map at the **Philip A. Hart Visitor Center** and follow the route to **Pierce Stocking Scenic Drive,** a steep 7.4-mile route for cars and bicycles, to a high bluff overlooking the dunes. It also offers an impressive view of North and South Manitou islands, about 17 miles offshore. Wonder how the dunes got their fanciful name? The legend of the Sleeping Bear tells it this way:

> Long ago, along the Wisconsin shoreline, a mother bear and her two
> cubs were driven into Lake Michigan by a raging forest fire. The
> bears swam for many hours, but eventually the cubs tired and lagged

behind. Mother bear reached the shore and climbed to the top of a high bluff to watch and wait for her cubs. Too tired to continue, the cubs drowned within sight of the shore. The Great Spirit Manitou created two islands to mark the spot where the cubs disappeared and then sculpted the top of a mainland dune to represent the faithful mother bear.

Near the northwest arm of Glen Lake is the **Dune Climb**. Climbers labor to reach the crest of this 400-foot dune and start out eager enough, but it doesn't take long for them to shuffle into a sand dance that lasts all the way to the top—if they make it that far. It's two steps forward and one step back. Kids know how to do it best. They climb for a while, then fall down and roll back to the bottom.

■ **MANITOU ISLANDS** *map page 205, A-4*
From May through October, ferries run from Leland on the west shore of the Leelanau Peninsula to South Manitou Island, which is part of Sleeping Bear Dunes National Lakeshore. Guided walking tours depart from the ferry docks, and they make for great outings. Late one evening I tried hiking along the beach toward the 104-foot South Manitou Island Light, intrigued by a little map that showed an

---

TOO MUCH OF A GOOD THING?

When you first see the Sleeping Bear Dunes rising massive and golden two hundred feet above a grassy plain, you think you're in the Serengeti or someplace equally strange, not the Midwest. On its eastern slope, this mountain of flesh-colored sand rises like the Taj Mahal to be mirrored in the placid, cattail-bordered Mill Pond below.

I never thought too much about it, growing up there. When you're a child your environment is your environment; it could be the far side of the moon and you wouldn't think about it. The Sleeping Bear Dunes were where we always took our end-of-the-school-year picnics, the red, white, and blue school buses of the 1950s lining up at the base of the dunes from all over Michigan. It got so that by third grade we'd complain about going to the dunes *again*—as in vanilla ice cream, *again*. We didn't know that our vanilla ice cream was everyone else's pistachio nut ripple.

—Kathleen Stocking, *Letters from the Leelanau: Essays of People and Place*, 1990

Sleeping Bear Dunes in winter.

abandoned farm and a "Valley of the Giants," with a stand of virgin white cedar trees. However, I missed them—I was chased back to the boat by ferocious sand flies that stung like little devils.

To the northeast is South Manitou's rustic cousin, North Manitou Island, which shares ferry service from Leland. Prepare for primitive camping, no island transportation, and on-your-own touring. To accommodate fall hunters, ferries make runs to North Manitou through November, or as long as weather permits. *Sleeping Bear Dunes National Lakeshore; 9922 Front Street, Empire; 231-326-5134; www.nps.gov/slbe.*

■ LEELANAU PENINSULA *map page 205, B-4*

This 35-mile-long peninsula between Lake Michigan and Grand Traverse Bay, with Lake Leelanau extending up the middle, is circled by sand beaches and cliffs. Lake breezes blow gently across the vineyards and herb farms. A drive around the Leelanau in autumn is an annual pilgrimage for those familiar with the burst of

A view of Sleeping Bear Dunes from Empire Bluff.

Leland, a historic fishing town along the Leelanau Peninsula, is today the jumping-off point for ferries to the Manitou Islands.

colors in the forest and the crispness in the air. Set up along the roadsides are fruit and vegetable stands staffed by folks who find time to chat. It seems that every small town has a winery, galleries and gift shops, a restaurant, and a bed-and-breakfast inn, but each town is unique in its offerings. The most interesting and certainly the most ambitious of the B&Bs is **Black Star Farms** at Suttons Bay, which also has a winery, a creamery, and an equestrian training center. *231-271-4886; www.blackstarfarms.com.*

The town of **Leland,** along the west side of the Leelanau Peninsula, began in 1853 as a cluster of shacks hastily built by lumbermen and seasonal fishermen. The main attraction is still **Fishtown**—gray weathered shacks along the Carp River that have been converted to gift shops and boutiques. Some of the other original buildings are still ice- and smokehouses for local fishermen. **Manitou Island Transit** (231-256-9061; www.leelanau.com/manitou) runs ferries to North and South Manitou islands on a daily basis in summer, less frequently in spring and fall.

For more information: *Leelanau Peninsula Chamber of Commerce; 5046 South West Bayshore Drive, Suite G, Suttons Bay; 231-271-9895; www.leelanauchamber.com.*

■ TRAVERSE CITY AND ENVIRONS *map page 205, B-5*

It wasn't until 1839 that the Grand Traverse region, so named by the French *voyageurs*, was settled. First to come was the short, hardworking Rev. Peter Dougherty, who established a Presbyterian mission at the tip of what is now called the Old Mission Peninsula, a narrow strip of land that divides Grand Traverse Bay into its east and west arms. The mission has been reconstructed as the **Old Mission** and sits in the midst of a kind of living museum, the core of which is the **Old Mission Store,** which began serving settlers—out of a wigwam—shortly after Peter Dougherty arrived. It has remained in continuous operation ever since, essentially unchanged for a century or so. To enter the store is to take a remarkable step into the past. *18250 Mission Road; 231-223-4310; www.oldmission.com.*

The **Old Mission Light**, a working lighthouse that is also the official marker for the 45th parallel, perches on the northern tip of the peninsula. Mid-century brought settlers to the head of the bay, with Horace Boardman's sawmill on Kid's Creek buzzing out lumber for new housing. Then came more people, more mills, and nearby settlements. After the pine was cut for lumber and the homesteaders planted flourishing cherry orchards, the first Blessing of the Blossoms was held in 1924. Two years later this ritual became part of the **National Cherry Festival**, still celebrated annually during the first part of July with parades, cherry treats, orchard tours, fireworks, and much more. *800-872-8377; www.cherryfestival.org.*

Clinch Park, in Traverse City at the bottom of Grand Traverse Bay's west arm, is so green I want to instantly plop down on a park bench and gaze north along the bay at the sailboats and other watercraft cutting patterns in the waves. Kids head for the park's zoo, aquarium, or beach. You can also stroll along the Boardman River to the downtown district and take in its nautical shops and sidewalk cafés.

Vineyards have replaced many of the apple and cherry orchards, spreading an old-world pattern across the rolling hills. Along with other wineries in the area, **Chateau Chantal** offers tours and tastings and also has a fine B&B. *15900 Rue de Vin; 800-969-4009; www.chateauchantal.com.*

■ TALL SHIP *MANITOU*

Few things are more romantic than boarding the windjammer Tall Ship *Manitou* for a sail across Grand Traverse Bay. In spring and fall the 114-foot, two-masted, gaff-rigged replica of an 1800s schooner operated by Traverse Tall Ship Company runs charters to nearby islands and through the Straits of Mackinac. In July and

(above) A crow's-nest view of the deck of the Tall Ship Manitou. *(opposite) Students practice in the woods at Interlochen.*

August the ship schedules regular sails that include optional picnic lunches to be enjoyed as the schooner scuds along Grand Traverse Bay, often accompanied by live entertainment. My favorite sail is the floating B&B. After the last sail of the evening, with all lines secured dockside and the last day-sailor debarked, it is sheer joy to climb below, where red geraniums, petunias, and trailing vines brighten the skylights, and choose one of the 12 cabins equipped with double bunks, wash basin, and electric bedside reading lights as my quarters for the night. Or, sometimes I pack my sleeping bag and spread it topside, where the gentle shore waters rock me to sleep. When dawn streaks across the bay, the tangy scent of wood smoke from the galley awakens me: the crew is preparing a hearty breakfast on the wood-fired stove. Later, with sea legs steady, I reluctantly head for land. *13390 South West Bay Shore Drive; 231-941-2000 or 800-678-0383; www. tallshipsailing.com.*

■ INTERLOCHEN *map page 205, B-6*

Interlochen, 16 miles southwest of Traverse City, is one of the nation's premier art centers. The 1,200-acre campus of the **Interlochen Center for the Arts** includes the **Interlochen Arts Academy,** a boarding school for gifted students in grades 9 through 12, and the **National Music Camp,** which attracts students from around the world in summer. If you stroll along the wooded paths in summer, you may hear young musicians practicing under the trees, oblivious to everything except their music. The **Interlochen Arts Festival** (box office: 231-276-7800 or 800-681-5920) brings internationally known artists to the north woods year-round. *4000 Highway M-137; 231-276-7200; www.interlochen.org.*

■ MUSIC HOUSE MUSEUM *map page 205, B-5*

Back along the east arm of Grand Traverse Bay, follow U.S. 31 north for 6 miles to the **Music House Museum** at Acme. It verges on the hokey, but the variety of melodic sounds everywhere, from small music boxes to player pianos to a 97-key pipe organ, makes it fun. Linger to sip a soda in the museum's Hurry Back Saloon while old-fashioned tunes play on nickelodeons. *7377 U.S. 31; 231-938-9300.*

While in the area, watch for roadside fruit stands. At **Amon Orchards,** climb aboard a wagon for a tour of the orchards or pick your own fruit. The gift shop offers samples from its vast array of cherry and apple jams, spreads, butters, and relishes, all lined up on the counter. The fruit pies? To *die* for. Open June–November. *8066 U.S. 31; 231-938-1644 or 800-937-1644; www.amonorchards.com.*

For more information: *Traverse City Convention & Visitors Bureau; 101 West Grandview Parkway; 800-873-8377; www.mytraversecity.com.*

■ FISHERMAN'S ISLAND STATE PARK *map page 205, C-3*

Six miles from Charlevoix, watch for the sign directing you to Fisherman's Island State Park. The park runs for several miles along the Lake Michigan shoreline and also encloses a small island, thus its name. The island can't be seen from the park's main beach and campground, but the beach running alongside your campsite is a great place to find Petoskey stones, Michigan's official state stone: strolling along this pebbly stretch is like walking barefoot on jellybeans. The brown and tan stones patterned in hexagonal polyps are fossilized pieces of the 350-million-year-old Devonian-Era coral reef offshore, polished and deposited along the beach by waves. Their various shapes and colors show up best where the sand is damp.

Several homes in Charlevoix were designed by architect Earl Young, known for his unique use of boulders and Lake Michigan stones.

Keep an eye out also for fulgurites—cigar-shaped glassy tubes formed when lightning strikes high-silica sand. They can be several inches long. *231-547-6641; www.dnr.state.mi.us/parksandtrails.*

■ **CHARLEVOIX** *map page 205, C-3*

It's no wonder that Charlevoix is known as Charlevoix the Beautiful. A wide-open view of the cobalt-blue water of Lake Michigan stretches to the north and west. Inland is Lake Charlevoix, which begins 12 miles to the southeast at Boyne City and here empties into the 150-acre circular Round Lake, which is only one street down from Charlevoix's main business section and lined with a marina, businesses, and homes. Round Lake's outlet to Lake Michigan is another attraction: the navigable Pine River, which ducks under the city's lift bridge and the boardwalk that stretches the length of two football fields to the lakeshore and the Charlevoix South Pier Light.

Summer visitors, including boaters, stroll the waterfront streets through the lingering twilight hours. Stop by **Koucky Gallery**; its silly and funky art offerings can run as high as $55,000. *325 Bridge Street; 231-547-2228.*

Charlevoix's Venetian Festival in full swing.

Charlevoix's inland lakes make it a perfect place to throw a water festival. For the past 74 years it has done just that every July with the **Venetian Festival,** when there are regattas, festivals of lights, games along the lakeshore, music, and food, and the entire area is fitted out for a carnival. *www.venetianfestival.com.*

For more information: *Charlevoix Area Convention & Visitors Bureau; 408 Bridge Street; 800-367-8557; www.charlevoix.org.*

■ BEAVER ISLAND *map page 205, B-2*

Beaver Island has the dubious distinction of having been, in the mid-19th century, the site of one of the more bizarre interludes in American history: the brief and self-proclaimed kingdom of Mormon rebel James Strang. Today 100 miles of road laid down by the island's Mormon colonists wind through green forests to pristine beaches. Old-model cars and bicycles are for rent in St. James, the island's only village, which overlooks the bowl-shaped natural harbor. As I wend my way along the roads, it takes a great stretch of the imagination to picture Beaver Island as a kingdom of anything but natural beauty.

To reach the 13- by 6-mile island, catch the **Beaver Island Ferry** (103 Bridge Park Drive; 231-547-2311; www.bibco.com) in downtown Charlevoix. The trip is an enjoyable 32-mile jaunt. Or board the 15-minute **Island Airways** (111 Airport Drive; 231-547-2141; www.islandairways.com) flight from the Charlevoix Municipal Airport and enjoy the view of the entire Beaver chain of islands.

For more information: *Beaver Island Chamber of Commerce, 231-448-2505; www.beaverisland.org.*

■ HORTON BAY *map page 205, C-3*

Don't come looking for the slapstick Fourth of July parade that once attracted attention to this one-store village along County 56. The **Horton Bay General Store** is still worth a stop, however. It's more or less like any other rural general store now, but not completely. They call it a deli, with fresh seafood and smoked fish. But ghosts of the past still linger around the soda fountain and in the back room, where there is a collection of memorabilia devoted to Ernest Hemingway.

(above) The interior of the Horton Bay General Store. (following pages) On Beaver Island, the town of St. James awaits visitors.

STRANG'S KINGDOM

The only kingdom ever established in the United States belonged to James Jesse Strang, King of Beaver Island. Born on March 21, 1813, in western New York State, Strang early on harbored visions of grandeur, comparing himself to Caesar and Napoléon. He became a lawyer noted for his hypnotic oratorical skill, but left the profession to join the Mormon Church, where he was baptized by its founder, Joseph Smith. The murders of Joseph and Hyrum Smith (in 1844 in Carthage, Illinois, by a mob inflamed, in part, by Smith's presidential ambitions) created a vacuum of leadership that Strang leapt to fill, producing an apocryphal letter from Joseph Smith endorsing him as his true successor. Excommunicated for his efforts, Strang established a rival church at Voree, in southeastern Wisconsin, and sanctified his community with the miraculous discovery of a set of ancient tablets—much as Smith had done. The tablets could be read only by using magic "peep stones," and doing so, Strang generated *The Book of the Law of the Lord*—a direct challenge to *The Book of Mormon*.

Persecuted and harassed in Wisconsin, Strang found refuge for his church on remote Beaver Island, inhabited by a few Irish fishermen. The industrious Strangite Mormons built roads, acquired land, appropriated the better fishing grounds, renamed the harbor St. James, and generously bestowed biblical names on geographic features. The resident Irish were not amused. When President Millard Fillmore refused Strang's petition for title to all the uninhabited islands in Lake Michigan, Strang pronounced them his by God's decree. This wonderment was announced during Strang's coronation on July 8, 1850, a costume pageant in which Strang wore a crimson robe and was crowned by an actor turned "saint" for the occasion.

Hostilities with the Irish persisted, and the conflict came to a head when President Fillmore learned of Strang's kingdom and ordered his arrest. Acting as his own lawyer, Strang won an acquittal, then rigged a local election to gain a seat in the Michigan legislature. The end came when two disgruntled followers, Thomas Bedford—who had been whipped for allegedly supporting his wife's refusal to wear bloomers—and Alexander Wentworth, shot the king one June evening in 1856. The resulting chaos invited invasion, and on July 5, 1856, a mob of drunken rowdies descended upon the kingdom, burning the tabernacle and ferrying 2,600 men, women, and children off the island. A turn-of-the-20th-century historian, Byron M. Cutcheon, called it "the most disgraceful day in Michigan history." Today all that remains of Strang's kingdom are a few names such as King's Highway, Lake Geneserath, and Mount Pisgah, and the **Old Mormon Print Shop Museum** (231-448-2254), now the headquarters of the Beaver Island Historical Society.

This is Hemingway country; the writer, who spent the summers of his youth at the family's cabin on nearby Walloon Lake, liked to hang around here, and the general store is listed on the National Register of Historic Places. *Boyne City Road; 231-582-7827; hortonbaygeneralstore.com.*

■ **BAY HARBOR** *map page 205, C-3*

Until 1994, the shoreline along Little Traverse Bay was lined with industrial smokestacks, silos, buildings, and gravel pits left behind by a cement factory that operated here from 1910 to 1981. In 1995 the site became the largest land reclamation project in the nation. Today the vista takes one's breath away.

Surrounded by green lawns and golf courses, the upscale development of Bay Harbor has its own lake, marinas, shops, restaurants, and condominiums. The sprawling white **Inn at Bay Harbor,** with its staggered raspberry-red roofline outlined against the blue waters of the bay, offers elegant seclusion. From the dining room of **Sagamore's**, the inn's restaurant, the beauty of the bay pulls me outside, where patios and walkways afford more expansive views. Settling into one of the Adirondack chairs on the beach, I am lulled into daydreams, feeling as lazy as the waves that gently lap the shore. *3600 Village Harbor Drive; 231-439-4003; www.innatbayharbor.com.*

■ **PETOSKEY** *map page 205, D-3*

Petoskey earned its reputation as a resort town early, but it started out in the usual manner of other Michigan river-port settlements. Lumbermen came to harvest timber and establish mills and then moved on once the forest was leveled—typical of the boom-and-bust pattern all along the Lake Michigan shore.

On the evening of November 25, 1873, the Pennsylvania Central Railroad chugged into Petoskey with officials onboard to celebrate the completion of the 193-mile line from Grand Rapids. George Gage, reporter for the *Grand Rapids Times,* rode along. Later he wrote stories describing the village at the end of the line and the million-dollar sunsets over Little Traverse Bay. Soon three trains a week were bringing tourists from "down below." By the turn of the century, 13 hotels were accommodating tourists in downtown Petoskey, with more in Charlevoix, Harbor Springs, and Mackinac Island. The Petoskey area remains one of Michigan's prime tourism destinations.

Downtown Petoskey, dressed up for Christmas.

The flower-banked **Little Traverse Historical Society History Museum,** housed in the town's restored 1892 railroad depot, traces the area's history through the lumber industry, transportation, and the tourism of today. Hemingway aficionados gravitate toward displays of his books and memorabilia, including a childhood chair—in his early life, Hemingway summered in the Petoskey area, at his family's cabin on nearby Walloon Lake. *100 Depot Court; 231-347-2620; www.petoskeymuseum.org.*

In Petoskey's **Gaslight District** you'll find Victorian buildings, modern-art galleries, brick sidewalks, softly glowing streetlights, park benches, flower boxes, canopied doorways, and—my favorite—the 1879 redbrick **Simons General Store** (401 East Lake Street; 231-347-2438). Inside, pots, pans, baskets, and other wares hang from the high tin ceiling, and the aisles are stocked with a plethora of cheeses, wines, and ethnic foods, all begging to hop into your picnic basket.

■ **Bay View** *map page 205, D-3*

Around the same period that Petoskey was developing into a tourist town, the Methodists of Michigan were searching for a summer campground site. In 1875 they purchased land for it and founded the Bay View Association side by side with

Victorian "cottages" in Harbor Springs.

Petoskey on Little Traverse Bay. The Methodists started out in tents, and eventually built more than 400 Victorian summer homes in the hills above the bay, opened a summer university, and established Chautauqua programs. It's easy to identify where Petoskey ends and Bay View begins by Bay View's salmon-colored street curbing.

■ HARBOR SPRINGS *map page 205, D-3*

North of Bay View, U.S. 31 is intersected by M-119, which leads to Harbor Springs and continues along the lakeshore to Cross Village. In winter Harbor Springs is almost deserted, virtually all of its summertime "cottage" mansions shuttered. Indeed, Harbor Springs is so deserted out of season that those remaining hold a bowling tournament down Main Street on the first of April and shoot off a cannon to celebrate the end of winter.

When the French explorers and fur traders arrived, Harbor Springs was one of dozens of Ottawa villages that stretched for 30 miles up the coast from Little Traverse Bay to what is now Cross Village. L'Arbre Croche, or Crooked Tree, near the present village of Good Hart, was the seat of the Ottawa nation. A tall white pine with a twisted crown once stood along the cliff above Lake Michigan, marking the Great Lakes Indian chiefs' council place and serving as a landmark for paddlers on the lake.

Ottawa tribe member Andrew J. Blackbird grew up in L'Arbre Croche in the 19th century, went away to what is now Eastern Michigan University, and returned to serve as postmaster. In one of his two books on Michigan Indians, *History of the Ottawa and Chippewa Indians of Michigan,* Blackbird describes the area in the early 1800s:

> In my first recollection of the country of L'Arbre Croche, which is sixty years ago, there was nothing but small shrubbery here and there in small patches, such as wild cherry trees, but the most of it was grassy plain; and such an abundance of wild strawberries, raspberries and blackberries that they fairly perfumed the air of the whole coast with fragrant scent of ripe fruit. The wild pigeons and every variety of feathered songsters filled all the groves, warbling their songs joyfully and feasting upon these wild fruits of nature; and in these waters the fishes were so plentiful that as you lifted up the anchorstone of your net in the morning, your net would be so loaded with delicious whitefish as to fairly float with all its weight on the sinkers. As you look towards the course of your net, you see the fins of the fishes sticking out of the water in every way. Then I never knew my people to want for anything to eat or to wear, as we always had plenty of wild meat and plenty of fish, corn, vegetables, and wild fruits. I thought (and yet I may be mistaken) that my people were very happy in those days.

Boyne Highlands Resort in the hills northeast of Harbor Springs offers excellent accommodations and so many outdoor enticements both summer and winter that one has to return time and time again. For summer fun there are 162 holes of world-class golf within a 30-mile radius that includes sister resorts at **Boyne Mountain,** at Boyne Falls, 14 miles south of Petoskey, and the Crooked Tree and Bay Harbor golf clubs, all part of Boyne USA. When snow covers Boyne Highlands' hills, with their 550-foot vertical drop, the resort gives skiers their choice of 46 downhill ski slopes or 40 kilometers of Nordic trails. *600 Highland Drive, Harbor Springs; 231-526-3000; www.boynehighlands.com.*

Tunnel of Trees Scenic Drive.

■ TUNNEL OF TREES SCENIC DRIVE

Although the road is narrow, a drive along M-119 north of Harbor Springs to Cross Village is one of the most scenic in Michigan. It twists, turns, dips, and climbs through the thick forest of birch, maple, and evergreens that form a tunnel over it, offering occasional glimpses of Lake Michigan to the west. Spring brings out the fresh mint-greens of the forest with splashes of flowering sugarplum and pin cherries; autumn cocoons the road in radiant shades of red, gold, and orange.

For more information: *Petoskey–Harbor Springs–Boyne Country Visitors Bureau; 401 East Mitchell Street; 800-845-2828; www.boynecountry.com.*

■ INLAND DIVERSION

■ GRAYLING *map page 205, D-6*

We'll begin our inland journey along the I-75 corridor at Grayling, which was named for the beautiful trout-like fish that vanished in the face of overfishing, logging, and fire. The Au Sable River flows fast through the city and gets top billing as a catch-and-release trout stream. Some fishermen still use the flat-bottom Au Sable riverboat, guided with a long pole, made popular during logging drives of the late 1800s.

For more information: *Grayling Area Visitors Council, 213 North James Street; 800-937-8837; www.grayling-mi.com.*

■ **HARTWICK PINES STATE PARK** *map page 205, D-5*

Seven miles northeast on M-93 lies Hartwick Pines State Park, the fifth largest in Michigan. What makes this park unique is an 86-acre remnant of Michigan's original white pine forest. Standing tall, cool, and dark, these trees are all that remain of the glorious forest that once covered Michigan. Why this tract wasn't logged is something of a mystery. In 1893 the Salling Hanson Company of Graying purchased the land and logged all of it except for this small area. Was the market weak or were the trees too small back then? No one is really sure. *989-348-7068; www. dnr.state.mi.us/parksandtrails.*

■ **GAYLORD** *map page 205, D-4*

Designed after its sister city, Pontresina, Switzerland, downtown Gaylord offers ornate clock towers, flower boxes, sidewalk canopies, and shake-shingled rooftops. The popular **Alpenfest** fair is held the third week of July. At the **Otsego Club**, the wildly-colored **Pontresina Ristorante**, reminiscent of a Swiss chalet, treats its diners to a breathtaking view of the Sturgeon Valley (696 M-32 East Main Street; 989-732-5181 or 800-752-5510; www.otsegoclub.com).

The Treetops Signature golf course was designed by Robert Trent Jones Sr.

GOLFING IN GAYLORD

One of America's premier golfing destinations is the area in and around the Otsego County town of Gaylord, which lies off I-75, 57 miles south of Mackinaw City and 35 miles southeast of Petoskey. Clustered here within a 30-mile radius are no fewer than 15 separate golf resorts and a total of 24 courses—some of which are rated among the best in the country. Following is a brief list of what we consider the top courses, along with their basic amenities. For a virtual tour, go to www. gaylordgolfmecca.com.

BEAVER CREEK RESORT & GOLF CLUB *map page 205, D-5*
This Jerry Mathews–designed course, on the west side of Otsego Lake, is called the Natural. It has a beautiful clubhouse that overlooks all 18 holes and a wetlands wildlife preserve. Open year-round. *5004 West Otsego Lake Drive, 5 miles south of Gaylord; 989-732-1785 or 877-295-3333; www.beavercreekresort.org.*

BLACK FOREST GOLF RESORT AT WILDERNESS VALLEY *map page 205, D-5*
The Black Forest course—one of the highest-ranked courses in Michigan—features difficult bunkers and sculptured greens. Open April–October. *7519 Mancelona Road, 15 miles southwest of Gaylord; 231-585-7090; www. blackforestgolf.com.*

ELK RIDGE GOLF CLUB *map page 152, B-3*
This course was designed by Jerry Mathews and is relatively expensive, but it's in lovely surroundings. Watch for bull elk in the fall. Open May–October. *9400 Rouse Road, Atlanta, 35 miles east of Gaylord on M-32 and then north 6 miles on M-33; 989-785-2275; www.elkridgegolf.com.*

The boardwalk on the back nine at Elk Ridge Golf Course.

The Robert Trent Jones Sr. Masterpiece course at Treetops, pictured above at hole 15.

FOX RUN COUNTRY CLUB *map page 205, D-6*
This course has a reputation for having a knowledgeable staff, with lessons available from a PGA pro. It's a nice course out in the middle of nowhere. Open April–October. *5825 West Four Mile Road, 3 miles south of Grayling, 31 miles south of Gaylord, at I-75 Exit 251; 989-348-4343; www.foxruncc.com.*

GARLAND RESORT *map page 152, B-3*
Here there are four courses. The Fountains, opened in 1999, offers six par-fives and the "longest single-span log bridge in the world" (it crosses CR-489 to connect two holes). A *Golf Digest* reader avows that the Monarch is the "Augusta of northern Michigan" (he also says that this resort has the "most luxurious lodge rooms in Michigan"). Water hazards come into play on 14 of the 18 holes. The Swampfire course winds its way through, well, swamps. It's a challenging course with lots of wildlife to view. The Reflections course is considered the easiest of the four and is perhaps the most scenic. Open April–October. *4700 North Red Oak Road, Lewiston, 30 miles southeast of Gaylord, east on M-32 about 20 miles to CR-491, then south for 10 miles; 989-786-2211 or 877-444-2726; www.garlandusa.com.*

TREETOPS SYLVAN RESORT *map page 205, D-4*

Perhaps the premier Gaylord-area golf resort, Treetops features five courses, two of them considered world-class links, as well as indoor-outdoor pools with spas and two restaurants. Tom Fazio's Premier course, rated the best at Treetops and also the most difficult, is considered by some to be the best course in Michigan for its wide fairways and imaginative holes. *Golf Digest* ranks the Robert Trent Jones Sr. Masterpiece course among the top 30 courses in America. In October the extraordinary fall foliage may divert you from your bogeys.

Rick Smith's award-winning Signature course is another challenging set of links with fabulous views. His Tradition course is described as having a "classic look," perhaps because Smith designed the course for golfers who walk between holes: there's less hilly terrain and shorter distances between holes. His par-three, 9-hole Threetops course is geared toward the beginning golfer. Open April–October. *3962 Wilkinson Road; 989-732-6711 or 888-873-3867; www.treetops.com.*

OTSEGO CLUB *map page 205, D-4*

The three world-class courses here were all designed by William H. Diddel but are at different locations. The Loon, opened in 1994, has proved to be one of northern Michigan's most popular courses. It's listed as one of the top fairways by *Golf for Women* magazine for its "user-friendly" landscaping. The Classic, the founding course in the "Gaylord Golf Mecca," is considered to have some of the finest greens in Michigan. The Lake combines three distinct terrains: six alpine holes around ski hills, six Scottish holes (tall and plentiful roughs), and six holes over and around water hazards. Open April–October. *Loon, 4400 Championship Drive, Gaylord. Classic, 696 M-32 East, Gaylord. Lake, 5750 Opal Lake Road, Gaylord. 989-732-5181 or 800-752-5510; www.otsegoclub.com.*

GAYLORD COUNTRY CLUB *map page 205, D-4*

Following the rolling hills 5 miles west of Gaylord are 18 holes of scenic golf. A spacious practice range and budget-friendly greens fees make the place a favorite. Open April–October. *M-32 West, Gaylord; 231-546-3376; www.northguide. com/gaylordcc.*

Gaylord prides itself on being a "swinging" region—that is, swinging golf clubs. With 24 major courses, Gaylord offers more world-class golf per square mile than any other place in the United States. Among the sterling attractions are two of the courses at **Treetops Sylvan Resort**: one, the Masterpiece, was designed by Robert Trent Jones Sr.; the Premier was designed by Tom Fazio. At **Beaver Creek Resort** another golf course, the Natural, has been declared a wildlife sanctuary by the National Audubon Society. Most courses are open for play from April to October.

There is also great fishing here, on the Sturgeon, Pigeon, Black, and Manistee rivers, and on the North Branch of the Au Sable.

For more information: *Gaylord Area Convention & Tourism Bureau; 101 West Main St.; 800-345-8621; www.gaylord-mich.com.*

■ MACKINAW CITY *map page 205, D-1*

First, the name. Most historical names in the Straits are spelled "Mackinac," except for the city and a few other local namesakes, which became "Mackinaw." But they're all pronounced the same: "Mackinaw" (as in "saw") and never "Mackinak" (as in "sack"). Mackinaw City was originally a low sand beach of swamp grasses, with an Indian village along the shore. In 1715 the French built a fort here, the *second* Fort Michilimackinac, which was eventually taken over by the British and was finally abandoned when, in 1779–80, they sought a more strategic location and built the *third* Fort Michilimackinac on Mackinac Island.

Michilimackinac in the 18th century was both a military outpost and a fur-trading center. Today Mackinaw City's business is tourism: its population of 875 full-time residents swells to the thousands with the influx of visitors during the summer months. Of interest are the town's historic sites, the 5-mile-long **Mackinac Bridge,** and the waters of the Straits of Mackinac, where Lake Huron meets Lake Michigan.

Until the introduction of ferries, and later the Mackinac Bridge, people either paddled or sailed across the Straits, except in winter, when the Straits froze into icy slabs like jagged concrete, cutting off water transportation altogether. In 1881 the passenger and freight ferry *Algomah*—which was designed to tow the barge *Betsy,* with a capacity of four railroad cars, behind it—became the first such link between the two peninsulas. The most popular passenger-car-rail ferry was the *Chief Wawatam*, which operated between St. Ignace and Mackinaw City from 1911 until it retired from passenger service in 1958. During hunting season, travelers sometimes lined up for more than 20 miles, with drivers napping at the wheel. Finally, construction of the Mackinac Bridge began in May 1954; the first driver to pay the toll and drive across it did so on November 1, 1957.

■ **MACKINAC BRIDGE** *map page 205, D-1*

A pair of towers rises 552 feet above the water of the Straits of Mackinac to support a web of cables for the bridge that became the only ground-transportation link between Michigan's Upper and Lower peninsulas when it was completed in 1957. Commonly called Big Mac, the bridge measures 8,614 feet in length and ranks among the world's longest suspension bridges. Every Labor Day the two east lanes are used for the **Mackinac Bridge Walk,** which begins in St. Ignace, on the Upper Peninsula, and ends in Mackinaw City, on the Lower Peninsula. Tens of thousands of walkers participate, including politicians shaking hands, parents pulling tired kids in red wagons, and folk dancers and a ballerina or two who dance their way across. At 7:30 A.M., when the walk begins, sunlight streaks across Lake Huron, casting long shadows of the bridge toward Lake Michigan. *www. mackinacbridge.org.*

■ **MACKINAC STATE HISTORIC PARKS**
Mackinac State Historic Parks includes Colonial Michilimackinac, Historic Mill Creek, and Old Mackinac Point Lighthouse in Mackinaw City, as well as other historic attractions on Mackinac Island: Fort Mackinac, Historic Downtown, and Mackinac Island State Park.

■ **COLONIAL MICHILIMACKINAC** *map page 205, D-1*
When the British built a new fort on Mackinac Island in 1779–80, they dismantled their old one at Mackinaw City, salvaged its usable parts, and burned the remainder down. Now archaeologists are excavating the area, and the old Fort Michilimackinac has been reconstructed and opened to the public as a living-history museum under the name Colonial Michilimackinac. Visitors see a British trading post, a French church where a colonial wedding is re-enacted daily, a guardhouse, a blacksmith shop, colonial homes with gardens, and other structures. There are frequent reenactments from the late-18th-century days of the fort's British occupation and the American Revolution.

Fort Michilimackinac was the scene of perhaps the most dramatic episode of the French and Indian War. The great Ottawa chief Pontiac had assembled a large "secret" confederation of tribes with the aim of ousting the British and returning control of the fur trade to the French. His "rebellion" involved simultaneous assaults at forts all along the Great Lakes and the Ohio Valley—what was then the western frontier.

On June 2, 1763, two bands of Chippewas and Sauks, part of Pontiac's confederation, gathered in front of Fort Michilimackinac to stage a game of baggataway (lacrosse). Although he had been warned of possible trouble, fort commander George Etherington took the warning lightly. On that June morning, soldiers leaned idly at their posts along the stockade and watched as the game heated up. They cheered as the wooden ball went back and forth in a near frenzy of plays. Suddenly the ball sailed over the stockaded walls. The Indian teams swarmed through the open gate, grabbed tomahawks and knives hidden under the blankets worn by their women waiting inside the walls, and started hacking, stabbing, shooting, and scalping every English soldier to be found.

Civilians watched or cowered in their houses. A British fur trader, Alexander Henry, was sitting in his room at the fort writing a letter when the massacre began.

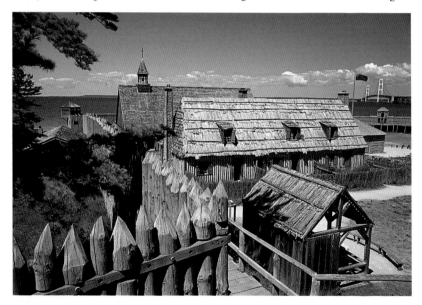

(*above*) *A view of Colonial Michilimackinac with the Mackinac Bridge in the background.*
(*opposite*) *A sawyer in early Federal-period costume works the mill at Historic Mill Creek.*

A Game of Baggatiway

In this passage, Alexander Henry, a British trader who traveled in the Great Lakes area in the mid-18th century, describes a lacrosse-like game played by Indian tribes in the Northeast. The Indian chief Pontiac used a baggataway match as a ploy to catch the British soldiers unprepared to defend their fort.

The game of *baggatiway* . . . is necessarily attended with much violence and noise. In the ardor of contest the ball, as has been suggested, if it cannot be thrown to the goal desired, is struck in any direction by which it can be diverted from that designed by the adversary. At such a moment, therefore, nothing could be less liable to excite premature alarm than that the ball should be tossed over the pickets of the fort, nor that having fallen there, it should be followed on the instant by all engaged in the game, as well the one party as the other, all eager, all struggling, all shouting, all in the unrestrained pursuit of a rude athletic exercise. Nothing could be less fitted to excite premature alarm—nothing, therefore, could be more happily devised, under the circumstances, than a stratagem like this; and this was in fact the stratagem which the Indians had employed. . . .

—Alexander Henry, *Travels and Adventures in Canada and the Indian Territories Between the Years 1760 and 1776,* 1809

Although a servant girl hid him, he was nevertheless captured. Henry, Etherington, his lieutenant, and 12 privates were loaded in canoes bound for Beaver Island, where supposedly they were to be killed, boiled, and eaten.

Meanwhile, the Ottawas at L'Arbre Croche heard about the massacre and were furious, in part because they had not been consulted. They gathered a band of a hundred warriors and set out for Michilimackinac. They met the Chippewas and Sauks en route, and in the ensuing fight the Ottawas prevailed and Henry and nine of the other soldiers were rescued. Henry lived to tell the story in graphic detail. The drama is reenacted at Colonial Michilimackinac every Memorial Day weekend. *Colonial Michilimackinac Visitor's Center: 102 Straits Avenue.*

■ **Old Mackinac Point Lighthouse** *map page 205, D-1*
Near Colonial Michilimackinac, near the south end of the Mackinac Bridge, the 1892 **Old Mackinac Point Lighthouse** has been restored and was opened to the

public in June 2004 for the first time since its decommissioning in 1957. Tours of the keepers' quarters are given. *North Huron Avenue.*

■ **HISTORIC MILL CREEK** *map page 205, D-1*
This reconstructed 1790 lumber mill along Mill Creek three miles east of Mackinaw City is a replica of the state's first industrial complex. Given the sparse forests on Mackinac Island, it was this mill that furnished lumber for village homes. Today the water-powered mill is especially interesting for children, who are called on to assist interpreters in their outdoor demonstrations. Historic Mill Creek also has forest trails and a visitors center. *9001 South U.S. 23.*

Mackinac State Historic Parks are open daily from mid-May to mid-October. *Year-round information for Colonial Michilimackinac, Old Mackinac Point Lighthouse and Historic Mill Creek: 231-436-4100, www.mackinacparks.com.*

■ **MACKINAW CITY—STAY AND PLAY**
Mackinaw Crossings is a Disneyesque web of shops, replete with fountains, park benches, parkside entertainment, live theater, and a nightly laser show. It draws visitors throughout the main May to mid-October tourist season. *248 South Huron Avenue; 231-436-5030; www.mackinawcrossings.com.*

With the largest outdoor wave pool in Michigan, the **Thunder Falls Family Water Park** is making a big splash. The 20 acres include the Lazy River, winding among a dozen wet and wild thrill slides. Open mid-May–mid-September. *1028 South Nicolet Street, 231-436-6000; www.thunderfallswaterpark.com.*

For more information: *Mackinaw Area Visitors Bureau; 10300 U.S. 23; 800-666-0160; www.mackinawcity.com.*

■ **MACKINAC ISLAND** *map page 205, D-1 and map page 241*

As you arrive by ferry from St. Ignace or Mackinaw City, the limestone bluffs of Mackinac Island are crowned by the long white 19th-century Grand Hotel and Fort Mackinac, flanked by Victorian summer mansions (called cottages) replete with gingerbread trim, turrets, and wraparound porches. The Chippewa Indians called the island Michilimackinac, or Land of the Great Turtle, referring to its oval humpbacked shape, and considered it a holy place for all tribes. Their belief holds that the great god Manitou ascended from his home in the depths through the imposing limestone sweep of Arch Rock that overlooks Lake Huron. The French honored that tradition, but the British viewed the island in more practical terms—as a strategic point of defense against the Americans. In 1779–80, the British moved Fort Michilimackinac from Mackinaw City to the island (and shortened its name to Fort Mackinac). The Americans nevertheless gained possession in 1813 at the close of the War of 1812. Abandoned in 1894, the military outpost, along with half of Mackinac Island, became Michigan's first state park one year later. Through acquisitions over the years, it now encompasses 1,800 acres, or 82 percent of the island.

In the early years of the island's development, a few of its wealthy cottage owners brought automobiles with them, but because their explosive banging and rattling continually frightened the horses, automobiles were banned in 1898. The effect of stepping onto the island, with its horse-drawn carriages, false storefronts, and Victorian extravagance, is like walking through a portal into the past. As though mesmerized by this effect, about 75 percent of the visitors never explore beyond the souvenir shops (which range from T-shirt emporiums to upscale art galleries), the restaurants (which lure with irresistible aromas), and the comforts found in the

A costumed reenactor plays his flute at Fort Mackinac.

Arch Rock on Mackinac Island

island's 12 hotels and 20 tourist homes and inns.

There is a lot more, however, including Fort Mackinac and other Mackinac State Historic Parks sites. You can orient yourself by taking one of the tours offered by **Mackinac Island Carriage Tours** (906-847-3573; www.mict.com), the oldest livery service in the country. The narrated tour provides an insider's view of the island, including stops at Arch Rock, cemeteries, and the Surrey Hills Museum, which contains antique carriages and more souvenir shops. The company's office is on Main Street across from the Arnold Ferry Dock. You can also take a private carriage tour, rent a drive-your-own carriage or a bicycle, go horseback riding, or hike the island's 61 miles of roads and trails.

■ MACKINAC ISLAND HIGHLIGHTS

From Main Street, walk up Fort Street and the white ramp that gradually ascends the 150-foot cliff to the 14 original buildings of **Fort Mackinac,** grouped within thick stone walls. The enactments and displays here are more than history—they provide entertainment for all ages. When youngsters tire of soldiers in 1880s dress uniforms firing muskets and playing fife and drum, they are often called upon to

MACKINAC ISLAND

For a while, Mackinac Island was the biggest trading post in the New World—John Jacob Astor's fur trading company was based here—but its real glory dates from the late nineteenth century when wealthy people from Chicago and Detroit came to escape the city heat and enjoy the pollen-free air. The Grand Hotel, the biggest and oldest resort hotel in America, was built and the country's wealthiest industrialists constructed ornate summer houses on the bluffs overlooking Mackinac village and Lake Huron. I walked up there now. The views across the lake were fantastic, but the houses were simply breathtaking. They are some of the grandest, most elaborate houses ever built of wood, twenty-bedroomed places with every embellishment known to the Victorian mind—cupolas, towers, domes, dormers, gables, turrets, and front porches you could ride a bike around. Some of the cupolas had cupolas. They are just incredibly splendid and there are scores of them, standing side by side on the bluffs flanking Fort Mackinac. What it must be to be a child and play hide-and-seek in those houses, to have a bedroom in a tower and be able to lie in bed and gaze out on such a lake, and to go bicycling on carless roads to little beaches and hidden coves, and above all to explore the woodlands of beech and birch that cover the back three-quarters of the island.

—Bill Bryson, *The Lost Continent: Travels in Small-Town America,* 1990

Mrs. Potter Palmer, queen of Chicago society, here enjoys a carriage ride on Mackinac Island, circa 1890.

help the soldiers fire the canon. Then interpreters in period costumes introduce them to pioneer games or the Kid's Quarters for more play. Other family members tour officers' quarters with period furnishings, barracks, and the jail. In one barracks, an informative exhibit traces the island's history from the Indians and missionaries through the fur trade, fishing, the War of 1812, and into the tourism era. Stop at the Fort Tea Room overlooking the village and marina for lunch or afternoon lemonade.

Five sites downtown are under the aegis of Mackinac State Historic Parks and known collectively as Historic Downtown. Besides two 18th-century houses— **McGulpin House** and **Biddle House**—the **Mission Church,** and the **Benjamin Blacksmith Shop,** they include the **Dr. Beaumont Museum,** housed in a building at Market and Fort streets that was once the American Fur Company's retail store. In the early 1800s it was frequented by voyageurs pausing on their long canoe paddles between Montreal and western suppliers. While in the store on June 6, 1822, the 19-year-old Canadian voyageur Alexis St. Martin sustained an accidental gunshot to his stomach, and post surgeon Dr. William Beaumont rushed to assist him. Beaumont saved St. Martin's life, but the wound never closed, leaving a "window" into his digestive system. Along with interpreting life in the fur company store, the museum interprets Beaumont's extensive experiments with St. Martin. The doctor was later heralded as the "leader and pioneer of experimental physiology in America."

Tickets to Fort Mackinac, open from mid-May to mid-October, include admission to the Historic Downtown sites (open mid-June to late-August). *For information on all the above Mackinac State Historic Parks located on Mackinac Island, call 906-847-3328 from May to mid-October, 231-436-4100 the rest of the year; www. mackinacparks.com.*

Stuart House Museum

The two-story white **Stuart House Museum** was one of the four warehouses built by fur trader John Jacob Astor in the early 1800s. It was named for the American Fur Company's resident manager, Robert Stuart. Now owned by the City of Mackinac Island, it is being furnished with mementos of the fur trade and historic Mackinac, such as a scale for weighing baled furs, a cannonball from the War of 1812, and a soldier's flintlock rifle with horn and shot. Open from mid-May to mid-October. *Market Street, next door to Community Hall; 906-847-3307.*

The Grand Hotel's front porch stretches more than 600 feet along the lakefront.

Grand Hotel

The front porch of this stunning, world-famous 1887 Victorian hotel is lined with classic columns, white wicker rockers, and flower boxes that hold 2,500 red geraniums. Throughout the salons, hallways, dining area, and private rooms, the hotel takes on the quality of a living museum. Guests lounge on antique sofas, enjoy viewing fine art, and often sleep on antique beds. Open from May through October. *One Grand Drive; 906-847-3331; www.grandhotel.com.*

Don't leave Mackinac Island without sampling its most famous export—fudge—from any of the dozen or more shops along Main Street. Then you're a "fudgie," the island residents' name for tourist. Granted, fudge is no substitute for lunch or dinner, but you're not a visitor to Mackinac Island until you've indulged.

For information: *Mackinac Tourist Bureau, Main Street; 800-454-5227; www. mackinacisland.org.*

■ Travel Basics

Area Overview: This area—from Grand Traverse Bay to Mackinac Island—is the heart of Michigan's most scenic, and most visited, vacationland. Included are the popular Mackinac Island and Gaylord, one of America's golf meccas.

Travel: The main north–south travel arteries are U.S. 31 and U.S. 131. Interstate-75, the mid-state corridor, borders the region on the east. Interconnecting highways form a network of good road systems. Air travel is available from Traverse City and Pellston.

Getting to Mackinac Island

Mackinac Island is serviced by three ferry lines. All depart from the docks at St. Ignace and at Mackinaw City and charge about the same round-trip fare ($18 adults, $8 children). Schedules change with the seasons, so be sure to confirm departure times.

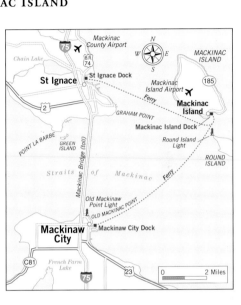

Arnold Transit Co.
Catamaran ferries. *906-847-3351 or 800-542-8528; www.arnoldline.com.*

Shepler's Mackinac Island Ferry. Hydroplane ferries. *906-643-9440 or 800-828-6157; www.sheplersferry.com.*

Star Line. Hydro-jet ferries. *906 643-7635 or 800-638-9892; www.mackinacferry.com.*

Great Lakes Air operates between St. Ignace and Mackinac Island Airport, which has a paved 3,500-foot runway. Reservations are recommended. $40 round-trip. *Airport Road; 906-847-3231; www.greatlakesair.com.*

Weather: The weather is generally mild with prevailing westerly winds. As in the rest of Michigan, summertime highs can reach the 90s, with low humidity and gentle breezes. Fall can bring temperatures in the upper 70s and one-blanket nights. Winters, with the westerly lake effect, average an annual snowfall of 130 inches, with freezing temperatures that can reach zero.

Food & Lodging: Some of Michigan's best places to dine and to stay are found here. From the vineyard B&Bs on the Leelanau Peninsula to the ultraluxurious Grand Hotel on Mackinac Island, the choices are many. *Refer to the listings, which begin on page 274.*

UPPER PENINSULA

Three of the largest freshwater lakes in the world—Superior, Huron, and Michigan—draw the 1,100-mile boundary of Michigan's Upper Peninsula, which reaches 384 miles from Drummond Island in the east to Ironwood in the west and 233 miles from Menominee in the south to Copper Harbor at the tip of the Keweenaw Peninsula far out in Lake Superior. Yet in all this vastness only three cities have a population of more than 13,000: Marquette, Sault Ste. Marie, and Escanaba.

The Upper Peninsula, locally called the U.P. (residents call themselves Yoopers), is larger than the states of Connecticut, Delaware, Massachusetts, and Rhode Island combined. Its western border is as far west as St. Louis, Missouri, and most of the peninsula including Isle Royale is farther north than Montreal. In fact, the distance between Detroit and Isle Royale is about the same as that between Detroit and New York City.

The U.P. includes Michigan's largest wilderness, its largest state park, and all but two of the state's 152 significant waterfalls. There are 200-foot cliffs, beaches, dunes, 4,300 inland lakes, and 12,000 miles of trout streams. It's no wonder the peninsula appeals so strongly to nature lovers and sportsmen.

Along Lake Michigan, wide bands of fine, squeaky sand stretch undisturbed for 15 miles; along Lake Superior's shore, sheer sandstone cliffs loom 200 feet above the waves. Between the two lakes there are 49 warning lights and lighthouses, including seven lighthouse museums, two lighthouse bed-and-breakfast inns, and one light station with lighthouse and overnight accommodations.

The U.P. is the Michigan frontier, where most residents are aggressively provincial; diners wearing jackets and ties sit comfortably alongside those in swamper boots and Mackinaw jackets. Yoopers are known for their dedicated work ethic as well as their high tolerance for eccentricity. They teasingly refer to people living below the Mackinac Bridge as Trolls. The U.P. economy is based on forest products, tourism, and health care. Temperatures from May through October are especially pleasant, but Yoopers joke about having "10 months of winter and 2 months of poor sledding."

The first day of whitetail deer season is considered a Yooper holiday. Most winter events include dogsled races. Depending on their mood, Yoopers root for the Green Bay Packers or the Detroit Lions. They favor pasties—the meat pie in a crust introduced by miners who immigrated from Cornwall, England—and cudighy, a spicy Italian sausage brought to the U.P. by Italian immigrants.

■ HISTORY

In the early 1600s—while the English were dropping anchor from the *Mayflower* in Plymouth Harbor, the Dutch were building New Amsterdam (New York), and the Spanish were claiming lands on the Gulf and Pacific coasts, having already settled along the southern Atlantic coast—French explorers and missionaries were paddling up the St. Lawrence River headed for what is now Michigan's Upper Peninsula. Chippewa (Ojibwa) Indians inhabited the eastern end of the peninsula; the Menominees inhabited the western end.

Young Étienne Brûlé might have been the first European to see the Upper Peninsula. Sent by Samuel de Champlain to search for water routes to China, which he believed lay just to the west of the lakes, Brûlé found neither China nor the fabled Northwest Passage, but he did find Native Americans, in this case Hurons. A talented linguist, Brûlé was soon speaking their language and, as was often the case in those years, was accepted into the Huron world as part of an extended family. But the warm feelings soured. Following a fierce argument, the Hurons killed and ate him.

A family strolls along windswept Twelvemile Beach at Pictured Rocks National Lakeshore.

Lake Superior

Ferry to Isle Royale
Sand Hills Light
Eagle Harbor 26
Copper Harbor
Fort Wilkins Historic State
MANITOU ISLAND
Keweenaw National Historical Park
Phoenix
Mohawk
Calumet
Old Bete Grise Light
Keweenaw Pt
F J McLain State Park
Keweenaw Upper Entrance Light
41
Laurium
Mount Bohemia
Mont Ripley
203
26
Hancock
Houghton
KEWEENAW PENINSULA

Fourteen Mile Pt
Toivola
Quincy Mine Hoist Museum
41
Pt Abbaye
Huron River Pt
Keweenaw Bay

Ontonagon Light
Ontonagon
Porcupine Mountains Wilderness State Park
107
Adventure Mtn
26
Huron River Pt
Big Bay Pt Light
Porcupine Mtn
Silver City
38
Baraga
HURON MTS
Big Bay Pt Light
PORCUPINE MTS
White Pine
Mass City
38
L'Anse
Big Bay
519
64
Bergland
Bruce Crossing
41
Alberta
Dear River Basin
Marquette History
Blackjack
Indianhead Mtn
28
Lake Gogebic
Covington
41
Three Lakes
US National Ski Hall of Fame
Negaunee
Marqu
Big Powderhorn
Bessemer
Wakefield
64
45
Bond Falls Flowage
28
Champion
Ishpeming
Marquette Mtn
2
Ironwood
Marenisco
2
141
95
Michigan Iron Industry Museum
77
51
Watersmeet
Amasa
Michigamme Res
Witch Lake
Gwinn
35
Land O'Lakes
Lac Vieux Desert
45
Crystal Falls
Sagola
Bewabic State Park
Ski Brule
70
Brule
Mary Lake
69
95
G30
Rap
139
Iron River
Norway Mtn
Iron Mountain
Vulcan
Glad
2
Escana

N
W E
S

Following in Brûlé's
footsteps came other explorers, traders, and zealous, black-
robed priests. Among this group were
Jean Nicolet, Father René Menard, Father
Claude Allouez, Louis Jolliet, and René-Robert
Cavelier, Sieur de La Salle. In 1668 Jesuit missionaries Jacques Marquette and Claude Dablon built a
mission at St. Marys Rapids, naming Michigan's first settlement Sault Ste. Marie for the Virgin Mary.

WISCONSIN
Carney
Is
41
35
Ingalls
Cedar Ri
J W Wells State Park
141
CHAMBERS ISLAND
64
Menominee
41
Marinette

Two years later, when Marquette moved south to the
Straits of Mackinac, he built a mission at the straits among the
villages of the Hurons and the Ottawas. With its strategic loca-
tion, the settlement attracted fur traders. Marquette named it St.
Ignace for St. Ignatius of Loyola, founder of the Jesuit order, but it was better
known by its Algonquian name, Michilimackinac. By 1681 New France had built
Fort de Buade along the St. Ignace waterfront, and the concomitant growth made
St. Ignace Michigan's second oldest settlement.

The compulsion to claim more souls for God—and, incidentally, more land for
France—soon drove Marquette and Jolliet westward into the wilderness. Willis F.
Dunbar and George S. May write in *Michigan*:

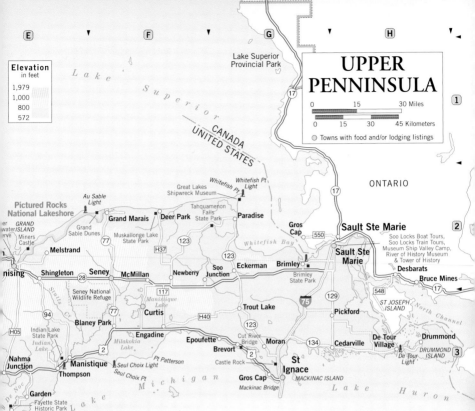

On May 17, 1673, Jolliet and Marquette, together with five other Frenchmen, departed from St. Ignace. Following the Lake Michigan shore of the Upper Peninsula into Green Bay, they ascended the Fox River, portaged to the Wisconsin, and on June 17, a month after the start of the trip, they entered the Mississippi "with a joy which I am unable to make known," Marquette later declared.

After the commander of Fort de Buade, Antoine de la Mothe Cadillac, left it at the end of the 17th century to construct the more strategically placed Fort Pontchartrain at Detroit, little was heard of the U.P. until Michigan began seeking entry into the Union; then the U.P. regained prominence, even notoriety. In 1835–36, as politicians and business leaders clamored for statehood—all the while engaged in a heated argument with Ohio over a strip of land around Toledo—Congress offered the Upper Peninsula to Michigan in return for its recognition of Ohio's claim to the disputed Toledo Strip. With statehood the prize, Michigan's politicos grudgingly accepted the 16,538-square-mile "barren waste" of the Upper Peninsula.

In 1841 state geologist Douglass Houghton presented the legislature with a report on the copper along the Keweenaw Trap Range, fueling a copper rush to the north. Three years later, state surveyor William Austin Burt discovered iron on Teal Lake in what is now Negaunee, and soon a stampede for iron was on. To become a state, Michigan had been forced to cede a slice of itself to Ohio, receiving in return the "godforsaken wilderness" of the Upper Peninsula. That wilderness, however, turned out to contain some of the richest mineral deposits in the world, generating more wealth than did the goldfields of California and Alaska combined.

■ ST. IGNACE *map pages 244–245, G-3*

As you drive across the Mackinac Bridge toward St. Ignace, you are presented with vast expanses of water on either side. To the east is Lake Huron, with Mackinac Island seeming to float on its blue-green waters. To the west is Lake Michigan, with three small islands in the distance. On clear summer days the lakes turn azure, with low, whitecapped waves when the wind is up. Impressive "big salties" (seafaring freighters) dwarf the lake freighters as they pass under the bridge through the Straits of Mackinac.

St. Ignace is not visible from the bridge, but on the west side, beyond the toll booth, is the Michigan State Police post, and to the east are the bridge headquarters and the **Travel Michigan St. Ignace Welcome Center** (401 I-75; 906-643-6979). U.S. 2 becomes State Street as it goes through town. It can be slow going during the peak summer months, when tourists come to enjoy Mackinac Island, and budget-minded vacationers seeking quarters cheaper than those on the island turn St. Ignace into a bedroom community. Low-key and friendly, St. Ignace offers convenient dining and lodging. Many establishments have been operating since the 1920s. **Straits State Park,** overlooking the Straits of Mackinac and the Mackinac Bridge, offers camping, picnicking, boating, and hiking. Most lodgings and attractions operate from May through October; some remain open for the busy winter snowmobile season.

Ferries bound for Mackinac Island maintain docks downtown along State Street, which parallels Moran Bay. Shepler's and Star Line operate May through October; Arnold Transit runs until ice freezes the bay (usually January through March). Great Lakes Air flies year-round from St. Ignace to Mackinac Island.

For more information: *St. Ignace Convention & Visitors Bureau; 560 North State Street; 800-338-6660 ; www.stignace.com.*

■ CUT RIVER BRIDGE AND CASTLE ROCK

West of St. Ignace, U.S. 2 wanders for 18 miles past numerous low dunes and miles of Lake Michigan beaches to the shallow Cut River, meandering through a deep forested gorge. It is spanned by the 641-foot-long cantilevered Cut River Bridge, and roadside parks on either side of the bridge offer scenic views. Known as the "million-dollar bridge over a 10-cent river," it is, at 147 feet, the second-highest bridge in Michigan. (Big Mac, at 199 feet, is the highest.)

Four miles north of St. Ignace on I-75 is the 195-foot-high Castle Rock, once a lookout for Great Lakes Indians. The climb to the top rewards you with a dramatic panorama of Lake Michigan and the Straits of Mackinac.

■ SAULT STE. MARIE *map pages 244–245, H-2*

The "twin Soos," as Sault Ste. Marie, Michigan, and Sault Ste. Marie, Canada, are called, share friendly waters where Lake Superior and Whitefish Bay's St. Marys River make a 21-foot drop before flowing on to Lake Huron. Soo, Michigan, has numerous historical attractions, but it lives somewhat in the shadow of its larger Canadian neighbor across the **International Bridge**, Soo, Canada, a city with busy shopping malls, fine restaurants, and industrial successes. What brings most visitors to Soo, Michigan, are the Soo Locks and the numerous attractions along Portage Avenue, which parallels the locks and river to form an east–west artery through the city. Attractions include souvenir shops, galleries, restaurants, and lodging.

For centuries, Great Lakes Indians fished the half-mile-long rapids that were long known as the Gathering Place. In 1668, noting the large encampments of Chippewas there, Fathers Marquette and Dablon built a mission on the east side of St. Marys Rapids in the hope of making converts. The founding of the mission makes this city of 14,700 the oldest European settlement in the Midwest (and, if one accepts local claims that the visit by Brûlé in 1620 marks its founding, the third oldest in the nation). The mission was abandoned in 1670, but in the late 1760s it was resurrected as a fort to protect the fur traders.

Activities in faraway Detroit affected the Soo. After France lost Fort Pontchartain to the British in 1760, the British renamed it Fort Detroit. The British in turn lost their naval dominance of the Great Lakes—at the hands of U.S. Commodore Oliver Hazard Perry in 1813 in the Battle of Lake Erie—and abandoned their fort to the Americans. In 1853, in response to expanding industries, particularly the ores being extracted in the north, construction began on the first two navigational locks. Today a total of five locks—four parallel U.S. and one Canadian—connect Lake Superior to Lake Huron and the rest of the St. Lawrence Seaway, and the Soo Locks rank as one of the world's busiest waterways.

The **Soo Locks Visitors Center** displays a working model of the locks and offers a history of the locks system. From any of three observation platforms outside you can watch the huge freighters ease their way through the locks. "We all rush dockside when the big salties lock through," says Soo native Bud Mansfield. Open mid-May to mid-October. *300 Portage Avenue; 906-632-3311; www. soolocksvisitorscenter.com.*

Soo Locks Boat Tours
To observe this close-up, take a narrated boat tour or sunset dinner cruise, both two hours, along the river and through the American and Canadian locks. *515 and 1157 East Portage Avenue; 800-432-6301; www.soolocks.com.*

Soo Locks Train Tours
For an interesting perspective on the locks, take the Soo Locks Train Tours hourlong narrated tour of the locks area. The trip takes you across the 2.8-mile International Bridge to Soo, Ontario, giving you a bird's-eye view of ships passing

The locks at Sault Ste. Marie in 1905.

An ore freighter passes through the Soo Locks.

through the five locks and of the St. Marys Rapids that necessitated them. A 2½-hour trip includes stops for a visit of the Canadian lock and lock museum as well as a tour of the Canadian city. For the longer tour, take a photo I.D. for customs; a birth certificate is suggested for children and is, in fact, required for some tours into Canada. In the current climate, it's best to call ahead for exact customs requirements. *317 West Portage Avenue; 906-632-4000 or 866-766-5625; www. soolockstraintours.com.*

Museum Ship Valley Camp

This 550-foot Great Lakes freighter has been transformed into a museum. Included among the exhibits are lifeboats recovered from the *Edmund Fitzgerald*, which sank in Lake Superior in 1975. Open mid-May to mid-October. *501 East Water Street; 906-632-3658 or 888-744-7867; www.thevalleycamp.com.*

River of History Museum

Displays capture the history of the St. Marys River and its people from early Chippewa days to modern times. Open mid-May to mid-October. *209 East Portage Avenue; 906-632-1999; history.eup.k12.mi.us/local/river.*

Tower of History
Ride the elevator up the 210-foot-tall Tower of History for a panorama of the locks, rapids, and river and a view of Ontario. The history museum on the first floor also has a nice gift shop. Open mid-May through mid-October. *326 East Portage Avenue; 888-744-7867 or 906-632-3658; www.towerofhistory.com.* For more information: *Sault Ste. Marie Welcome Center, 943 West Portage Avenue; 906-632-8242. Sault Ste. Marie Area Convention & Visitors Bureau, 2605 I-75 Business Spur; 800-647-2858; www.saultstemarie.com.*

■ GREAT LAKES SHIPWRECK MUSEUM
For a truly haunting experience of Great Lakes history, go west from Sault Ste. Marie on M-28 about 20 miles to M-123; then head north on M-123 to Paradise. At Paradise follow Whitefish Point Road north for 11 miles to the **Whitefish Point Light Station,** standing on the lake at a point where more than 300 ships have met a violent end. Among them was the most dramatic Great Lakes shipwreck of modern times, the iron-ore carrier *Edmund Fitzgerald,* which broke apart in a violent storm on the night of November 10, 1975, and sank below the waves, taking the entire crew of 29 with it. The lighthouse is now part of the **Great Lakes**

One of many victims of Lake Superior's unpredictable storms and hazardous shoals, the George M. Cox *ran aground on Isle Royale in May 1933.*

Shipwreck Museum, which includes the adjoining light keeper's quarters, built in 1861, and the museum proper, in a modern building. The artifacts from the *Edmund Fitzgerald* on view here are sobering, especially the ship's 200-pound bronze bell, which was recovered from the shipwreck at the request of the crew's families. Each time I visit, I recall lines from Gordon Lightfoot's song "Wreck of the *Edmund Fitzgerald*":

The legend lives on from the Chippewa on down,
Of the big lake they called Gitchigumi.
"Superior," they said, "never gives up her dead
"When the gales of November come early."

A quiet walk past the lighthouse raised above the grounds on iron pilings, then along the lonely beach scattered with driftwood, banded agates, and other collectible beach stones, continues the mood of reflection. The museum offers overnight accommodations year-round in the crew's quarters of the 1923 Coast Guard Lifeboat Station, another building on the property. Other than for overnight guests, the museum-complex season is from May to mid-October. *18335 North Whitefish Point Road, Paradise; 888-492-3747; www.edmundfitzgerald.org.*

■ TAHQUAMENON FALLS *map pages 244–245, G-2*

South of Paradise on M-123 at **Tahquamenon Falls State Park,** the tea-colored Tahquamenon (Ta-*kwah*-me-non) River meanders through Michigan's largest swamp, which is thick with tamarack trees and other species of the northern forests. The river then sheets over the Upper Falls' 200-foot-wide sandstone ledge to a fury of foam and bubbles 40 feet below. Pathways follow the river, leading to overlooks and continuing to a stairway down the riverbank to a deck that stretches to the very lip of the falls. In his famous poem *Hiawatha,* Henry Wadsworth Longfellow describes Hiawatha voyaging on the Tahquamenon:

And thus sailed my Hiawatha
Down the rushing Tahquamenaw,
Sailed through all its bends and windings,
Sailed through all its deeps and shallows.

Four miles north, at the park's Lower Falls, the river drops in cascades to circle an island accessible by paddleboats. The 40,000-acre Tahquamenon Falls State Park has campgrounds, hiking trails, fishing, cross-country skiing, and snowmobile trails. *906-492-3219; www.dnr.state.mi.us/parksandtrails.*

The tannin-dyed waters of Lower Tahquamenon Falls.

Add more adventure to your Tahquamenon River's Upper Falls visit with the **Toonerville Trolley and Riverboat Tour,** a 6½-hour tour that includes a 35-minute ride through the forest on a narrow-gauge railroad, followed by a two-hour (each way) wilderness riverboat tour that docks half a mile above the falls. There is time for a hike to the Upper Falls. Food and beverages are available on the riverboat. The trolley leaves from Soo Junction, 15 miles east of Newberry. Follow signs from the intersection of M-28 and Soo Junction Road. *888-778-7246.*

■ **SENEY** *map pages 244–245, F-2*

In the heyday of tall timber, Seney, at the junction of M-28 and M-77, was as wild as any western cow town, with brawls in crowded saloons when lumberjacks came to their "hell town in the pines." In *Call it North Country,* John Bartlow Martin describes the town's legendary ladies of pleasure: "Many of them chewed 'Peerless' [tobacco]. One was called Razorback; her peculiar forte, perfected at bagnio dances, was to waltz her partner near the door so the pimps could seize him and drag him outside and beat and rob him."

Seney is a peaceful village now, with the only evidence of its wild past the wooden "Died Fightin' " markers in a half-forgotten cemetery on the north side of town. How it used to be is vivid in the mind of the Hemingway aficionado who, reading the short story "Big Two-Hearted River," is with Nick Adams as he steps down from the train in a deserted, burned-out Seney and stands on the little bridge looking down at the trout swimming in the Fox River before hiking on to the Big Two-Hearted River. A note of caution, however: Hemingway was spinning a fish story. Actually, Seney is located some miles southwest of the Big Two-Hearted River, and Adams would have faced quite a hike. And although Seney endured two disastrous forest fires in the 1890s, it did not completely burn to the ground.

Five miles south on M-77, in the Great Manistique Swamp, is **Seney National Wildlife Refuge**, more than 95,000 acres, approximately two-thirds of it wetland. Within its maze of marshes, swamps, and forests can be found a multitude of rare and endangered species, including the bald eagle and the timber wolf. There are hiking trails, 80 miles of biking trails, canoeing on the Manistique and Driggs rivers, and the 7-mile self-guided Marshland Wildlife Drive. In the evening, if

---

Big Two-Hearted River

The train went on up the track out of sight, around one of the hills of burnt timber. Nick sat down on the bundle of canvas and bedding the baggage man had pitched out of the door of the baggage car. There was no town, nothing but the rails and the burned-over country. The thirteen saloons that had lined the one street of Seney had not left a trace. The foundations of the Mansion House hotel stuck up above the ground. The stone was chipped and split by the fire. It was all that was left of the town of Seney. Even the surface had been burned off the ground.

Nick looked at the burned-over stretch of hillside, where he had expected to find the scattered houses of the town and then walked down the railroad track to the bridge over the river. The river was there. It swirled against the log spiles of the bridge. Nick looked down into the clear, brown water, colored from the pebbly bottom, and watched the trout keeping themselves steady in the current with wavering fins. As he watched them they changed their positions by quick angles, only to hold steady in the fast water again. Nick watched them a long time.

—Ernest Hemingway, "Big Two-Hearted River," 1924

You Can't Go Home Again—Or Can You?

The life of Jim Harrison—novelist, poet, screenwriter, gourmand—has taken him far from his Michigan farmland roots: from New York to Hollywood to France and many places in between, such as Arizona and Montana, where he hunts and fishes and savors his love of literature. In his 2002 memoir Off to the Side, *Harrison recalls how his Swedish mother insisted, "We were never hungry during the Great Depression," along with other bittersweet memories he cherishes, and takes care not to leave behind.*

What have I forgotten? Waking to the animal sounds that seem to comfort one, easing the soul into consciousness. There were no alarm clocks in the house. . . . My young aunt bathing in a tin tub in the kitchen. . . . Reading with a pillow on the floor next to the wood-stove. . . . Salt-pork gravy. Churning sweet butter. The heaviness of the rye bread eaten with herring. The sip of my father's beer, the wet straps of his undershirt as he plowed with horses wearing an old fedora for the sun. . . . The long country funerals. The gush of blood at pig butchering. You could hear it.

Over fifty years later this life still lives within me . . . in the small village near my cabin in Michigan's Upper Peninsula, a location I found and moved to because it reminded me of the ambience of my childhood cabin. People who used to live in the village, were children there, come up for the holidays, usually Memorial Day weekend, or the Fourth of July, from what is called "down below," the cities far to the south of the Mackinaw Bridge that connects Michigan's two sections and where they make their livelihoods. When they first arrive back home there is often jubilant drinking, then the next day fishing or hunting, and by the second evening a vague unrest often settles in. Things, of course, are not what they were in the old days and though these feelings are bearable the disappointment is always there.

— Jim Harrison, *Off to the Side,* 2002

you're lucky, you may hear wolves howling in the distance—unforgettable. *906-586-9851; midwest.fws.gov/seney.*

Heading west from Seney across northern swamplands, highway M-28, known locally as the **Seney Stretch,** makes a 25-mile beeline across the flat landscape for the village of Shingleton. Voted Michigan's dullest highway by readers of the *Detroit Free Press,* it shoots as straight and monotonous as a West Texas two-lane, but as it approaches Munising, M-28 enters another gorgeous portion of the U.P.

■ MUNISING *map pages 244–245, E-2*

Grand Island, the largest island off Lake Superior's south shore, stands guard at Munising's front door, protecting the town from the wrath of storms. Nowhere is Superior more spectacular, but if you choose to venture forth, make certain that you understand its moods. It takes a brave soul to enter the water more than big-toe deep—the lake seldom comes within 40 degrees of body temperature, even on an August day. Despite clear waters as smooth as glass and cool breezes that caress, attesting to Superior's temperamental nature are at least 30 shipwrecks that lie in the **Alger Underwater Preserve** around the island and in Lake Superior's Munising Bay, a favorite site for scuba divers. From June to mid-October, **Shipwreck Tours** runs two-hour narrated cruises in glass-bottomed boats out to the wrecks, including that of the 150-foot wooden schooner *Bermuda,* which sank in 1870. *1204 Commercial Street; 906-387-4477; www.shipwrecktours.com.*

■ PICTURED ROCKS NATIONAL LAKESHORE *map pages 244–245, E-2*
The frenzied, Paul Bunyan–size Ice Age sculptor who carved the shores of Michigan's peninsulas was particularly inspired when he created Pictured Rocks. Rising more than 200 feet above Lake Superior, Pictured Rocks National Lakeshore extends about 45 miles eastward from Munising. Among the picturesque natural formations carved into its sandstone cliffs is one called Miners Castle.

At the eastern end of the lakeshore are the 4-square-mile Grand Sable Dunes. Notable here is the Log Slide Overlook, which marks the top of a 300-foot-long trough down the dunes to Lake Superior, cut by load after load of timbers that were slid down to the water to be rafted to southern markets during the harvest of the virgin forests in the 1800s. Visitors enjoy running down the dunes, but remember: it's a joyous 3 minutes down and a grueling 30-minute climb back up. Another popular site here is the 1874 Au Sable Light Station.

For more information: *Pictured Rocks National Lakeshore and Hiawatha National Forest Visitors Center, 400 East Munising Avenue; 906-387-3700; www.nps.gov/piro.*

Pictured Rocks Cruises offers two-hour boat trips along the painted cliffs, passing more than a dozen weather-sculpted formations. In the fall the bluffs are topped with blazing autumn foliage. The cruises depart from the Munising City Pier from May to mid-October. *906-387-2379; www.picturedrocks.com.*

(following pages) The spectacular sweep of the Grand Sable Dunes at Pictured Rocks National Lakeshore.

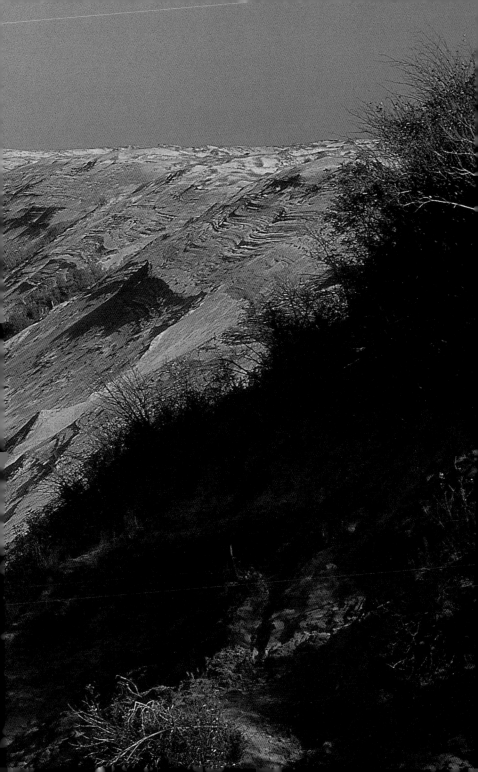

Lake Superior Lighthouse in Marquette.

■ **MARQUETTE** *map page 242, D-2*

Marquette, the peninsula's largest city (population 22,000), hugs the mouth of a wide harbor along Lake Superior about halfway between Sault Ste. Marie and the tip of the Keweenaw Peninsula, with a fiery-red lighthouse promoting safe passage to the harbor. Some people see comparisons here with the Oregon coast: the beaches, rocky cliffs, and blue waters that can brew ocean-type storms. Fine old brownstone buildings line Marquette's Washington Street and the historic East Ridge Street residential district, called Big Bug Hill in the early days for the wealthier mining and lumbering barons—big bugs—who built the Victorian homes there.

Beginning as a port city for shipping the iron that was discovered in the nearby hills in 1849, Marquette now prospers as a regional medical center and the home of Northern Michigan University, appealing to visitors year-round with its natural beauty, ski hills, and snowmobile trails.

■ IRON MINING

State surveyor William Austin Burt found the first iron mountain in 1844, when the deposits of ore near what is now Negaunee made his magnetic compass begin to dance erratically. He developed a solar compass to get around the problem, reported the iron discovery, and continued his work. When news of his discovery reached eager investors downstate, the rush was on.

Once metals were discovered, miners arrived. They dug into the earth, shored up tunnels with heavy timbers, and followed the veins for miles with picks and blasting powder. A miner worked by the light of a candle placed in a "sticking Tommy," a candleholder equipped with a metal spike that a miner could stick through his canvas or oilcloth hat and, once underground, into an outcrop or a shoring timber. The miners came from all over Europe, first the English, from the tin and copper mines of Cornwall, then Norwegians, Swedes, Finns, Slovenians, Irish, and Germans, contributing to the ethnic mix of today. They were clannish, with their own churches, customs, baseball teams, holidays, and communities. Mines worked round the clock. Beds in crowded boarding houses were never empty; as soon as one miner rolled out, another rolled in.

From Cornwall, miners brought the tradition of the pasty (it rhymes with *nasty*, not with *hasty*), the meat-pie-in-a-crust they carried underground in tin buckets. Pasties remain the area's regional dish, and are available at many shops, restaurants, and church suppers.

The **Marquette County History Museum** displays Burt's solar compass, which he invented after his magnetic compass failed in the presence of iron. *213 North Front Street; 906-226-3571; www.marquettecohistory.org.*

Eight miles west of Marquette, at Negaunee, on the Carp River, the **Michigan Iron Industry Museum** features interactive displays and a replica of an iron mine that guide visitors through the history of the industry on the U.P. Outside, take a short walk down the slope and along the river to the site where the Jackson Mining Company's forge once stood, marking the site where iron was first wrought in Michigan. Open from May through October. *73 Forge Road, Negaunee; 906-475-7857.*

For more information: *Marquette Welcome Center, 2201 U.S. 41 South, Marquette; 906-249-9066. Marquette Country Convention & Visitors Bureau, 2552 West U.S. 41, Suite 300; 800-544-4321, www.marquettecountry.org.*

CORNISH PASTIES

Miners' wives made these meat pies in a crust for the men to take into the mines.

Crust:	Filling:
1⅓ cup flour	cup each, diced; potatoes, turnips, carrots
tablespoon salt	1 medium onion, diced
cup lard or shortening	2 tablespoons minced parsley
cup cold water	1 pound boneless beef, cubed
	Salt and pepper, to season
	Pat of butter, if desired

Sift together the flour and salt. Cut in the shortening, and add water a little at a time, just enough to moisten. Mix and knead lightly (do not overwork); then divide the dough into two parts. Roll each into a 9-inch circle.

Mix the filling ingredients and season with salt and pepper. Put half the filling on each pastry circle. A pat of butter (optional) set on top of the filling adds richness and flavor. Moisten edges of dough with water and fold in half to enclose filling. Crimp edges to seal, and slit the top. Bake at 375 degrees F for 45–60 minutes. *Makes two pasties.*

■ SKIING

On the snowy, hilly U.P., ski resorts abound: **Marquette Mountain** at Marquette, **Indianhead** at Wakefield, **Powderhorn** and **Blackjack** at Bessemer, **Porcupine Mountains** at Ontonagon, **Mont Ripley** at Hancock, **Mount Bohemia** at Lac La Belle, **Norway Mountain** at Norway, and **Ski Brule** at Iron River. There are also ski jumps at **Suicide Hill** in Negaunee and **Pine Mountain** at Iron Mountain.

At Ishpeming, the **U.S. National Ski Hall of Fame and Museum** presents the history of local skiing from its birth on the iron-ore tailings of Ishpeming and Negaunee, where European immigrants made skis from barrel staves, to the early ski runs down the taller hills. The museum also interprets skiing history across the United States and around the world, with a spotlight on the role of the U.S. Army's 10th Mountain Division ski troops in World War II. The U.S. National Ski Hall of Fame features 342 inductees from across the nation. *610 Palms Avenue; 906-485-6323; www.skihall.com.*

Cross-country skiing at Al Quaal Recreation Area in Ishpeming.

■ KEWEENAW PENINSULA *map page 242, C-1*

Call it Copper Country: the 100-mile-long crook of land that curves into Lake Superior at Michigan's northernmost point is a land apart for more reasons than geography. Bony ridges give way to lakes, streams, waterfalls, hills that burn with autumn colors, and in winter the dancing aurora borealis. The mining towns have all but disappeared; garden flowers struggle in the wild, and mine-shaft houses crumble amid heaps of rusting machinery near piles of leftover copper ore. Many abandoned mine shafts have become the winter home of hundreds of thousands of hibernating bats, and the shaft openings are being modified and fenced to protect these habitats.

■ COPPER'S HISTORY

Shallow mining pits on Isle Royale and the Keweenaw Peninsula and in the area around the Ontonagon River date back at least 3,000 years to the Old Copper Indians, credited as being the first people in the Western Hemisphere to work with metals. Pits ranged from shallow indentations to holes as deep as 12 feet. The copper, some of the purest in the world, lay close to the surface. Prehistoric Michigan copper artifacts have been found as far east as New York and as far south as Kentucky, demonstrating that a widespread trading network connected these Indian groups.

Although the French explorers of the 1600s knew about the copper, it went ignored until state geologist Douglass Houghton submitted his report of its presence to the legislature in 1841. Ransom Shelden, one of the first promoters, advertised the Keweenaw in words not found in any dictionary, describing it as a "veritable Ophir of delitescent, metalliferous treasure."

How one of the world's richest mines was discovered is a matter of some debate. Old-timers say a man named Billy Royal was standing in a dusty road in front of his bar near Calumet when along came a man named Ed Hulbert. Royal's pigs had escaped their pen, and Hulbert offered to join the search for them. Following a faint squealing sound, they found the pigs trying to scramble out of a 12-foot-deep ancient mining pit. In their scrambling and snorting around the bottom of the pit, the pigs had uncovered a 20-ton chunk of conglomerate copper ore, thus launching the Calumet & Hecla mine at Calumet. Until the Depression years, the C&H was reported to be the richest metal mine in the world.

Stunning fall colors on U.S. 41 north of Hancock.

When copper ruled, men sank vertical shafts 2 miles deep and bored 2,000 miles of horizontal tunnels to produce 95 percent of the nation's copper. After almost 120 years in production, this mine closed in the 1980s following a prolonged and bitter strike.

■ HOUGHTON *map page 242, C-1*

Separated by the Portage Canal, which flows into Lake Superior, and connected by the Portage Lift Bridge, the twin cities of Houghton to the south (named for Michigan's first state geologist, Douglass Houghton) and Hancock to the north (named for John Hancock) face each other from 500-foot hills. Houghton is the home of **Michigan Technological University,** known for its graduating engineers, ice-hockey games, and winter ice carnivals with campus competitions for intricate ice statues that are smoothed to perfection with an electric iron. Also on campus is the **A. E. Seaman Mineral Museum** (1400 Townsend Drive; 906-487-2572), the state's official mineralogical museum. One-third of its collection of 60,000 specimens is on display, and they include a comprehensive sampling of minerals from Michigan's copper- and iron-mining districts.

■ ISLE ROYALE NATIONAL PARK *map page 266*

It's a big deal for home folks and visitors alike to pause and wave a hearty bon voyage to passengers when the 165-foot MV *Ranger III* pulls away from the docks at the Isle Royale National Park Headquarters and heads down the Portage Canal bound for the northwestern part of Lake Superior and Isle Royale National Park. The roadless, wilderness archipelago, made up of Isle Royale, the 45-mile-long and 9-mile-wide main island, and about 400 surrounding islands (if you count the rocks rising above the waves), is the best place I know to read the bones of the earth. Isle Royale's stone spine is 1.2 billion years old, with many parallel ridges of the archipelago made up of ancient lava flows.

Isle Royale boasts the largest island in a lake on an island in a lake—Ryan Island in Siskiwit Lake on Isle Royale in Lake Superior. Around Rock Harbor, as on other parts of the island, the terrain is rocky, with low shrubs, spruce, fir, cedar, and mixed northern hardwoods. Wave-stained boulders, covered with orange lichen, line the coves and bays. There is evidence here and there of failed mining operations of the late 1800s, such as a small cemetery all but hidden under the trees where a few crosses, encrusted with an inch of moss, mark the graves of forgotten residents.

In summer Isle Royale is a mass of wildflowers, and you may very well encounter a moose as you take an afternoon stroll. In fact, with the island's large moose population it's hard not to see a few. The famous Isle Royale wolves are a different story. Given their wild nature and their fear of humans, they are sometimes heard but rarely seen.

Hiking tours and cruises on board the MV *Sandy* leave from the park's **Rock Harbor Visitor Center** and the Rock Harbor Lodge. My favorites include the boat tour of the **Edisen Fishery,** interpreted by a fisherman, and the short walk through the woods to visit **Rock Harbor Lighthouse and Museum.**

■ HISTORY AND LEGENDS OF ISLE ROYALE

As the ferry approaches Rock Harbor, the first sign of the island is long, spiny Greenstone Ridge, which runs the island's length and towers over the hundreds of timbered islands, boulders, and ledges scattered offshore. After swinging through the channel at Rock Harbor Lighthouse, the ferry enters the still waters of 7-mile-long Rock Harbor. To the right is Mott Island, park headquarters and the point where the ferry offloads supplies and the occasional passenger before reaching its final docking point farther east. Mott Island is where, in the summer of 1845, copper speculators dropped off former *voyageur* Charlie Mott and his Chippewa bride, Angelique. The prospectors had hired the Motts to protect their find on the deserted island while they made a run back to Sault Ste. Marie for supplies, promising that they would return before winter. The Motts' rations of a few beans, rancid butter turned white like lard, and a bit of salt and flour were soon spent, snow was falling, and still the prospectors did not return. Charlie starved to death, and Angelique pulled hairs from her head to weave a snare to catch a rabbit now and then. Eventually, she built a lean-to with fallen tree limbs nearby, moved her fire, and left Charlie in the cabin so she wouldn't be tempted to eat him. The prospectors returned on the spring wind, but Angelique never forgave them. Her story is well documented in newspapers of the time. For the rest of her years, nightmares often wakened her at night as she screamed, "I did not eat Charlie!"

Scandinavian fishermen discovered the bounty of the island's waters in the late 1800s. The island reminded them of their homeland, and they brought their families to join them. It was a rough yet idyllic life, where men fished and women gathered rare greenstones (chlorastrolite, the state gemstone, now protected) from the beaches to sell to the agent from Tiffany in New York City, who came to the island to purchase them each spring. In winter everybody moved back to the

ISLE ROYALE: GETTING THERE AND WHERE TO STAY

ACCESS

Isle Royale National Park is open from mid-April through October and is accessible only by boat or seaplane; on the island, visitors get around by foot or by boat.

MV *Ranger III.* Operated by the National Park Service, this 126-passenger ferry makes the six-hour trip from Houghton to Rock Harbor on Isle Royale on Tuesdays and Fridays from June to mid-September and returns from Rock Harbor to Houghton on Wednesdays and Saturdays. The ferry leaves from Isle Royale National Park Headquarters. *800 East Lakeshore Drive, Houghton; 906-482-0984.*

MV *Isle Royale Queen IV.* Privately owned, this ferry travels to Rock Harbor, Isle Royale, from Copper Harbor, at the tip of the Keweenaw Peninsula. Departures are from mid-May through September, with a frequency varying from twice weekly in May and September to daily in August. The trip takes 3 hours each way. *Isle Royale Line Waterfront Landing, Copper Harbor; 906-289-4437; www.isleroyale.com.*

Both the MV *Ranger III* and the MV *Isle Royale Queen IV* dock in the vicinity of the **Rock Harbor Visitor Center** (no phone), the starting point for guided nature walks. Other ferry service to Isle Royale departs from Grand Portage, Minnesota, including the *Voyageur II,* which circumnavigates the island, stopping first at the **Windigo Visitor Center,** at the western end, and proceeding clockwise to Rock Harbor, at the eastern end, to overnight there and return to Grand Portage the following day.

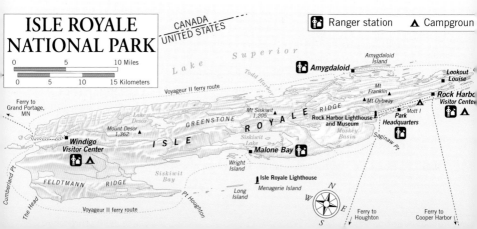

Royale Air Service Inc. operates five-person seaplane service from the Houghton County Memorial Airport to Isle Royale daily except Sundays from mid-May to mid-September, costing $230 per person round-trip. Houghton County Memorial Airport is 4 miles northeast of Hancock. *U.S. 41 North, follow signs; 877-359-4753.*

ACCOMMODATIONS

Rock Harbor Lodge and Marina. The only accommodation in the park (except for camping) offers rooms in the motel-style lodge or housekeeping cottages tucked into the forest and along the lakeshore. The lodge has a dining room and provides a range of services, including water taxis, boat rentals, fishing charters, and sightseeing tours aboard the MV *Sandy.* Open mid-May–mid-September. *906-337-4993 in summer; 270-773-2191 in winter; www.isleroyaleresort.com.*

Camping. Isle Royale has 36 official campgrounds, one of which is next to Rock Harbor, connecting with 165 miles of trails. Reservations and permits are mandatory. Camping is "leave no trace": no trash left behind, no fires, no pets.

Things to remember: The islands of Lake Superior (the coldest of the Great Lakes) attract cool breezes. On Isle Royale in August the maximum temperature averages 69 degrees F, with lows of 54 degrees F; a jacket and gloves are always recommended.

mainland—but to Wisconsin or Minnesota, which are closer to Isle Royale than the Michigan mainland.

The big cruise boats of the early 1900s found the island a tour destination. They sailed up and down the long finger peninsulas to enjoy the rugged beauty of boulder-strewn cliffs and moss-covered ridges and anchored offshore near one of the small resorts.

Then in 1931 Congress authorized the designation of Isle Royale as a national park. Plans moved forward to its establishment in 1940, then to its dedication six years later. Wilderness designation came in 1976. Homeowners were permitted to retain their homes until that generation died or moved away. Now, only memories remain as these homesites slowly return to nature, with their sagging roofs, and

(following pages) A view from Lookout Louise: the Canadian shoreline is visible in the distance.

Copper miners on strike in Calumet in 1913.

beside the door almost always a clump of roses or lilacs that bloom in spring. In 2004 the park service remained dedicated to maintaining this island for limited public use while protecting the wilderness and wildlife and continuing ongoing studies in this living laboratory and U.S. Biosphere Reserve.

For more information: *Isle Royale National Park Headquarters, 800 East Lakeshore Drive, Houghton; 906-482-0984; www.nps.gov/isro.*

■ HANCOCK *map page 242, C-1*

Back on the mainland and across the Portage Canal, Hancock is the home of **Finlandia University**, founded in 1896 as Suomi College by Finnish immigrants. While in Hancock, check out the interesting art shops, which include Finnish art. Follow U.S. 41 north up Quincy Hill to the **Quincy Mine Hoist Museum,** which interprets the history of copper mining. The key exhibit is the 880-ton steam-powered hoist used to lift ore cars to the surface of the 2-mile-deep copper mine. Also featured is a mineral collection from the A. S. Seaman Mineralogical Museum in Houghton. Don a hard hat and climb aboard a tram that takes riders down Quincy Hill for tours of the underground copper mine. *49750 U.S. 41 North; 906-482-3101; www.quincymine.com.*

■ CALUMET *map page 242, C-1*

The village of Calumet is a study in sandstone. The 1900 **Opera House** and **Calumet Theater** (the only place John Philip Sousa played twice) are particularly excellent examples of the use of the material. In fact, the entire five-block downtown is part of the **Keweenaw National Historical Park,** which comprises 12 cooperating sites along the peninsula from Ontonagon to Copper Harbor that tell the story of copper mining on the Upper Peninsula.

"The park is more than technology," explained a ranger, referring to the mining equipment. "It is miners who lived and sometimes died here, women who made and kept their families going, children who played in the streets, slapping mosquitoes, dodging the wagons, and sometimes going underground to work beside the men." *25970 Red Jacket Road; 906-337-3168; www.nps.gov/kewe.*

■ SNOWMOBILE COUNTRY

Along U.S. 41, 5 miles north of Mohawk, Keweenaw County's 33-foot-tall snow gauge is an attraction in itself. For a memento of this area of deep snows, tourists stop to photograph the gauge, which records annual snowfalls. The whopping 390.4 inches (more than 32 feet) in 1978–79 tops them all—so far.

In Michigan lots of snow means lots of snowmobiles, and networks of groomed trails are spread like highways, complete with trail signs throughout northern Michigan. These trails connect with others across the snow country that lead all the way to Alaska.

Most snowmobilers relish the speed and comfort of today's snowmobiles, along with the trails that ensure easy rides for countless miles, but I fondly recall our first adventures on the early motorized sleds, when groomed trails were a dream of the future and bumps were part of the ride. When snowmobiles were introduced, the ability to ride atop 3 or 4 feet of powder with no thought of trails was freedom, as heady as champagne, opening up hills and valleys otherwise sealed off by snow from all except snowshoers and cross-country skiers. Sure, the engine was loud, but with the rush of wind past my ears, the cold nipping at my cheeks, and friends riding alongside me, I hardly noticed. I loved crossing frozen lakes in the moonlight, packing a picnic lunch to spread below a frozen waterfall, and going on safari where we drove all day and gathered around a roaring fire at night in some remote lodge.

■ **COPPER HARBOR** *map page 242, C/D-1*

The drive along U.S. 41 up the Keweenaw Peninsula leads through almost forgotten mining communities, crosses sparkling streams, and cuts through deep forests. The peninsula is glorious in September, when autumn erupts in red, orange, and gold. From atop 700-foot Brockway Mountain, there is a wonderful view of the vast stretch of Lake Superior and the village of Copper Harbor, the white barracks of Fort Wilkins toylike in the distance. *Take Brockway Mountain Drive from Copper Harbor for the 9.5-mile drive to the top of the mountain.*

In 1844, after copper mining began, the U.S. Army built Fort Wilkins and sent in soldiers, ostensibly to protect miners from Indians. But the only people from whom the miners needed protection were themselves. On payday they flocked to bars to let off steam, became rowdy, and inevitably found reason to take great umbrage with one another. Now **Fort Wilkins Historic State Park,** the stockade with its 21 historic buildings was restored in the 1930s by the Work Projects Administration. There is also a narrated cruise to the park's Copper Harbor Lighthouse and keeper's quarters. *Park displays and lighthouse open Memorial Day to mid-October. U.S. 41, 1 mile east of Copper Harbor; 906-289-4215; www.dnr.state. mi.us/parksandtrails.*

For more information: *Keweenaw Convention & Visitors Bureau, 56638 Calumet Avenue, Calumet; 800-338-7982; www.keweenaw.org.*

■ **PORCUPINE MOUNTAINS WILDERNESS STATE PARK**
map page 242, A-1

Traveling back down the Keweenaw Peninsula, at Houghton take M-26 through more small towns that owe their beginnings to copper but now mainly rely on renewable resources from the forest as their economic base. At Mass City, turn northwest onto M-38 to Ontonagon; then follow M-64 to Silver City and County 107 to the Porcupine Mountains.

Viewed from the rocky escarpment 600 feet above it, the long finger of Lake of the Clouds stretches teal blue against the multi-green forest that carpets the mountains. There are many jewels in this 58,000-acre park, including rivers for canoeing, dramatic waterfalls, and campgrounds. For instance, follow the park trail to the mouth of the Carp River, where a short walk leads to a low, rocky ledge that stretches into Lake Superior. If you rise early enough, you are treated to a special show: sunrise over the Queen of the Great Lakes. *Three miles west of Silver City on M-107. Park headquarters: 412 South Boundary Road; 906-885-5275; www.dnr. state.mi.us/parksandtrails.*

■ **FAYETTE HISTORIC STATE PARK** *map pages 244–245, E-3*
On the sandstone bluff that rises above Lake Michigan's Snail Shell Harbor are overlooks providing a view of a green hillside dotted with 20 weathered structures—the ghost town of Fayette. From 1867 to 1891 the Jackson Mine Company shipped crude iron ore from the mines to this smelting town to be made into bars of charcoal pig iron. The town site includes a company store, a hotel, and the outdoor furnaces (kilns), as well as a modern visitors center. *Turn off US. 2 at Garden Corners; continue south for 17 miles. 13700 13.25 Lane, Garden; 906-644-2603; www.dnr.state.mi.us/parksandtrails.*

■ **TRAVEL BASICS**

Area Overview: Surrounded on three sides by lakes Superior, Huron, and Michigan, the Upper Peninsula, or U.P., begins to the east with low rolling hills, climbing to the "Midwest mountains" in the west. It is a land of rivers, waterfalls, and lakes with long stretches of sandy beaches interrupted by sandstone cliffs.
Travel: Main travel routes are east–west, by way of US. 2 and M-28, intersected by US. 41 running north–south. Commuter air service is offered at Sault Ste. Marie, Marquette, Escanaba, Hancock, Iron Mountain, and Ironwood.
Weather: Visitors have traditionally come to the U.P. to escape the summer heat. Nights are refreshingly cool, and humidity is generally low. The drawback? Summers are blackfly and mosquito season. September and October, however, can be idyllic, with cool northern air bringing autumn's palette to the hardwoods. The first snow is expected in November. Annual snowfall averages 200 inches.
Food & Lodging: Chains dominate the landscape, but as in so many other places in Michigan, small-town diners and B&Bs often prove surprisingly good. Refer to the listings that begin on page 274; another key source of information is the Upper Peninsula Travel & Recreation Association (800-562-7134; www.uptravel.com).
Time Zones: Most of the Upper Peninsula is in the Eastern time zone; the counties bordering Wisconsin (Menominee, Dickinson, Iron, and Gogebic) are in the Central zone.

L O D G I N G &
R E S T A U R A N T S

LODGING RATES

Per night, one room, double occupancy

$ = under $80   **$$** = $80–$130   **$$$** = $130–$200   **$$$$** = over $200

RESTAURANT PRICES

Average dinner entrée

$ = under $10   **$$** = $10–$17   **$$$** = $17–$25   **$$$$** = over $25

ALPENA *map page 152, D-3*

⊡ **Holiday Inn Alpena.** Nicer than is usually the case in a medium-priced chain, and more like a small hotel. Niceties include 148 rooms, indoor recreation area, heated pool, restaurant, and gift shop. 1000 Highway 23 North; 989-356-2151. **$$**

✗ **John A. Lau Saloon & Steakhouse.** Want steak? In Alpena, this is the place. Named for its original 19th-century owner, this historic saloon is famed for serving slab-sided cuts of American beef at its finest. There's a decidedly masculine atmosphere, with dark wood paneling, wall photos of Alpena's beginnings, and a huge, eclectic menu. Try the 20-ounce porterhouse. Other cuts include sirloin and Kansas City steak, plus prime rib on Fridays and Saturdays. Fresh-fish lovers are soothed, too, with baked whitefish, panfried perch, and even farm-raised bluegill. Its location (next to the Thunder Bay Theater, Alpena's professional playhouse) makes it perfect for a pre- or post-show bite. *414 North Second Avenue; 989-354-6898.* **$$–$$$**

ANN ARBOR *maps page 83, A/B-4 and page 103*

⊡ **Ann Arbor Bed & Breakfast.** This B&B occupies a unique chalet-style building on the edge of campus, right off State Street; there are four rooms for guests. *921 East Huron Street; 734-994-9100; www.annarborbreakfast.com.* **$–$$**

⊡ **Artful Lodger.** Just four guest rooms in a mid-19th-century Victorian house full of cool theater memorabilia. Breakfast and private baths, of course. *1547 Washtenaw Avenue; 734-769-0653; www.artlodger.com.* **$–$$**

✕⊡ **Bell Tower Hotel.** A seeming world of its own in the midst of the U of M campus, the Bell Tower is elegantly restored and appointed. Make reservations to dine in the **Earle Uptown,** known for its French menu. *300 South Thayer Street; 734-769-3010 or 800-562-3559; www.belltowerhotel.com.* **$$$**

✕⊡ **Dahlmann Campus Inn.** One of Ann Arbor's finest. The 200-plus guest rooms in this inn and conference center uniformly guarantee a good night's sleep—and excellent access to both downtown and campus. **Victors** (734-769-2282) does fine renditions of classic beef, seafood, and chicken dishes, with an occasional surprise. Open for breakfast, lunch, and dinner. *15 East Huron Street; 800-666-8693; www.campusinn.com.* **$$–$$$**

⊡ **Embassy Hotel.** Downtown and inexpensive. Most rooms have a microwave and a mini-fridge. It's the Embassy, and it'll outlive us all. *200 East Huron Street; 734-662-7100.* **$**

⊡ **First Street Garden Inn.** A nifty little—and we do mean little—B&B just southwest of the Main Street area. Homey, comfortable, and low-key. Highly recommended, so call early. *549 South First Street; 734-741-9786; www.firststreetgardeninn.com.* **$–$$**

⊡ **Vitosha Guest Haus.** It's hard to resist a guesthouse whose hosts send forth this message: "You are invited for afternoon tea, feathered duvets, and owls in the rafters!" Ten rooms with private baths in a nearly 90-year-old Swiss-chalet home, including Continental breakfast and afternoon tea. *1917 Washtenaw Avenue; 734-741-4969; www.vitosha.org.* **$–$$**

✕ **Amadeus Café & Patisserie.** Amadeus features authentic central European–style dinners. Highly recommended. *122 East Washington Street; 734-665-8767.* **$$**

✕ **BD's Mongolian Barbeque.** Pick your own polyglot of meats, seafoods, cut vegetables, and spices, and then have it stir-fried to your specifications. It's a tricky idea and can be fun. Long waits for a table can be a minus. *200 South Main Street; 734-913-0999; www.bdsmongolianbarbeque.com.* **$$**

✕ **Brown Jug.** A university hangout for more than 60 years, the Brown Jug gives students, profs, and locals homemade cooking at hard-to-beat prices. From sandwiches to specials, this place is all right. *1204 South University Avenue; 734-761-3355.* **$**

✕ **Café Felix.** Coffee and cappuccino, accompanied by light sandwiches, soups, and pastries. Watch for the tapas specials. *204 South Main Street; 734-662-8650.* **$**

✕ **Café Zola Crepe and Coffee Bar.** Plenty of room here to nurse a caffe latte. And if you're dining, Café Zola offers unique veggie omelets, crepes with a multitude of fillings, and generous sandwiches. *112 West Washington Street; 734-769-2020.* **$**

✕ **Dominick's.** Relaxing outdoor seating and sublime sangria combine to make a fine experience. *812 South Monroe Street; 734-662-5414.* **$**

✕ **The Earle.** Considered by many to be Ann Arbor's most romantic restaurant, the award-winning Earle is dark and cozy—with an inventive rotating French and Italian menu. *121 West Washington Street; 734-994-0211; www.theearle.com.* **$$$**

✕ **Fleetwood Diner.** An A² institution, the Fleetwood is always open. At this classic diner you're never quite sure who you'll see or what short-order specialty they'll be having. The wall-to-wall conversation that comes with your meal is on the house. *300 South Ashley Street; 734-995-5502.* **$**

✕ **Gypsy Café.** This is more than just a coffeehouse with some good sandwiches. Live music on weekends and some week nights, along with poetry, performance art, original art on the walls, AA meetings, and writers' forums, make Gypsy Café atypical—and engaging—every time you enter. *214 North Fourth Avenue; 734-994-3940.* **$**

✕ **Le Dog.** These are some darn good hot dogs, even when they compete with the surprising roast duck. An unusual and fun place for lunch—but since it opens late and closes early, only for lunch. *410 East Liberty Street; 734-665-2114.* **$**

✕ **Original Cottage Inn.** Ann Arborites take this pizza joint to heart. The deep-dish is measured in fathoms, the thin-crust in micrometers. Expect good pizza and a boisterous atmosphere. *512 East William Street; 734-663-3379; www. cottageinn.com.* **$**

✕ **Red Hawk Bar & Grill.** The locals love the sandwiches here. A better-than-average selection of microbrews doesn't hurt. *316 South State Street; 734-994-4004; www.redhawkannarbor.com.* **$**

✕ **Thano's Lamplighter.** The world is blasting past Thano's, and that's all right. This Italian-Greek place will put an excellent pizza or moussaka in front of you, minus the lights, noise, and fanfare of newer, more happening places. Thanks, Thano. *421 East Liberty Street; 734-996-0555.* **$**

✕ **Zanzibar.** The chefs take culinary risks at this place, and some are bound to work better than others. But if you love new and different dining, there may be no better place in Ann Arbor to find it. *216 South State Street; 734-994-7777; www. zanzibarannarbor.com.* **$**

✕ **Zingerman's Delicatessen.** One-of-a-kind in these parts, legendary Zingerman's brings New York City to the shores of the Huron River. The sandwiches are stacked high and the place is never empty. This is not fast food. *422 Detroit Street; 734-663-3354; www.zingermans.com.* **$**

Au Train, *see Munising*

BATTLE CREEK *map page 171, D-4*

⊞ **Greencrest Manor.** This romantic sandstone, slate, and copper mansion was built in 1925 in French Normandy style. Set on the highest elevation of St. Marys Lake, about 5 miles north of downtown, it has eight rooms with double, king, or queen beds. Explore the 20-acre grounds with formal gardens that include fountains and stone urns. Breakfast includes fresh fruit, cereal (this is Battle Creek, remember), breads and coffee, and juice. *6174 Halbert Road; 269-962-8633; www. greencrestmanor.com.* **$$–$$$$**

⊞ **McCamly Plaza Hotel.** There are 242 rooms in 16 stories, with an indoor pool and exercise room. All rooms have irons and ironing boards and free cable TV. *50 Capital Avenue SW; 269-963-7050 or 888-622-2659; www.mccamlyplazahotel.com.* **$$$**

✕ **Clara's on the River.** In a former train station along the Kalamazoo River. Clara's is known for a wide variety of offerings, including, a favorite, the chicken Caesar salad. *44 North McCamly Place; 269-963-0966; www.claras.com.* **$– $$$**

BAY CITY *map page 126, A-2*

✕ **Hereford and Hops Restaurant.** Party it up while charcoal-grilling your own steaks, seafood, chicken, or kabobs. *804 East Midland Street; 989-891-4677; www. herefordandhops.com.* **$$**

✕ **Krzysiak's House Restaurant.** This restaurant on the southeast side of town has been nourishing Bay City's Polish roots proudly for almost 25 years. Before that, it was a Polish neighborhood bar. Polka up the entrance ramp to Polish music emanating from outside speakers; turn right through the small store that sells Polish beer, breads, and other items; and take your place in the dining room, decorated with murals depicting the old country. Prices are cheaper than cheap. The all-you-can-eat buffet includes sausage in kraut, chicken, vegetables, ham, salad, and dessert. On the menu are Polish platters—*pierogi* (stuffed dumplings), *golabki* (cabbage rolls), homemade kraut and sausage—as well as steaks, including Delmonico and strip. *1605 Michigan Avenue; 989-894-5531.* **$–$$$**

BAY HARBOR *map page 205, C-3*

✕▢ **Inn at Bay Harbor.** Corporate, neoclassical, over-the-top elegance is the theme. Golf, spa, and upscale dining are the rule at this bastion of conspicuous consumption. In **Sagamore's** restaurant, every table has a view of Little Traverse Bay, and white pillars frame the dining area adjacent to the terrace. In summer choose from the "alfresco menu" and dine indoors or outdoors on the terrace. *3600 Village Harbor Drive, Bay Harbor; 231-439-4000 or 800-462-6963 (reservations); www.innatbayharbor.com.* **$$$–$$$$**

BAY VIEW, *see Petoskey*

BIG BAY *map pages 244–245, D-2*

▢ **Big Bay Point Lighthouse B&B.** This converted 1896 brick lighthouse on a Lake Superior bluff 25 miles northwest of Marquette has seven guest rooms, some with fireplaces and whirlpools. From the 60-foot light tower one can view both sunset views across the lake and the aurora borealis in the night skies. Hiking trails, full breakfast. *3 Lighthouse Road, Big Bay; 906-345-9957; www.bigbaylighthouse. com.* **$$$–$$$$**

BIRMINGHAM *map page 83, D-3*

▢ **Hamilton Hotel.** This well-kept hotel on the northern outskirts of downtown Birmingham has 64 rooms and a fitness center. Rates include an extensive breakfast buffet including fruit, eggs, juice, and cereals. *5270 Woodward Avenue; 800-334-8086.* **$$$**

▢ **Townsend Hotel.** Birmingham's premier hotel, with a distinct European boutique atmosphere. There are 87 rooms in four stories, and afternoon tea is served in the lobby. Elegance wraps its arms around you from the first step through the entrance. It's no wonder that the Townsend consistently makes Condé Nast's

"Top 100 Gold List." *100 Townsend Street; 248-646-7300; www.townsendhotel. com.* **$$$$**

✕ **Big Rock Chop & Brew House.** In the former Birmingham passenger train station, the restaurant brews its own beers and offers steak, lamb chops, and fish, plus gourmet pizzas. *245 South Eton Street; 248-647-7774.* **$$$$**

✕ **Forte.** In the heart of downtown Birmingham, this restaurant specializes in northern Italian food, including pasta with seafood. *201 South Old Woodward Avenue; 248-594-7300.* **$$$**

CADILLAC *map page 197, D-2*

✕⊡ **Hermann's European Café & Inn.** Austrian-born owner-chef Hermann Suhs has brought a touch of Europe to this quiet, romantic restaurant, which is a mixture of a French bistro and Austrian *gasthof.* It's very continental, with exposed-brick walls, pressed tin ceiling, and mauve tones. There are both booths and tables. Suhs's eclectic menu reflects his travels and his homeland, including applewood-smoked pork loin with potato dumplings. Traditionally in Europe, wild game such as pheasant, venison, or reindeer is served in the fall, and Suhs does so here, too. He also runs the deli and bakery next door, which serves breakfast, and, next to that, the wine and butcher shop. Upstairs there's a seven-room hotel furnished in country style with lots of natural wood, high ceilings, and private baths. *214 North Mitchell Street; 231-775-9563; www.chefhermann.com.* **$$–$$$**

⊡ **McGuire's Resort & Conference Center.** Perched atop one of the highest hills overlooking the Manistee National Forest and Lakes Cadillac and Mitchell, McGuire's has been a fixture in many families' vacation plans for both summer and winter for more than 30 years. Several buildings spreading from the lobby contain 122 rooms, some with whirlpools. Visitors may reach the sauna, whirlpool, and indoor pool through an enclosed walkway. In winter there is snowmobiling and lighted cross-country skiing, while golfers take over in summer to play 27 holes. *7880 Mackinaw Trail; 800-634-7302; www.mcguiresresort.com.* **$$–$$$**

CHARLEVOIX *map page 205, C-3*

⊡ **Weathervane Terrace Inn & Suites.** From a distance, it looks like a castle. Stone turrets pop up like mushroom caps at this 68-room city landmark on a hill on the north side of the Pine River channel. Oversized rooms come in three versions, including some with a patio. All include a small refrigerator, microwave, VCR, hair dryer, iron, and cable TV. There are two rooms with whirlpool tubs and one-bedroom suites with a fireplace and kitchenette. Relax in the hot tub or the outdoor pool surrounded by stonework. Breakfast is included in the rate. *111 Pine River Lane; 231-547-9955 or 800-552-0025; www.weathervane-chx.com.* **$$$**

✕ **Stafford's Weathervane Restaurant.** Not under the same ownership as the Weathervane Terrace Inn up the hill, the restaurant is under the tutelage of Stafford Smith, who also operates Stafford's Bay View Inn in Petoskey. Views of the Pine River channel and Round Lake provide a constantly changing panorama for dining. There's a decidedly nautical theme in the decor, and the menu also reflects the waterfront location. The planked whitefish is baked on an oak plank and served with plank-baked duchess mashed potatoes. *106 Pine River Lane; 231-547-4311; www.staffords.com.* **$$$**

✕ **Whitney's of Charlevoix.** One of the region's best places to enjoy a summery evening. All three floors offer views of Round Lake. On top is an open-air deck with an awning to protect diners from the weather. The decor is nautical: sailboat cloths on the tables and old boats built in below the high tin ceiling in both bar areas. The restaurant is famed for its seafood, including oysters, Maryland crab cakes, and New England clam chowder. *305 Bridge Street; 231-547-0818.* **$$**

CHEBOYGAN *map page 152, A-1*

✕⊡ **The Gables Bed and Breakfast.** Ken and Annetta Coates run this comfortable, restored, multi-peaked Victorian inn, built in the 1890s as a lumber baron's home. The six guest rooms include one with a private bath, two with half-baths, and the rest with shared facilities. There's also an eight-person hot tub in the Queen Anne gazebo. Complimentary desserts—cakes, pies, and various berry treats—are served each evening on the wraparound porch, in the fireplace room, or in the parlor. Ken, who has run several fine kitchens, prepares the food and will even make dinner for B&B guests by arrangement. Parking in the back. *314 South Main Street; 231-627-5079; www.mich-web.com/gablesbb.* **$$$**

✕⊡ **Hack-Ma-Tack Inn.** Moored beside the Cheboygan River and the east end of Mullett Lake, this century-old log lodge was built as a fishing and hunting retreat. *Hack-matack* is Native American for tamarack, and lots of tamarack went into the lodge's construction, says Mike Redding, whose family has owned the inn for the last two decades. Stroll through the dining room and read the local Native American legends inscribed on ceiling beams; check out the various display cases as well as two canoes and two rowing skulls that hang from the ceiling. House specialties include the Lake Huron whitefish amandine and prime rib that's been roasted then lightly char-grilled, imparting a unique, smoky flavor. Six spartan rooms are also available for rent. Open May to mid-October. *8131 Beebe Road; 231-625-2919.* **$$$**

✕🏠 **The Boathouse.** Watch the boats go by and enjoy the summery evenings Michigan's north country is famous for. This was originally built as a vacation house with an attached boat garage, and local old-timers like to tell about the 1920s and '30s, when it housed one of northern Michigan's principal whiskey distributors and was controlled by Detroit's infamous Purple Gang—then it was rum-runners with fresh shipments from Canada that tied up outside, not pleasure boaters. Look up at the windows overlooking the Cheboygan River, and you'll notice the original boat hoists. The boathouse became a restaurant in the 1980s, and it's known for Lake Huron walleye sautéed in honey and sprinkled with pecans, and breast of duck drizzled with cherries jubilee sauce. *106 Pine Street; 231-627-4316.* **$$–$$$**

CROSS VILLAGE *map page 205, C-2*

🏠 **Legs Inn.** The family-owned inn on a bluff overlooking Lake Michigan has been a traditional stop for tourists on the Tunnel of Trees Highway (M-119) since 1921. The stone house was named for the row of inverted white cast-iron stove legs along the roof ledges. Inside are log walls and an eccentric mix of tables and chairs handmade from tree trunks and twisted limbs. The full-service menu features Polish dishes such as golabki, pierogi, kielbasa, and sauerkraut. Mid-May to mid-October, with indoor and outdoor dining in summer. *6425 Lake Shore Drive; 231-526-2281.* **$–$$**

CURTIS *map pages 244–245, F-3*

🏠 **Chamberlin's Ole Forest Inn Bed & Breakfast.** This 19th-century railroad-passenger hotel on a bluff overlooking Big Manistique Lake holds on to the charm of yesteryear while offering guests up-to-date conveniences. It's open all year, with a dining room. *Big Manistique Lake; 906-586-6000 or 800-292-0440; www. chamberlinsinn.com.* **$$**

DEARBORN *map page 83, D-4*

⌕ **Dearborn Bed & Breakfast.** Close to shops, museums, and fine dining in west Dearborn, this brick house was built in 1927 and is listed on the Michigan Register of Historic Places. Rooms—including one suite—are furnished with Victorian Renaissance antiques. Guests enjoy down comforters and fine lace and linens in a romantic, relaxing atmosphere *22331 Morley Street; 313-563-2200; www.dearbornbb.com.* **$$$**

✕⌕ **Dearborn Inn-A Marriott Hotel.** Built in the 1930s by Henry Ford to house visitors and to serve his airport across Oakwood Boulevard (now part of a Ford vehicle test area), the hotel is across from the Henry Ford Museum and Greenfield Village. There are 222 rooms, some of them within five replicas of homes owned by famous Americans. Two restaurants, heated pool, and tennis courts. *20301 Oakwood Boulevard; 313-271-2700; www.marriotthotels.com.* **$$$**

✕⌕ **Hyatt Regency Dearborn.** Now, this is class! Stepping into the lobby's subdued lighting against the elegant mix of glass, stainless steel, and wood is like walking onto a Hollywood set. This all-glass-sided, 13-story hotel is opposite Ford's world headquarters. Its 772 well-appointed rooms bend around an open atrium. Pool, sauna, whirlpool, and three restaurants. *Michigan Avenue and M-39; 313-593-1234.* **$$–$$$$**

✕ **Big Fish.** One of the region's best seafood restaurants, on the south edge of Fairlane Town Center mall. Entrées include whole fish, and pasta with shrimp, scallops, and chunks of salmon surrounded by mussels in a light garlic sauce. Can be noisy. *700 Town Center Drive; 313-336-6350.* **$$**

✕ **La Pita.** Dearborn's Middle Eastern presence is apparent in the crop of good, inexpensive restaurants that have been opened in recent years. Combination plates of lamb, dolmas, shish kebab, and hummus with flat bread prevail in this west Dearborn establishment. Good pureed fresh fruit drinks also. *22435 Michigan Avenue; 313-565-7482.* **$$**

✕ **Mati's on Monroe.** Housed in a former service station, this deli stacks some of the best sandwiches on the planet. Try the Ellen's—corned beef, coleslaw, and Swiss on rye. Finish off with carrot cake or a cream cheese brownie. *1842 Monroe Street; 313-277-3253.* **$**

DETROIT *maps page 83, D-4, and page 51*

✕⊡ **Atheneum Suite Hotel.** The anchor of Greektown, this 10-story hotel has 174 rooms, including some suites and 160 two-bedroom units. Restaurants on the premises include the highly regarded **Fishbone's Rhythm Kitchen Café** (313-965-4600; **$–$$$**), serving New Orleans Cajun specialties including barbecued ribs and chicken gumbo. *1000 Brush Street; 313-962-2323.* **$$$–$$$$**

⊡ **Courtyard by Marriott.** Comfortable 21-story downtown hotel: 250 rooms, heated pool, health club, and tennis courts. It's connected by covered walk to the RenCen and also has a People Mover stop connecting it to the rest of downtown. *333 East Jefferson Avenue; 313-222-7700; www.marriott.com.* **$$$**

✕⊡ **Detroit Marriott Renaissance Center.** The pièce de résistance of the RenCen, this 72-story hotel has 1,298 rooms overlooking the Detroit River and downtown. Restaurants in the hotel include the RiverCafe, with expansive views of the river and Windsor, Ontario. The hotel also has an exercise area. *In the Renaissance Center; 313-568-8000 or 800-228-9290; www.marriott.com.* **$$$$**

✕ **Hockeytown Café.** The bright, neon-lit downtown café has a street-level bar lined with a ring of ice and Detroit Red Wings hockey memorabilia on display. Menu items include crab cakes, grilled pork chops, and salmon in tomato-thyme barley. Outdoor dining on the upper levels. *2301 Woodward Avenue; 313-965-9500; www.hockeytowncafe.com.* **$$**

✕ **Opus One.** Generally considered one of the best restaurants in the city. The seasonally changing menu lists chef Tim Giznsky's imaginative, beautifully presented American regional dishes. Extensive wine list. *565 East Larned Street; 313-961-7766; www.opus-one.com.* **$$$$**

✕ **Rattlesnake Club.** With chef Jimmy Schmidt in charge, this windowed dining room in a renovated warehouse offers great meals served with flair in a sophisticated setting. The menu might include perch sautéed with citrus, capers, sweet peppers, and thyme. The wine list is super, as are the views of the Detroit River and Windsor skyline. *300 River Place at Joseph Campau Avenue, in Rivertown district; 313-567-4400.* **$$$$**

✕ **Traffic Jam & Snug.** College students rub elbows with professors and professionals here, just south of Wayne State University and the University Cultural Center. The menu stretches from vegetarian to turkey Reubens. Beer brewed in-house. *511 West Canfield Street; 313-831-9470; www.traffic-jam.com.* **$$**

DOWAGIAC *map page 171, B-5*

✕ **Wicks' Apple House.** Enjoy a taste of Michigan on a 120-year-old farm 8 miles northwest of Dowagiac. The farm market, open for 50 years, sells fresh produce, jams, jellies, preserves, local honey, and maple syrup; the bakery makes pies from local fruit and family recipes. There's also a cider mill, a gift shop, and the Orchard View Room restaurant, serving breads, soups, quiche, and salads. Open from Memorial Day to Halloween. *52281 Indian Lake Road; 269-782-7306; www. wicksapplehouse.com.* **$**

EAST LANSING, *see Lansing*

ELLSWORTH *map page 205, C-4*

✕ **Rowe Inn.** With a dining room captained by Wes Westhoven and chef Todd Veenstra, the Rowe is in a former 1940s fast-food roadhouse. Now a fine-dining restaurant, whose menu changes weekly. Entrées may include such delights as rainbow trout with shrimp stuffing or chicken and portobello crepes with mushroom crème. Morel mushroom dishes are a specialty. Desserts might include delicate white-chocolate brownies. *6303 East Jordan Road; 231-588-7351 or 866-432-5873; www.roweinn.com.* **$$$**

✕ **Tapawingo.** The tiny town of Ellsworth holds one of the best restaurants in the Midwest. Chef-owner Harlan "Pete" Peterson's spot is generally booked months in advance. The food, the ambience of the rambling country home, and the bright, simple dining room with windows nearly floor to ceiling (summer lunch is served on the patio) are all part of the reason. Recent dishes on the daily-changing menu have included roasted parsnip and apple soup, sautéed lemon sole with seared sea scallops, Israeli saffron couscous, and sautéed spinach in a red pepper coulis. Desserts include wonders like molten chocolate—a warm chocolate mousse cake with a molten bittersweet chocolate center, served with vanilla ice cream and blood-orange sauce. Wonderful. *9502 Lake Street; 231-588-7971; www.tapawingo. net.* **$$$$**

FENNVILLE *map page 171, B-3*

✕ **Crane's Pie Pantry.** In the back of a barn on a working fruit farm southeast of Saugatuck-Douglas, Crane's is perhaps best known for its apple cider and its pies full of fresh orchard fruit, but it also serves good food for lunch and dinner. Take 196/U.S. 31 south to Exit 34; then drive 4 miles east on M-89. *6054 124th Avenue; 269-561-2297; www.cranespiepantry.com.* **$**

EAST TAWAS *map page 152, C-5*

🛏 **Bambi Motel.** A well-kept mom-and-pop motel with lake access. Rooms aren't fancy but are clean and the price is right. *1100 East Bay Street (U.S. 23); 989-362-4582.* **$**

🛏 **East Tawas Junction B&B.** Ask innkeeper Leigh Mott about the history of this turn-of-the-century home built by a president of the Detroit and Mackinac Railroad (on whose tracks—albeit under a different name—trains still rumble nearby, but well out of range now). All rooms have fireplaces and private baths, and a guest house has been added. Relax on the sundeck, next to the fireplace, or in the library. Breakfasts are sumptuous, including raspberry crepes or cheese soufflé, with homemade bread and rolls. The inn is a short walk from downtown and across U.S. 23 from the beach. *514 West Bay Street (U.S. 23); 989-362-8006; www.east-tawas.com.* **$$$**

🛏 **Holiday Inn Tawas Bay Resort.** Heading for the beach and want a place to stay? Select one of these 103 rooms, many with shoreside views of the 900-foot sand beach on Tawas Bay, where there is great swimming. There's also an indoor pool. Walk to downtown's shops or the small local movie theater. *300 East Bay Street (U.S. 23); 989-362-8601 or 800-336-8601.* **$$–$$$**

✕ **Genii's Fine Foods.** Genii's has been an East Tawas fixture for more than 40 years, serving American, Chinese, and Thai food, open for breakfast, lunch, and dinner. *601 West Bay Street (U.S. 23); 989-362-5913.* **$**

✕ **Marion's Dairy Bar.** After dinner, head here for dessert, because Marion's specializes in ice cream—more than 32 flavors of it. Cones, malts, sundaes. *111 East Bay Street (U.S. 23); 989-362-2991.* **$**

FRANKENMUTH *map page 126, A-3*

⊞ **Drury Inn.** This modern, 78-room motel in the heart of downtown offers access to everything. Indoor pool and complimentary breakfast. *260 South Main Street; 989-652-2800.* **$$**

⊞ **Frankenmuth Bavarian Inn Lodge.** This 354-room hotel is the city's largest and one of the most popular with families. It offers five indoor pools, three whirlpools, an 18-hole indoor mini-golf course, jogging trails, tennis courts, and an exercise area, as well as two restaurants. *One Covered Bridge Lane; 989-652-7200; www.bavarianinn.com.* **$$–$$$**

⊞ **Zehnder's Bavarian Haus Motel.** Away from the crowds just south of downtown are 137 rooms to choose from in a quiet setting, along with indoor and outdoor pools, exercise room, and breakfast nook. *1365 South Main Street; 989-652-0470; www.zehnders.com.* **$$**

✕ **Frankenmuth Bavarian Inn Restaurant.** First, stand outside to watch a 35-bell glockenspiel tell the story of the Pied Piper of Hamelin. Then, although this place is as famous for its all-you-can-eat chicken dinners as its neighbor across the street, head in to try such German dishes as *kasseler rippchen* (smoked pork loin) or sauerbraten (tender, spicy marinated beef). *713 South Main Street; 989-652-9941 or 800-228-2742; www.bavarianinn.com.* **$$–$$$**

✕ **Zehnder's Restaurant.** It's America's largest family restaurant, and the menu is also huge, but most folks chow down on its famous family-style, all-you-can-eat chicken dinners with all the fixings—stuffing, potatoes, giblet gravy—and fresh German stollen and ice cream for dessert. Order a sample of fried chicken livers too: you'll be hooked. *730 South Main Street; 989-652-0450 or 800-863-7999; www.zehnders.com.* **$$–$$$**

FRANKFORT *map page 205, A-6*

⊞ **Harbor Lights Motel and Condos.** Located on 400 feet of Lake Michigan beach are 120 units, including 48 one-, two-, and three-bedroom condominiums, some with two-person whirlpools. All have full kitchens and decks overlooking the lake. Rooms are air-conditioned and have satellite television and free HBO. Rent by the week in July and August. *15 Second Street; 231-352-9614 or 800-346-9614; www.harborlightsmotel.com.* **$$$**

▥ **Knollwood Inn.** Hosts Al and Irene Rice welcome guests to their turreted Victorian beauty. Four antiques-filled guest rooms have private baths and queen beds. Breakfast is served by candlelight in the formal dining room. There's also a two-bedroom carriage house, rentable by the week. The Sleeping Bear Dunes are close by; Traverse City is about 45 minutes away. *219 Leelanau Avenue; 231-352-4008.* **$$**

GAYLORD *map page 205, D-4*

▥ **Treetops Sylvan Resort.** One of northern Michigan's best four-season resorts, so named because it sits atop a hill outside Gaylord and looks over the Pigeon River valley, home of Michigan's wild elk herd. There are 252 rooms, suites, condos, and homes, along with two restaurants, two pools, sauna, and fitness center. In summer more than 81 holes of designer golf—on courses by Robert Trent Jones Sr., Tom Fazio, and Rick Smith—beckon. In winter enjoy downhill and cross-country skiing. *3962 Wilkinson Road, Treetops Village; follow the signs along M-32; 989-732-6711 or 888-873-3867; www.treetops.com.* **$$**

✕ **Sugar Bowl.** Tucked amid a cluster of businesses downtown, this eatery is easy to miss, but don't. Opened in 1919 by the family that runs it today, it's among the oldest such restaurants in Michigan. If visiting during morel season (usually in May), be sure to ask if those prized mushrooms are on the menu. Great breakfasts. Steak and fish specials at lunch and dinner; children's menu available. *216 West Main Street; 989-732-5524; www.sugarbowlrestaurant.com.* **$$**

GRAND HAVEN/SPRING LAKE *map page 171, B-1/2*

▥ **Best Western Beacon Inn.** A small-scale hotel with 107 rooms, an indoor pool with whirlpool, and whirlpools in some rooms. *1525 South Beacon Boulevard (U.S. 31), Grand Haven; 616-842-4720 or 800-528-1234.* **$$$**

▥ **Grand Haven Holiday Inn.** Formerly the Grand Harbor Resort and Yacht Club and long a fixture of the Grand Haven scene, the hotel has 120 rooms, indoor and outdoor pools, exercise area, whirlpool, and restaurant. It's 2 miles from the Lake Michigan beach. *940 West Savidge Street, Spring Lake; 616-846-1000 or 888-788-8411.* **$$$**

⊡ **Lakeshore B&B.** Three rooms are open to guests at this 4,500-square-foot mansion, built in 1941, with 200 feet of Lake Michigan beach out its front patio. Rooms are named after former U.S. presidents for good reason: locks of hair from Washington, Lincoln, and Kennedy; the Bible on which Harry Truman took the Oath of Office; and other presidential memorabilia are on display. A beach bungalow is available, as is a guest house (rentable by the week). Dan and Jackie Hansen are innkeepers. *11001 Lakeshore Drive, Grand Haven; 616-844-2697 or 800-342-6736; www.bbonline.com/mi/lakeshore.* **$$$$**

✕ **Bil-Mar Restaurant.** Watch from the deck as sailboats and 600-foot freighters alike arrive at Grand Haven's harbor to dine at this restaurant, which has stood here since the 1950s. Specialties include fish in a bag, salmon baked in parchment, scallops, and vegetarian dishes. The deck, with umbrella-shaded tables, offers simpler fare such as good burgers, including a veggie burger. *1223 Harbor Avenue, Grand Haven; 616-842-5920; www.grandhaven.com/~bil-mar.* **$$**

GRAND RAPIDS *map page 171, C-2*

✕⊡ **Amway Grand Plaza Hotel.** Next to the Grand River in downtown Grand Rapids, this wonderful marriage of the former Pantlind Hotel and a 30-story glass-exterior tower adds up to 682 rooms. The older high-ceilinged Pantlind section offers the elegance of a grand old hotel; in the west wing, modern rooms look out over city attractions across the river. Heated pool, saunas, whirlpool, racquetball and squash courts, tennis courts, three restaurants. In the **1913 Room ($$$$)**, a classy restaurant in period decor, the duck confit is a notable offering on the elegant menu (with prices to match). The must-have dessert is the Forbidden Apple, a mocha ice-cream confection wrapped in a sugar coating and colored to look just like an apple. *187 Monroe Avenue Northwest; 616-774-2000 or 800-253-3590 (reservations); www.amwaygrand.com.* **$$–$$$$**

⊡ **Fountain Hill B&B.** A beautiful Italianate home built in 1874 in the historic Heritage Hill district with four guest rooms, cable TV with video library access, down comforters, feather beds. A full breakfast with breads, yogurts, and entrée is served. *222 Fountain Street Northeast; 616-458-6621 or 800-261-6621; www.fountainhillbandb.com.* **$$**

⊡ **Peaches B&B.** This brick Georgian home was built in the Heritage Hill district in 1916. The living room is spacious, and breakfasts are special, with fruit, breads, and gourmet entrées. Five guest rooms with four baths on the second floor; each room has down comforters, TV, and telephone. Exercise and TV room downstairs. DaChien the dalmatian obligingly leads house tours. *29 Gay Avenue Southeast; 616-454-8000 or 866-732-2437; www.peaches-inn.com.* **$$**

✕ **BDs Mongolian Barbecue.** A fun restaurant. Choose from the selection of various meats and vegetables and one of the cooks will sear it all deliciously in a giant wok. Various recommended combinations are posted for the unsure. *2619 28th Street Southeast; 616-957-7500.* **$$**

✕ **B.O.B. Restaurants.** Standing for "Big Old Building," the B.O.B. is a four-level entertainment and dining extravaganza downtown. Five restaurants, a nightclub-standup showcase, and a brewpub offer everything from steaks to comedy. *20 Monroe Avenue Northwest; 616-356-2000.* **$$–$$$$**

✕ **Pal's Diner.** An old-time diner has been refurbished and once more hosts the hungry for solid American comfort food, from burgers to meat loaf. *6503 28th Street Southeast; 616-942-7257.* **$**

✕ **San Chez.** The menu of this "tapas bistro" is filled with exciting entrées, but there is no way I would order anything but tapas, the Spanish-style small servings that keep coming until the table is filled. Go with friends and pass the plates, mix hot and cold, zesty and tame. Decor is highlighted with Spanish tiles and paintings splashed with Mediterranean blue. *38 West Fulton Street; 616-774-8272; www. sanchezbistro.com.* **$$$**

GRAYLING *map page 205, D-6*

⊡ **Gates Au Sable Lodge.** Lovers of rivers, especially trout streams, and those who like to fall asleep indoors to the sounds of the outdoors, head here: 16 rooms on what many consider the best trout stream east of the Mississippi give you fly fishing right outside your door. Owner Cal "Rusty" Gates manages a well-stocked fly shop next to the small restaurant run by his wife, Julie. If you're not an angler, sit in the swinging chair and let the sounds of the river lull you to sleep. *471 Stephan Bridge Road; 989-348-8462; www.gateslodge.com.* **$$**

⊡ **Hanson House B&B.** Margarethe Hanson, wife of lumber baron Rasmus Hanson, wouldn't move from her home in Manistee to the wilds of Grayling unless her husband built her a "proper home." She approved of Hanson House, completed in 1883, and moved in. At 6,500 square feet, it's a picture of Victorian elegance. Guests can choose from four bedrooms, all furnished with period furniture, including antiques original to the home. Explore the library with its 12-foot ceilings and the rathskeller, where many a lumber deal was struck over brandy and cigars. *604 Peninsular Street; 989-348-6630; www.hansonhousebandb.com.* **$$**

✕ **Patty's Town House.** This A-frame-style restaurant is one of the town's favorite spots. Steaks and seafood dominate the dinner menu, and breakfast and lunch choices vary. *2552 South I-75 Business Loop; 989-348-4331.* **$$–$$$**

✕ **Stevens Family Circle.** The soda fountain in this former drugstore is presided over by Russ Stevens, patriarch of the family running the show. Pull up a stool or slide into a booth and prepare to be wowed by old-fashioned sodas, creamy malteds, and even phosphates that could be ranked as gourmet by any ice-cream aficionado. The sandwiches coming off the grill aren't bad, either. *231 North Michigan Avenue; 989-348-2111.* **$**

Harbor Springs *map page 205, D-3*

🏠 **Kimberly Country Estate.** This Colonial plantation-style house with wide sweeping lawns is adjacent to Wequetonsing Golf Course. Back verandas with view of the swimming pool; six guest rooms. Deluxe buffet breakfast. *2287 Bester Road; 231-526-7646.* **$$$$**

✕ **Juilleret's.** A family restaurant since 1906, this seat-yourself eatery has a casual atmosphere, linoleum floor, tin ceiling, and paper napkins and placemats. Planked whitefish with duchess potatoes is the house specialty. The ice-cream parlor—northern Michigan's first soda fountain—is famous for its homemade Thunder Cloud and Velvet sundaes. Open May–December. *130 State Street; 231-526-2821.* **$–$$**

✕ **Stafford's Pier Restaurant.** A nautical theme runs throughout this waterfront restaurant, where diners dress as formally or as casually as they choose. Waiters in tuxedos serve in the elite Pointer Room, while the Chart Room downstairs is casual. Catch views of the yacht harbor and Little Traverse Bay from either room. À la carte menu featuring fresh fish. *102 Bay Street; 231-526-6201; www.staffords. com.* **$–$$$$**

HARRISVILLE *map page 152, D-4*

⊡ **Alcona Beach Motel.** Owner Barbara Berl's great-great-grandfather—a farmer and the area's first justice of the peace—homesteaded the 56 acres surrounding this cozy six-unit motel in 1873. Berl's grandmother and brother built it in the mid-1950s, making sure it was a half mile from the highway noise of U.S. 23. Each room sleeps four and has a refrigerator, stove, and cable TV but no telephone. Pets are allowed. Stroll the footpaths and logging roads through the lush pine, cedar, and maple forest on the property or along its quarter-mile-long Lake Huron beachfront. Three-night minimum room rental. Open May–November. *700 North Lake Huron Shore Drive; 989-724-5471.* **$$**

⊡ **Widow's Watch Bed & Breakfast.** In 1990 Bill and Becky Olson took over Widow's Watch, named after the room that used to be on top of this Victorian home built by lumber baron George Caldwell in 1866. The watch proved too heavy and was moved to ground level close to 100 years ago, where it remains. Four guest rooms are furnished with a variety of antiques. Sit on the wraparound porch and watch the salmon charter boats moor up in the harbor; enjoy breakfasts of pancakes or quiche; go fishing (the Olsons can book local charters); head for the beach; or go antiquing. *401 Lake Street; 989-724-5465; www.thewidowswatch. com.* **$$**

HILLMAN *map page 152, C-3*

✕⊡ **Thunder Bay Golf and RV Resort.** In summer, Jack Matthias's resort in the woods just east of Hillman hosts cartsful of golfers. In winter cross-country skiers come to ski the 12 kilometers of trails on the course and along the Thunder Bay River, which flows along the northern edge of the fairways. Sleep in luxury villas near the restaurant or in log-cabin chalets dotting the course, which can be split into smaller rooms or set up for large groups (up to 12). Also drawing visitors during snowy months are sleigh-ride tours, which include delicious dinners of classic American food. Sign up for this unique trip and you'll be carried over snow and across the river to a 150-acre preserve of tangled primeval forest, where a herd of elk roam. Then you'll warm up before the fireplace at the **Elk Antler Log Cabin,** where dinner—five courses with an entrée of crown roast of pork—simmers over wood cookstoves under the eye of Jack's wife, Jan Matthias. After the meal you'll hop into the sleigh for more elk viewing on the trip back to the resort. *27800 M-32; 800-729-9375; www.thunderbaygolf.com.* **$$–$$$**

HOLLAND/MACATAWA *map page 171, B-2*

▣ **Bonnie's Parsonage.** Bonnie McVoy-Verwys has turned this white-sided 1908 home into a quiet neighborhood inn, where you can relax on the glassed-in front porch. Two rooms with private baths. Morning begins with a gourmet breakfast. *6 East 24th Street, at Central Avenue, Holland; 616-396-1316; www.bbonline.com/mi/parsonage.* **$$**

✕ **Backstreet Restaurant & Brew Pub.** Holland's only microbrewery pub. Menu items range from pizza and pastas to prime rib. *13 West Seventh Street; 616-394-4200.* **$$**

✕ **Piper Restaurant.** Along Lake Macatawa 5 miles west of Holland, this contemporary restaurant has a whimsical theme. Pastas and wood-fired-oven pizzas are its specialties. *2225 South Shore Drive, Macatawa; 616-335-5866; www.piperrestaurant.com.* **$$**

HOUGHTON *map pages 244–245, C-1*

✕▣ **Best Western Franklin Square Inn.** This seven-story, 104-room hotel has balcony suites, spa, whirlpool, indoor pool, sauna. The dining room in the hotel's **Northern Lights Lounge** offers panoramic views of the city and hills. *820 Shelden Avenue; 906-487-1700.* **$–$$$**

▣ **Charleston House Historic Inn.** A two-story early-1900s Georgian house with pillared double verandas and wicker chairs. Inside are a large library with fireplace, period furnishings, extensive woodwork, stained leaded-glass windows. There are four guest rooms; breakfast-in-a-basket at your door. *918 College Avenue; 906-482-7790 or 800-482-7404; www.charlestonhouseinn.com.* **$$–$$$$**

HOUGHTON LAKE/PRUDENVILLE *map page 152, A-5*

Looking for a cottage? Consult a map, available from local chambers of commerce. Some of the best places to stay here are on the lake's north side. Nearby Higgins Lake has some great lodgings, but they are harder to find and not widely advertised. Searching them out, however, can be well worth your time.

✕ **Brass Lantern.** A rustic, paneled "up north" atmosphere envelops this restaurant across the road from Michigan's largest inland lake. Steaks and seafood for lunch and dinner. *729 Houghton Lake Drive (M-55), Prudenville; 989-366-8312.* **$$**

✕ **Coyles Restaurant.** A pleasant, unassuming restaurant; good for an inexpensive family breakfast, lunch, or dinner. Entrées include crab and frogs' legs as well as beef. *9074 Old U.S. 27, on Houghton Lake's western shore; 989-422-3812.* **$**

HUBBARD LAKE *map page 152, C/D-3/4*

✕⊞ **Churchill Pointe Inn.** Some inns are former homes, but this one, built in 1926, has always been an inn, and Sharon and Donald Geib have looked after it since 1994. The summery, neatly trimmed blue-and-whitewood-frame building is nestled in the trees on the east side of the large lake. (Good swimming but no beach.) There are eight rooms and one apartment. Natural cedar paneling lends a woodsy feel to the interior common rooms. The nightly rate includes full breakfast for two. The inn's dining room features Lake Huron whitefish, walleye, perch, seafood, steaks, prime rib, and an expansive view of the lake. On balmy evenings, choose a table on the deck and watch the sunset over the lake. Boaters can place their orders to be delivered dockside for dining on board. *5700 Bennett Road; 989-727-2020; www.churchillpointeinn.com.* **$$**

KALAMAZOO *map page 171, C-4*

✕⊞ **Radisson Plaza Hotel.** This well-appointed and newly renovated downtown hotel, with shops on the first floor, has 280 rooms as well as a health club, heated pool, and whirlpool. **Webster's** restaurant is excellent; its extensive and sophisticated wine list, hard to find in this part of Michigan, has won acclaim from *Wine Spectator. 100 West Michigan Avenue; 269-343-7959 or 800-333-3333; www.radisson.com.* **$$$**

⊞ **Stuart Avenue Inn.** This B&B is actually *two* elegant pinnacled Victorian homes—the Bartlett-Upjohn House and the Chappell House—and a carriage house, in the Stuart Avenue historic district. Bartlett-Upjohn is the former residence of the Upjohn pharmaceutical family. One stroll through the adjacent McDuffee Gardens is never enough to absorb their beauty. Footpaths through the acre-size English garden lead through beds of blossoms and past a gazebo, a pergola, and a fountain. *229 Stuart Avenue; 616-342-0230; www.stuartaveinn.com.* **$$**

LAURIUM *map pages 244–245, C-1*

✕⊡ **Laurium Manor Inn.** This neoclassical 1908 mansion has a pillared wraparound porch and balcony, nine guest rooms, a 1,300-square-foot ballroom, and a library. One of the most opulent homes of its time, it has silver-leaf-covered ceilings in the music parlor and elephant-leather wall coverings in the dining room, and it is furnished in period antiques. Under the same ownership is the **Victorian Hall** B&B across the street, which has seven guest rooms. A full buffet breakfast for guests of either is served in the Laurium. *320 Tamarack Street; 906-337-2549; www.lauriummanorinn.com.* **$–$$$**

LANSING/EAST LANSING *map page 83, A-3*

⊡ **Radisson Hotel Lansing.** In the heart of Michigan's capital, this 11-story fullservice downtown hotel is close the state's political pulse. Amenities include a pool, whirlpool, and sauna. Restaurant on site. *111 North Grand Avenue; 517-482-0188; www.radisson.com/lansingmi.* **$$–$$$**

✕ **All Seasons Bistro.** Gourmet dining, featuring an American menu with a touch of French country. Closed Sundays and Mondays. *1500 West Lake Lansing Road, East Lansing; 517-336-9890.* **$$**

✕ **Clara's Lansing Station.** This restaurant occupying the old Michigan Central Railroad depot, built in 1903, is within an easy walk of downtown and the capitol complex. It's full of old-fashioned fixtures and fittings and has a thick menu with wide array of choices. Sunday buffet. A sister restaurant, Clara's on the River, is in Battle Creek. *637 East Michigan Avenue; 517-372-7120; www.claras.com.* **$$**

✕ **Carrabba's Italian Grille.** Italian decor. Large open kitchen. Watch cooks prepare Italian selections, from pizza to eggplant Parmesan. *6540 West Saginaw Highway; 517-323-8055.* **$$**

✕ **Michigan State University Dairy Store.** Ice cream to die for! Watch students making multiple flavors of ice cream and cheeses from the observation deck, then leave with big scoops of your favorite. The Dairy Store also creates some remarkable cheeses—suspend your disbelief and try the fudgelike chocolate cheese. *1140 South Anthony Hall, Farm Lane, East Lansing; 517-355-8466; www. dairystore.msu.edu.* **$**

LEELANAU PENINSULA *map page 205, B-4*

Between the sweeping orchard valleys of the Leelanau Peninsula lie scores of finger- and oval-shaped lakes, and nearly every one will have some sort of resort accommodations nestled along its shores. If you're searching for a cottage, check out the larger waters such as Glen Lake, Lake Leelanau, and Silver Lake, but don't ignore the smaller waters.

⊞ **Manitou Manor** B&B. Bordered by century-old willows and accented by fruit trees and blue spruce, Manitou Manor is a former farmhouse, built in 1873 and added onto several times. The lodge has catered to vacationers since the early 1900s, when they arrived by steamer. Explore the expansive lawn, rose garden, perennials, and trees or sunbathe on a deck on the house's west side. The dining room, where guests enjoy a five-course breakfast, has country accents, with maple hutches and windows on three sides. The living room features a granite fireplace, oak planking, and lots of Americana. Rooms are done in country style; queen beds with quilts, some with lace canopies. Open April–November. *147 North Manitou Trail, 2.5 miles south of Leland; 231-256-7712.* **$$$**

✕ **The Cove.** In Michigan's north country, at least one whitefish meal is a must, and whitefish is the specialty of this restaurant beside the Carp River and just upstream from the historic Leland Fishtown area—as you dine, you can enjoy a window or patio table and the great views of Lake Michigan and the Manitou Islands in the distance. After an appetizer of seafood chowder, take your pick from several preparations, such as garlic-Parmesan, macadamia-nut, or "campfire" whitefish—the latter baked and served with key-lime dressing and garnished with red and green peppers. *111 River Street, Leland; 231-256-9834; www.thecoveleland.com.* **$$**

✕ **Hattie's.** Owner-chef Jim Milliman creates unique dishes in this former storefront, which seats 78 for dinner. It's furnished in soft blues and grays, with white tablecloths, wood accents, and a display of works by Michigan artists that changes every two months. Popular menu items include sautéed lobster medallions with roasted red pepper butter sauce, and sautéed mushroom ravioli with locally picked morels. Wine list contains 180 labels. Reservations suggested. *111 St. Joseph (M-22), Suttons Bay; 231-271-6222; www.hatties.com.* **$$$**

LEWISTON *map page 152, B-3*

✕▣ **Garland Resort.** Luxury in the north country, with the feel of a woodsy European hunting lodge. With 182 lodge rooms, 84 log-cabin-style units from one to three bedrooms, and 16 two-bedroom villas on a lake or in the woods, Garland earns its reputation with outstanding lodging, dining, and services year-round. There are 72 holes of golf, a big-game hunting club, outdoor hot tub, and a small indoor pool on the main lodge's lower level; cross-country skiing and snowmobiling. Special winter weekend packages include one of Garland's romantic Zhivago Nights: a sleigh ride through the woods, followed by a gourmet dinner and live music. At Herman's, Garland's excellent restaurant, the hunting-lodge theme continues, with wild game—pheasant, salmon, and trout or venison—a specialty, as are locally picked morel mushrooms in season. In summer enjoy the view of the golf course or, in winter, of Nordic skiers gliding by. Be sure to take home a jar of Shelly's preserves—yum! *4700 North Red Oak Road; 877-444-2726; www. garlandusa.com.* **$$–$$$**

LUDINGTON *map page 197, A-3*

▣ **Inn at Ludington.** This 1890 Victorian bed-and-breakfast sits cozily along a street with other such mansions. Six guest rooms, full breakfast. *701 East Ludington Avenue; 231-845-7055 or 800-845-9170; www.inn-ludington.com.* **$$**
✕ **Scotty's Restaurant.** Good down-home cooking served in a nautical atmosphere. Mix with the locals who also come here. *5910 West U.S. 10; 231-843-4033; www.scottysrestaurant.com.* **$$**

MACATAWA, *see Holland*

MACKINAC ISLAND *maps page 205, D-1, and page 241*

▣ **Bay View Bed & Breakfast.** Stay in the island's only B&B directly on the water, a short walk from downtown. Built in 1891 for the Armour family, the house retains its Victorian charm. Guest rooms have period furnishings, air-conditioning, private bath, and phones. Three have TV and VCR (free movie library); three suites have in-room whirlpools. Enjoy the views over afternoon cookies and lemonade on the large second-floor deck. Breakfast might include quiche, freshly baked muffins, fruit, cereal, and the inn's own coffee blend. Open May–October. *Harborside; 906-847-3295; www.mackinacbayview.com.* **$$$**

▨ **Cloghaun.** Built by an Irish immigrant fishing family in 1884, the inn is one of the island's oldest homes. Its 11 rooms are furnished in period antiques. The common library has a TV and VCR. Take afternoon tea in the sitting room or in the swing on the wide front porch. Breakfast in the dining room includes fresh coffee cake, muffins, fruit salad, oatmeal bagels, and other breads. Open May–October. *Market Street, a block from the harbor; 906-847-3885 or 888-442-5929; www. cloghaun.com.* **$$$**

✕▨ **Grand Hotel.** Visitors to Mackinac Island can't do better than to stay at the Grand Hotel. Festive decor shows the touch of New York interior designer Carleton Varney. Awake each morning by the clip-clop of horses' hooves as carriages come and go on this car-free island. Enjoy cocktails and spectacular views in the fifth-floor Cupola lounge. Swim in the kidney-shaped Esther Williams pool and relax in a white rocker on the 660-foot-long front porch. Rates include breakfast and dinner. Do not, repeat, *do not* pass up the buffet lunch. Top off a five-course dinner with the Grand Pecan Ball. (Jacket and tie required at dinner.) Afterward, dance to a live orchestra. Open May through October. *One Grand Drive; 906-847-3331 or 800-334-7263; www.grandhotel.com.* **$$$$**

✕▨ **Island House.** Enjoy one of 97 rooms at the island's oldest hotel, built in 1852. Rooms range from modest to deluxe, with floor-to-ceiling windows giving onto the harbor. Three suites feature whirlpools; also an indoor pool and whirlpool. Relax on the porch overlooking the yacht harbor and have a casual meal at the Ice House Bar and Grill or dine more elegantly at the 1852 Grill Room. Open May–October. *Lakeshore Drive; 906-847-3347 or 800-626-6304; www. theislandhouse.com.* **$$$–$$$$**

✕▨ **Mission Point Resort.** This resort east of downtown reflects a northern Michigan-lodge-style decor in its 242 rooms and 92 suites. Amenities include feather beds, cable TV, coffee-makers, and hair dryers. There's a heated outdoor pool, also two hot tubs, a Kids' Club providing day care for 4- to 10-year-old guests, a theater, four restaurants, and a health club and spa; bicycles and in-line skates are available for rental. Children 12 and under stay free when sharing room with an adult. Open from late December through late October. *One Lakeshore Drive; 906-847-3312 or 800-833-7711; www.missionpoint.com.* **$$$$**

✕ **The French Outpost.** One of the island's most popular casual spots. Dine on the outside deck or indoors beside the stone fireplace, starting with bread topped with pesto, Parmesan, and goat cheese. A favorite entrée on the seasonally changing menu is their traditional roasted Mackinac whitefish with capers. Open May–October. *Cadotte Avenue; 906-847-3772; www.frenchoutpost.com.* **$$**

✕ **Pink Pony Bar and Grill.** Popular with islanders, this downtown spot specializes in light fare, from burgers to chicken. Open May–October. *Chippewa Hotel, One Main Street; 906-847-3341 or 800-241-3341; www.chippewahotel.com.* **$**

✕ **Pub Oyster Bar.** Dark paneling helps set the mood of this popular and intimate downtown eatery. The renovated interior retains much of the original decor, notably the pressed-tin ceiling and 120-year-old mirrored bar. Meals served around the clock start with a breakfast of Mr. Mike's biscuits and gravy, and dinner might include cold-water oysters and walnut-encrusted whitefish. End your day with a Pub Sub for a post-midnight snack. Open May–October. *Huron Street; 906-847-9901; www.puboysterbar.com.* **$$**

✕ **Woods.** Visiting this restaurant, run by the Grand Hotel and reachable via a shuttle carriage ride from Market Street or the Grand, is like discovering a Bavarian retreat. Bavarian dishes on the menu change seasonally, but the outstanding Austrian steak soup is a mainstay. Approach it carefully, for delightful entrées and "ooh-aah" desserts follow. A must! Open May–October. *About 1.2 miles from the Grand Hotel, near the Woods golf course; 906-847-3331 or 800-334-7263.* **$$–$$$**

MACKINAW CITY *map page 205, D-1*

▦ **The Beach House.** This cabin resort, with a sand beach and views of the Straits of Mackinac and Mackinac Island, has 25 small, vintage-1950s cabins with chenille bedspreads. Flowers bloom along the path to the outdoor grill. Heated indoor pool in the main lodge; coffee, juice, and hot muffins every morning. Beach toys on the clean swimming beach. Open mid-May–mid-October. *11490 U.S. 23; 231-436-5353 or 800-262-5353; www.mackinawcitybeachhouse.com.* **$$–$$$**

▦ **Brigadoon Bed & Breakfast.** This is like a small boutique hotel, with whirlpool baths, fireplaces, wet bars, and balconies; gourmet breakfast is included. The inn is within walking distance of the restaurants, shops, and beaches of Mackinaw City and of the Mackinac Island ferries. Open May–October. *207 Langlade Street; 231-436-8882.* **$$$**

⊞ **Comfort Inn Lakeside.** This family-oriented lodging lets kids stay free. Private balconies afford lakeside views, and folks like the indoor pool with oversized whirlpool. Wake to a deluxe Continental breakfast. *611 South Huron Street, 231-436-5057; www.comfortinnmackinaw.com.* **$–$$$**

✕ **Audie's Family Restaurant.** Casual dining and fast service at a very friendly restaurant that's been serving tourists for more than 25 years. Daily specials are served in the Family Room, where bacon and eggs are available all day. Leisurely dining in the Chippewa Room. *314 North Nicolet Street; 231-436-5744; www.audies.com.* **$–$$**

✕ **The Embers.** Since 1976, the Embers has been serving smorgasbord-style meals from breakfast through dinner, along with a full menu. Come hungry! *810 South Huron Avenue; 231-436-5773.* **$$**

MANISTEE *map page 197, A-2*

✕ **Four Forty West.** Dine on the bank of the Manistee River as boat traffic floats past. The full-service menu features local lake fish. *440 West River Street; 231-723-7902.* **$$$**

MARQUETTE *map pages 244–245, D-2*

✕⊞ **Landmark Inn.** Restored 1920s six-story hotel overlooking Marquette Harbor and Lake Superior, with 62 rooms and a health spa. Off the original lobby, serving breakfast, lunch, and dinner, is the **Heritage Room ($)**, distinguished by its tall, graceful windows and chandeliers. The Northland Pub is more casual; there's also a top-floor cocktail lounge. *230 North Front Street; 906-228-2580 or 888-752-6362; www.thelandmarkinn.com.* **$$–$$$$**

✕ **Northwoods Supper Club.** Renovated 1934 family-owned roadhouse. Gardens, full-service menu, and homemade breads and pies. Sunday brunch and Tuesday-night smorgasbord. This log-frame rustic lounge also offers weekend entertainment. *260 Northwoods Road; 906-228-4343.* **$–$$**

✕ **Vierling Restaurant & Marquette Harbor Brewery.** Local artwork adorns the brick walls of this renovated 1883 saloon, and its windows overlook Marquette Harbor. Menu features fresh, locally grown or gathered food (especially Lake Superior whitefish) for health-conscious diners. *119 South Front Street; 906-228-3533; www.thevierling.com.* **$–$$**

MARSHALL *map page 171, D-4*

▣ **Arbor Inn–Historic Marshall.** One-story economy motel with 48 rooms. *15435 West Michigan Avenue; 269-781-7772.* **$$**

✕▣ **National House Inn.** Michigan's oldest operating inn, a former stagecoach stop dating from 1835, overlooking Fountain Circle. Innkeeper Barbara Bradley cares for the 15 rooms named for historic Marshall figures and decorated with Victorian antiques; some rooms have half-baths and shared showers. A Continental breakfast is included, and dinner is catered by appointment. *102 South Parkview; 269-781-7374; www.nationalhouseinn.com.* **$$$**

✕ **Schuler's Restaurant & Pub.** Built to cater to Detroit–Chicago rail travelers in the early 1900s, Schuler's remains a traditional stop for today's auto travelers too. A state historic landmark, Schuler's prides itself on its warm atmosphere; poetic epigrams about food are inscribed on overhead beams. Favorites include prime rib and Lake Superior whitefish. *115 South Eagle Street; 269-781-0600 or 877-724-8537; www.schulersrestaurant.com.* **$$**

MONTAGUE, *see Whitehall*

MUNISING/AU TRAIN *map pages 244–245, E-2*

▣ **Pinewood Lodge.** This log lodge with five guest rooms, atrium, Finnish-style sauna, and porches is 12 miles west of Munising. Gardens, boardwalks, and gazebo under tall pines on a Lake Superior beach. You can walk for miles. Full homemade breakfast. *M-28, Au Train; 906-892-8300; www.algercounty.com/chamber/pinewood.* **$$–$$$**

✕ **Dogpatch.** A mural of the denizens of Li'l Abner's Dogpatch decorates this eatery, and the menu is also illustrated with characters from the comic strip. Generous portions with salad bar. *325 East Superior Street, Munising; 906-387-9948.* **$–$$**

MUSKEGON *map page 197, A-6*

▣ **Blue Country B&B.** Children are not usually welcomed at heirloom-laden B&Bs, but this one, run by John and Barbara Stevens, welcomes kids of all ages.

Infants stay in cribs equipped with stuffed animals. Toddlers wind down in the toy room. Older tykes play games, do puzzles, watch videos. Special kids' menus too. *1415 Holton Road, North Muskegon; 231-744-2555 or 888-569-2050.* **$$**

⌂ **Hackley-Holt House.** Built in 1857 for the father of lumber baron Charles Hackley, this stately Victorian has four first-floor rooms with king and queen beds and private baths. Lots of antiques; big parlor and common room. Full breakfast. *523 West Clay Avenue; 231-725-7303 or 888-271-5609; www.bbonline.com/mi/hhhbb.* **$$**

⌂ **Port City Victorian Inn.** This renovated 1877 home, now a B&B, has five beautifully decorated upstairs rooms; note the original glass in the living-room windows. Innkeepers Barbara and Frederick Schossau serve full breakfasts. Take time to relax in the rooftop pergola overlooking the park. *1259 Lakeshore Drive; 231-759-0205 or 800-274-3574; www.portcityinn.com.* **$$–$$$**

✕⌂ **Shoreline Inn at Terrace Point.** The 140-room Shoreline Inn towers above the shore of Muskegon Lake and the downtown area. Twelve of the accommodations are penthouse suites; antiques are found in many parts of the hotel, which is next door to Terrace Point Marina and the hotel's **Rafferty's Dockside Restaurant** (231-722-4461), a great place to enjoy casual fine dining. Entrées include pretzel-crumbed walleye and prime rib. In summer watch the sun go down while you dine on the outdoor deck. *701 Terrace Point Boulevard; 866-727-8483; www. shorelineinn.com.* **$$-$$$**

✕ **Doo Drop Inn.** Family owned for more than half a century, the restaurant offers good family meals, including lake perch. *2410 Henry Street; 231-755-3791.* **$**

NORTHVILLE, *see Plymouth*

OSCODA *map page 152, D-5*

⌂ **AmericInn Lodge and Suites of Oscoda.** Close to the Au Sable River, this inn features 47 rooms, some with water views and some with whirlpools. Some even have fireplaces. There's also a heated pool and sauna. Continental breakfast comes with your stay, and boat tie-up is available. *720 Harbor Street; 989-739-1986; www.amerinn.com.* **$$**

⊡ **Huron House B&B.** Innkeepers Denny and Martie Lorenz specialize in making the 14 rooms of this lodge retreats for couples. Private decks and hot tubs, two-person in-room whirlpool, and fireplace, along with breakfast served in your room, help make this a special getaway. *3124 North U.S. 23; 989-739-9255; www. huronhouse.com.* **$$$**

✕ **Charbonneau's Family Restaurant.** A family-style restaurant for breakfast, lunch, and dinner overlooking the pleasure-boat traffic on the Au Sable River. Try the roast chicken and weekend seafood buffet. *700 Lake Street; 989-739-5230.* **$$**

PETOSKEY/BAY VIEW *map page 205, D-3*

✕⊡ **Stafford's Bay View Inn.** An 1886 Victorian inn in the heart of the historic Bay View home district, with eight classic Edwardian-style rooms. Breakfast, lunch, dinner, and a large Sunday brunch are served in the bright **Roselawn** dining room, decorated in green, pink, and red, with clamshell-back chairs. Dinner entrées include cherry-pepper steak—twin medallions of beef tenderloin dredged in cracked peppercorns and quickly seared and served with a rich port wine demi-glace laced with dried tart cherries. *2011 Woodland Avenue (U.S. 31), Bay View; 800-258-1886; www.thebayviewinn.com.* **$$$**

⊡ **Stafford's Perry Hotel.** When the Perry Hotel was about to crumble from sheer neglect, Stafford Smith of the Bay View Inn (*see above*) stepped in to save this historic former vacation retreat in the heart of Petoskey's Gaslight District. Built in 1899, the Perry is the only hotel in Petoskey surviving from that era. Eighty rooms and the common areas are decorated in Victorian style. *Bay and Lewis Streets, Petoskey; 231-347-4000 or 800-737-1899; www.theperryhotel.com.* **$$$**

⊡ **Terrace Inn.** This charming 1911 inn, built in the Victorian style and located within the historic Bay View home district, is a designated National Historic Landmark. The white clapboard building's 43 rooms contain original furnishings. All have private baths; two have whirlpools. Interiors make extensive use of Michigan hemlock, and the floors are dark hardwood. Guests have access to Bay View Association facilities, including its private beach and tennis court. *1549 Glendale, Bay View; 231-347-2410 or 800-530-9898; www.theterraceinn.com.* **$$$**

✕ **Andante.** After a stroll down Andante's garden path, entering this two-level eatery is like stepping into the home of a good friend. Local artworks are displayed, and the north wall affords a panoramic view of Little Traverse Bay and the waterfront. Eclectic seasonal menu. *321 Bay Street, Petoskey; 231-348-3321.* **$$$**

PLYMOUTH/NORTHVILLE *map page 83, C-4*

⊞ **Embassy Suites.** Choose from 240 rooms in this hotel conveniently located just off I-275. Restaurant, an indoor pool, and other amenities. *19525 Victor Parkway, Livonia (just south of Northville); 734-462-6000 or 800-362-2779.* **$$$**

⊞ **Hilton Garden Inn Plymouth.** Located outside Plymouth, this six-story inn has 157 rooms and a small indoor pool. *14600 Sheldon Road, Plymouth; 734-354-0001 or 877-782-9444; www.hiltongardeninn.com.* **$$$**

✕ **Café Bon Homme.** A very French-American restaurant, rated one of the state's best. The frequently changing menu lists dishes like southern French lamb pie. Homemade desserts. *844 Penniman Avenue, Plymouth; 734-453-6260.* **$$$$**

✕ **Guernsey Farms Dairy.** Ice-cream eaters are always satisfied when they leave this spot. In addition to 55 flavors of ice cream, check out the dairy's restaurant, with its special "broasted" chicken and all kinds of burgers. *21300 Novi Road, Northville; 248-349-1466; www.guernseyfarmsdairy.com.* **$**

✕ **MacKinnons.** The menu varies from chops to lobster, but steaks take the spotlight in this restaurant with a country inn atmosphere. Desserts, such as chef Tom MacKinnon's famed Chocolate Chocolate Creation, are house-made, so save room. *126 East Main Street, Northville; 248-348-1991.* **$$$$**

✕ **Uncle Frank's.** Hot dog aficionados looking to transcend the limits of their usual Detroit coney dog come here to savor 15 types of franks, from Italian to turkey to tofu. *550 Forest Avenue, Plymouth; 734-455-4141.* **$**

PORT AUSTIN *map page 126, C-1*

⊞ **Captain's Inn.** This rambling white-frame, two-story 1859 home is a great spot to base your tour of Michigan's Thumb. The B&B's five period-decorated rooms are named after owners Dave and Debbie Ramey's four children and granddaughter. Charter-boat fishing for salmon or perch, as well as golf packages, can be arranged. Or just relax outside in a rocker or swing on the front porch, or inside in the library or living room, both of which have fireplaces, which the Rameys will light whenever anyone feels romantic. A full breakfast is served on a rear patio or indoors. *8586 Lake Street; 989-738-8321 or 888-277-6631 (reservations); www.thumbtravels.com/captains.htm.* **$$–$$$**

✕⊞ **Garfield Inn.** The innkeepers—the Pasant family—rent six rooms (three with private baths) here and serve lunch and dinner, too. Named after President James

Garfield, who once spoke from its balcony, this French Empire Revival–style building is on both the Michigan and the National Register of Historic Places. The most popular menu item is the reasonably priced prime rib; a children's menu is available as well. Breakfast is served for overnight guests. *8544 Lake Street (M-25); 989-738-5254 or 800-373-5254; www.garfieldinn.com.* **$$**

✕ **The Bank–1884.** What do you do with an old and unused bank that survived the fires that wiped out forestry here in 1881? Make it a restaurant. (It's also a National Historic Site.) Come here and dive into prime rib or fresh walleye. Children's menu available. *8646 Lake Street; 989-738-5353; www.thebank1884. com.* **$$–$$$**

✕ **The Farm.** Many hungry travelers who've stumbled across Jeff and Pam Gabriel's 100-year-old white-frame farmhouse return again and again, for the Gabriels prepare dishes spiced with herbs and accompanied by produce grown in their own garden. Recipes from the owners' grandmother inspired Grandma Lizzie's chicken with lemon-thyme dumplings and other "heartland" dishes. Open April through October. *699 Port Crescent Road; 989-874-5700; www. thefarmrestaurant.com.* **$$**

PORT HOPE *map page 126, D-1*

🏠 **Stafford House B&B.** After a day on the road, relax in this delightfully restored 1886 frame house with four rooms (full or queen beds), a third of a mile from Lake Huron. Woodwork is original. Sit by the marble fireplace to enjoy complimentary evening snacks. Full breakfast served. Borrow a bicycle to explore nearby lighthouses, or take in a historic walking tour. Owners Kathy and Greg Gephart are happy to help you. *4489 Main Street (M-25); 989-428-4554; www. staffordhousepthope.com.* **$$**

PORT HURON *map page 126, D-4*

✕🏠 **Thomas Edison Inn.** Among the inn's 149 rooms, best are the ones with views on the river side, with their lookout onto the Blue Water Bridge. Indoor pool, whirlpool, and exercise area. The restaurant serves breakfast, lunch, and dinner—at which the prime rib and paella are standouts. If you dine here in summer, you can watch the traffic on the St. Clair River plow through the fast current created where Lake Huron narrows into the river. *500 Thomas Edison Parkway; 810-984-8000 or 800-451-7991; www.thomasedisoninn.com.* **$$**

✕ **The Fogcutter.** Great views of Lake Huron, the Blue Water Bridge, and the St. Clair River. Steaks and seafood for lunch, dinner; children's meals available. *511 Fort Street, atop the Port Huron Office Center; 810-987-3300.* **$$**

PORT SANILAC *map page 126, D-3*

▦ **Raymond House Inn.** This 1872 Victorian gingerbread home is 500 feet from the Lake Huron shore. Gary and Cristy Bobofchak run the inn and the adjacent gift shop, and the art gallery that features Gary's photographs. Seven rooms (five with private baths) are decorated with antiques. Most have queen beds, one with canopy and some with antique frames. Stroll downtown to browse through the antiques shops, head to the beach, or visit the barn theater across the street for a performance by local talent. Salmon- and steelhead-fishing charter boats are moored nearby in the harbor, and a historic lighthouse is but 300 feet away. *111 South Ridge Street; 810-622-8800 or 800-622-7229; www.laketolake.com/raymond.* **$$**

PRUDENVILLE, *see Houghton Lake*

ROTHBURY *map page 197, A-5*

▦ **Double JJ Ranch and Golf Resort.** A lot more than trail rides is offered at this dude ranch, one of several in Michigan and the one that offers the most. Off U.S. 31 north of Muskegon, the ranch is divided into two sides—one adult-oriented, with rustic accommodations and no phones, TV, or air-conditioning; one family-oriented, featuring water slides and wagons, tepees where young ropers can sleep, and beautiful log cabins big enough for an entire family. Learn to handle cows on the range during a two-hour cattle drive; play on the Thoroughbred, an Arthur Hills–designed 18-hole course rated one of the nation's best; or just relax and fish on the lake. Weekly, weekend, or three-day stays; packages include meals. *5900 South Water Road; 231-894-4444 or 800-368-2535; www.doublejj.com.* **$$**

ROYAL OAK *map page 83, D-4*

✕ **Memphis Smoke.** Ribs here are great, but the menu also tempts with beef brisket, pulled pork, smoked turkey, pork ribs, and other meats slow-roasted over wood. When the sun goes down, the live music—often the blues—begins. *100 South Main Street; 248-543-4300.* **$$$**

✕ **Royal Oak Brewery.** Soups, salads, sandwiches, gourmet pizzas, and pastas can be washed down by any of six or seven house brews on tap daily at this casual eatery. *215 East Fourth Street; 248-544-1141; www.royaloakbrewery.com.* **$$**

ST. CLAIR *map page 83, D-4*

✕▣ **River Crab Restaurant.** The River Crab specializes in seafood: one of the best dishes is the pasta *pagliara*: shrimp, scallops, and chunks of salmon surrounded by mussels in a light garlic sauce over homemade linguine. Great Sunday brunch. Lots of waterfront memorabilia, including a racing shell hanging from the ceiling and paintings of freighters on the paneled walls. The adjacent **Blue Water Inn**, under the same ownership, has 21 rooms angled to face the river. *1137 North River Road; 810-329-2261 or 800-468-3727; www.muer.com.* **$$**

✕▣ **St. Clair Plaza Inn and Suites.** Many of this recently upgraded Tudor-style inn's 78 romantic rooms look out over the St. Clair River, with its parade of boats, freighters, and oceangoing "salties." In the **Riverwatch Restaurant**, dine on the boardwalk or inside by windows overlooking the river. Seafood, fresh lake fish (especially whitefish and perch) are specialties at this inn. Whirlpool, indoor pool. *500 North Riverside Avenue; 810-329-2222 or 800-482-8327; www.stclairplaza. com.* **$$–$$$**

ST. IGNACE *map pages 244–245, G-3*

▣ **Best Western Harbour Pointe Lakefront.** This 150-room lodge has balconies on Lake Huron, giving you a view of the nightly beach bonfires. Indoor and out-door pools, spas, game room, and yard games. Suites have hot tubs. Three stories, no elevator. Continental breakfast. Open May–October. *797 North State Street; 906-643-6000 or 800-642-3318; www.harbourpointe.com.* **$$$**

🛏 **K-Royale Motor Inn.** Summer lodge with 150 rooms on 600 feet of private sand beach on Lake Huron. Balconies overlook the lake, a large playground, and picnic area. Some 95 rooms and suites. Three stories, no elevators. Open April–October. *1037 North State Street; 906-643-7737 or 800-882-7122; www.stignace. com/lodging/kroyale.*

✕ **Galley Restaurant & Bar.** Views of Moran Bay and Mackinac Island. All-service menu specializing in fish fresh from the bay; hard-to-find whitefish livers. Open May to mid-October. *214 North State Street; 906-643-7960.* **$–$$**

ST. JOSEPH *map page 171, A-5*

✕🛏 **Boulevard Inn and Bistro.** The seven-story downtown hostelry features 82 one-bedroom suites on the cliff above Lake Michigan. The dining area is aptly named, with the decor of a French bistro and tall windows and chairs to assure perfect views of the Lake Michigan sunset. The full-service menu also includes French bistro specialties; there's a special three-course fixed-price choice at dinner and a popular Sunday brunch buffet. *521 Lake Boulevard; 269-983-6600 or 800-875-6600; www.theboulevardinn.com.* **$$$$**

🛏 **South Cliff Inn.** The brick exterior and formal perennial garden topping a Lake Michigan bluff call to mind an English cottage. Inside this B&B you'll find custom-made furniture and many antiques. Seven guest rooms: some have fireplaces, whirlpool tubs, and/or balconies; all have private baths. From the inn's decks overlooking the lake I have photographed more than one blazing sunset. Innkeeper Bill Swisher is a retired chef, so expect a great breakfast. Handicapped-accessible. *1900 Lakeshore Drive; 269-983-4881; www.southcliffinn.com.* **$$–$$$**

✕ **Clementine's Too.** Clementine's in South Haven (*see below*) proved to be so much fun that its owners, the Ruppert family, decided they had to do it twice! Marina view and huge club sandwiches. Try the lake perch: it's lightly dusted, pan-fried, then served with garlic bread and coleslaw. Children's menu is available. *1235 Broad Street; 269-983-0990; www.ohmydarling.com.* **$$**

✕ **Schu's Grill and Bar.** Cozy downtown location; traditional American fare from burgers to steaks to pasta. Rustic atmosphere, with outdoor dining. *501 Pleasant Street; 269-983-7248; www.schus.com.* **$$**

SAUGATUCK *map page 171, B-3*

This area must be Michigan's B&B mother lode: more than 30 are listed on the local visitors bureau Web site (www.artcoast.com). Most downtown Saugatuck businesses don't need an address, as the area is so compact. Just drive down Water Street and you'll see them.

⊡ **Park House Inn.** Built in 1857 by lumberman H. D. Moore, this is Saugatuck's oldest home. (Susan B. Anthony was once a guest here for two weeks, while she gave lectures in the area.) Eight rooms with queen beds, one family suite, and two suites with fireplaces and whirlpool tubs. All have private baths and air-conditioning; large continental breakfast. The Park House also has three cottages, including the oft-photographed Peterson's Mill on the north edge of town. *888 Holland Street; 269-857-4535 or 866-321-4535; www.parkhouseinn.com.* **$$$**

✕ **Coral Gables.** On the Kalamazoo River, this is the Saugatuck party place, with "Open till 3 A.M." taken seriously. Dining options range from casual burger joint and bar and grill to lower-level Rathskeller (with karaoke) to the nautically themed full service dining room. Docking along the river. *220 Water Street; 269-857-2162; www.coral-gables.com.* **$$**

✕ **Ida Reds.** Named for a variety of apple tree as well as the famous folk song on which Chuck Berry's "Maybellene" was based, Ida Reds serves good Italian and Greek dishes. Burgers, too. *631 Water Street; 616-857-5803.* **$**

SAULT STE. MARIE *map pages 244–245, H-2*

✕⊡ **Ramada Plaza Ojibway Hotel.** With 71 rooms and suites, this restored 1927 hotel overlooking the Soo Locks offers an indoor pool and spa. In **Freighters**, one of the hotel's two restaurants, tall windows give diners panoramic views of the locks and of ships traveling up and down the St. Marys River. Casual upscale menu. *240 West Portage Avenue; 906-632-4100 or 800-654-2929; www. waterviewhotels.com.* **$–$$**

✕ **The Antlers.** A rustic old bar decorated with bric-a-brac (canoes, logging tools, deer antlers) hanging from ceiling rafters and walls. Family-sized hamburgers, steak, and lobster. Gift shop on premises. *804 East Portage Avenue; 906-632-3571; www.antlersgiftshop.com.* **$–$$$**

SENEY *map pages 244–245, F-2*

✕ **Golden Grill.** The hearty country menu includes homemade pies, bread, pastries, and doughnuts. Breakfast buffet and 4 P.M. daily smorgasbord. *South side of M-28 in the village; 906-499-3323.* **$–$$**

SOUTH HAVEN *map page 171, A-4*

▣ **Carriage House at the Harbor Bed and Breakfast.** I have never felt so pampered! Antiques, gas fireplaces, endless cookies in the jar, balconies, gourmet breakfasts. Eleven guest rooms—none are finer. *118 Woodman Street; 269-639-2161; www.carriagehouseharbor.com.* **$$$-$$$$**
▣ **Inn at the Park.** At this Victorian-style country inn every room has a character of its own. Full breakfast. *233 Dyckman Avenue; 269-639-1776 or 877-739-1776; www.innpark.com.* **$$$–$$$$**
✕ **Clementine's.** The predecessor of Clementine's Too in St. Joseph. The Ruppert family opened Clementine's in 1982 and a few years later moved it into this charming setting, the old Citizen's Bank Building, built in 1897. Save room for the house special dessert—hot apple dumpling. *500 Phoenix Street; 269-637-4755; www.ohmydarling.com.* **$$**

SPRING LAKE, *see Grand Haven*

STEVENSVILLE *map page 171, A-5*

✕ **Grande Mere Inn.** An elegant restaurant, adept at preparing seafood and freshwater fish (including perch and bluegill) parboiled and served with house-made sauce, as well as ribs and steaks. Children's menu is available. *5800 Red Arrow Highway; 269-429-3591.* **$$**
✕ **Tosi's Restaurant.** Begun by Emil Tosi in 1948 using many of his mother's Old World recipes. No longer in the Tosi family, the restaurant serves excellent northern Italian cuisine and has an outstanding wine cellar. The huge menu includes pizza baked in a wood-burning oven, as well as pastas, seafood, steaks, and other meat dishes. *4337 Ridge Road; 269-429-3689 or 800-218-7745; www.tosis.com.* **$$**

TRAVERSE CITY *map page 205, B-5*

⌸ **Chateau Chantal.** Turn onto the private road off M-37 on the Old Mission Peninsula and you'll swear you were in California or France as you pass row upon row of grape trellises. Tour the winery and sample a few vintages before retiring to one of the two standard rooms, the eight suites, or the queen-sized two-bedroom suite dubbed the Palace in this B&B inspired by the great French chateaux. Guests sip wine by a majestic fireplace in the Great Room. Full breakfast. *15900 Rue de Vin; 231-223-4110 or 800-969-4009; www.chateauchantal.com.* **$$–$$$$**

⌸ **Grand Traverse Resort and Spa.** The gleaming blue-gray glass of this resort's 17-story tower, northern Michigan's tallest structure, can be seen for miles around. Choose from 660 rooms in the six-story hotel, in the tower, or in the condominiums scattered in various locations. Also on the property is the resort's main summer draw, 54 holes of golf (including the Jack Nicklaus–designed course called the Bear), along with indoor tennis, racquetball courts, exercise area, and a beach on Grand Traverse Bay. Located 6 miles northeast of Traverse City, off U.S. 31. *100 Grand Traverse Village Boulevard; 231-938-2100 or 800-236-1577; www. grandtraverseresort.com.* **$$–$$$**

⌸ **Great Wolf Lodge.** Water, water everywhere in a lodge that's also a popular indoor water park, with eight waterslides, five pools, two whirlpools, and more in a four-story atrium. The 281 guest rooms are all suites and fun for all, but ah, to be a 10-year-old again! Just south of Traverse City. *3575 North U.S. 31 South; 866-478-9653; www.greatwolflodge.com.* **$$$$**

✕⌸ **Waterfront Inn.** One of the best places to stay among the scores of places ringing the crescent necklace of a beach on the west arm of Grand Traverse Bay. Four-story building (127 rooms) surrounded by trees. Play on nearly 800 feet of beach or in the pool, saunas, and whirlpool. The restaurant atop the inn, **Reflections ($$–$$$)**, offers views of Grand Traverse Bay that suit the fine, sophisticated fare. Best dishes include seafood, whitefish, and brandy-pecan walleye. *2061 U.S. 31 North; 231-938-1100 or 800-551-9283; www.waterfrontinntc.com.* **$$$**

✕ **Boone's Long Lake Inn.** Traverse City's steak and seafood favorite has been feeding hungry locals and tourists for more than 20 years. The menu includes an 18-ounce New York strip that could convert the most ardent vegetarian. Finish with a slice of chocolate mousse pie. *7208 Secor Road; 231-946-3991.* **$$**

✕ **Bowers Harbor Inn.** The curved drive through stately pines sets the mood of elegance at this inn on Old Mission Peninsula. The decor befits royal guests, and the food is excellent. On most visits I go for the signature dish, Fish in a Bag, in which one may find all kinds of seafood surprises. Before you leave, ask about the resident ghost, Genevie. *13512 Peninsula Drive; 231-223-4222.* **$$$**

UNION PIER *map page 171, A-6*

▣ **Inn at Union Pier.** Choose from 16 spacious guest rooms in this lakeside retreat built in the 1920s as a summer resort. Bill and Madeleine Reinke purchased it in 1983, restored it, and in 1985 opened it as the area's first B&B. Each room is furnished with a mix of Danish and Swedish antiques and reproductions. Swedish wood-burning fireplaces in 13 of the rooms; all have private baths and air-conditioning, many with porch or balcony. As the inn is in Michigan's fruit belt, breakfast usually features blueberries. Chocolate chip–oatmeal cookies are set out each day along with seasonal refreshments (lemonade in summer, hot cocoa in winter). Relax in the hot tub or sauna, or borrow a bike from the inn to explore the countryside. *9708 Berrien Street; 269-469-4700; www.innatunionpier.com.* **$$$–$$$$**

✕ **Miller's Country House.** This "country house" is not so country anymore. After being a fixture of the area since the 1930s, when this roadhouse-style restaurant served travelers on the former main route from Michigan to Chicago, it has dressed itself up with new decor and a new menu. Entrées run from pastas to rack of lamb, seasoned with herbs from the restaurant's own garden. "Fresh" is the magic word here.*16409 Red Arrow Highway; 269-469-5950.* **$–$$$**

WHITEHALL/MONTAGUE *map page 197, A-5*

✕▣ **Lakeside Inn**. With fresh coats of white paint and tender care, this inn overlooking White Lake, serving travelers since 1913, looks as bright as the morning. There is housing to suit any occasion, from solo accommodations to a family reunion, in the main lodge, motel, and ranch house. The restaurant affords an expansive view of the lake and serves a full menu, from fresh fish to prime rib. Inn open April–mid-October (**$$$**); restaurant open Memorial Day–Labor Day (**$$**). *5700 North Scenic Drive, Whitehall; 231-893-8315 or 888-442-3304; www. lakesideinn.net.*

⊞ **Michillinda Lodge**. This rambling white four-story getaway lodge, with 500 feet of Lake Michigan beach, 53 guest rooms, and cabins, is right out of yesteryear. The former 1902 country estate also has a restaurant and ice-cream parlor, puts out freshly baked cookies at sunset, and arranges evening campfires. *5207 Scenic Drive, Whitehall; 231-893-1895; www.michillindalodge.com.* **$$$$**

✕ **Old Channel Inn**. I like to show up early at this restaurant in a cabin at the end of the trail, reserve a table, and then take the short path across the dunes to the beach to watch the sun set over Lake Michigan. Afterward I return for dinner beside the fireplace and enjoy some mighty good food. For dessert, be forewarned! Beth I's Pies—fruit or cheesecake made by Beth at her local bakery—are served here. *6905 Old Channel Trail, Montague; 231-893-3805 or 877-393-2433.* **$$**

YPSILANTI *map page 83, C-4*

✕ **Aubree's Saloon and Sticks Pool Hall**. Pretty good, as basic bar food goes (sandwiches, burgers, fish-and-chips, goulash, shepherd's pie, build-your-own pizza) and a great place to shoot stick and toss darts. *39 East Cross Street; 734-483-1870.* **$**

✕ **Cady's Grill and Bar**. Fun atmosphere, with food ranging from soup, salads, and sandwiches to seafood and pasta entrées. *36 East Cross Street; 734-483-2800; www.ypsilantirestaurants.com/cadys.* **$–$$**

✕ **Haab's Restaurant**. A local tradition since 1934. Under the beamed ceilings are just enough rustic touches to give it class. Any place that makes its bread from scratch gets my vote, but Haab's doesn't stop there. Most of the condiments, such as mayonnaise, are house-made, and ingredients used in the entrées are the freshest of fresh. To sample the wide variety of offerings, try the mixed grill. *18 West Michigan Avenue; 734-483-8200 or 888-431-4222; www.haabsrestaurant.com.* **$–$$**

✕ **Sidetrack Bar & Grill**. Award-winning burgers plus an eclectic decor make this a great place to linger a few hours beyond dinner. Local and international microbrews on tap. *56 East Cross Street; 734-483-1035; www.sidetrackbarandgrill.com.* **$–$$**

✕ **The Tap Room**. Music that's a bit bluesy in what's been called Ypsilanti's "hippest hangout." *201 West Michigan Avenue; 734-482-5320.* **$–$$**

INDEX

ACKNOWLEDGMENTS

■ FROM THE AUTHOR

I owe deep gratitude to so many fine folks of Michigan who so generously shared information when I called time and time again with the opening phrase of, "One more question on the book." A heart-felt thanks to all the historians who worked at keeping me posted on the facts of the past, tourism agencies, convention & visitors bureaus who helped define their main attractions, and so many more. So many friends and associates gave freely of their time and knowledge: Al Sandner, Bill Semion, Tom Nemacheck, Peter Fitzsimons, Renee Monforton, Chris Dancisak, Carolyn Artman. My thanks go to Leonard A. DeFrain whom I have never met and others like him who responded to my request for information by taking time to research almost forgotten ghost towns and other remnants of the past. Kay Boughner and other librarians at the small library in the village of Norway kept a constant flow of Michigan history books coming through interlibrary loans from Michigan to California. My thanks also go to the fine editorial staff of the original edition of this book, especially Kit Duane, Pennfield Jensen, and Chris Burt, without whose assistance it would not have been possible. Finally, I salute Kristin Moehlmann, senior editor of this edition who guided me through the web of facts and new attractions to bring this version of *Michigan* up to date. Thank you.

■ FROM THE PUBLISHER

Compass American Guides thanks Sara Wood for copyediting the manuscript of this edition, Russell Stockman for proofreading it, and Joan Stout for indexing it.

All photographs in this book are by Dennis Cox unless noted below. Compass American Guides would also like to thank the following individuals and institutions for the use of their photographs and illustrations:

Landscape & History:
Page 20, Library of Congress Prints and Photographs Division
Page 21, Art Gallery of Ontario
Page 24, Library of Congress Prints and Photographs Division
Page 26, Wisconsin Historical Society
Page 27, Library of Congress Geography and Map Division
Page 28, Library and Archives of Canada
Page 29, North Wind/North Wind Picture Archives
Page 30, Wisconsin Historical Society
Page 31, Collection of the New-York Historical Society
Page 32, Burton Historical Collection, Detroit Public Library
Page 33, State Archives of Michigan
Page 34, Bentley Historical Library, University of Michigan
Page 35, State Archives of Michigan

■ About the Authors

Dixie Franklin left her home state of Texas in 1963 and fell head-over-heels in love with Michigan and the Great Lakes. As a prize-winning, full-time freelancer, she roams the cities, byroads, and lakeshores, contributing to the *Chicago Tribune, Midwest Living, Lake Superior Magazine,* and AAA *Home & Away,* among others. Books she has written besides this volume in the Compass American Guide series include *Michigan, Faces of Lake Superior,* and *Haunts of the Upper Great Lakes.* She has won dozens of awards, including the Michigan governor's Ambassador of Michigan Tourism award in 1984 and the Society of American Travel Writers Central States Chapter Lifetime Achievement award in 2003. She has two daughters, three grandchildren, and two great-grandhcildren.

Bill Semion is an award-winning freelance writer who has lived in and explored Michigan all of his life and writes extensively about the state. He is a member of the Michigan Outdoor Writers Association, the Outdoor Writers Association of America, the Automotive Press Association, the North American Snowsport Journalists Association, and the Midwest Travel Writers Association. He lives in Canton Township.

After contributing to this book, freelance writer **Dan Stivers** moved back to Ann Arbor with his wife and daughter. His articles have appeared in a number of magazines, and he has co-authored books for Fodor's Travel Publications and *Cliffs Notes.*

■ About the Photographer

Dennis Cox is an Ann Arbor–based photographer whose work has appeared in more than 200 publications, including *Business Week, Forbes, LIFE, Newsweek, Time, Gourmet, National Geographic Traveler, Smithsonian,* and *Travel & Leisure,* as well as *Midwest Living.* He was the Society of American Travel Writers' Travel Photographer of the Year in 1997, and runner-up for the same honor in 1998 and 1999. He has taught photography, written for several photography magazines, leads photo tours to worldwide destinations, and is listed in *American Photographers: An Illustrated Who's Who among Leading Contemporary Americans.*